FAKE BOOK OF THE WORLD'S FAVORITE SONGS

WHAT IS A FAKE BOOK?

When a musician is asked to play a song he's never played before, he "fakes" it. One of the most valuable possessions any musician can have is a fake book which contains the melodies, lyrics, and chords for hundreds and hundreds of songs. With the access to the melody, lyrics, and chords, the musician can improvise his own arrangement of a song.

▼

ALPHABETICAL LISTING
PAGE 2

All songs are listed alphabetically with the page number on which each song can be found.

▼

CLASSIFIED LISTING
PAGE 6

Songs are grouped into popular categories to simplify locating various styles of music.

▼

BONUS SECTION
PAGE 337

ISBN 0-88188-879-6

HAL•LEONARD®
CORPORATION
7777 W. BLUEMOUND RD. P.O. BOX 13819 MILWAUKEE, WI 53213

Visit Hal Leonard Online at
www.halleonard.com

ALPHABETICAL LISTING

EDITOR'S NOTE TO GUITARISTS: If there is no X or O over a string in a chord diagram, the string(s) should not be played.

A

10	A-Hunting We Will Go
10	A-Tisket, A-Tasket
28	The Aba Daba Honeymoon
10	Abide With Me
11	Ach, Du Lieber Augustin
29	Adios Muchachos
12	After The Ball
338	After You've Gone
13	Ah! Sweet Mystery Of Life
14	Air (On The G String)
338	Ain't We Got Fun?
339	Alabama Jubilee
30	Alexander's Ragtime Band
340	Alice Blue Gown
340	All By Myself
15	All God's Children Got Shoes
15	All My Trials
16	All Through The Night
16	Aloha Oe
14	Alouette
15	The Alphabet Song
37	Also Sprach Zarathustra
17	Amazing Grace
17	America (My Country, 'Tis Of Thee)
18	America, The Beautiful
23	American Cadets March
18	The American Patrol
28	Anchors Aweigh
11	Andante Cantabile (Tchaikovsky)
19	Angels We Have Heard On High
19	Animal Fair
20	Annabel Lee
22	Annie Laurie
21	Anvil Chorus
341	Any Time
342	April Showers
23	Arkansas Traveler
22	As With Gladness Men Of Old
20	Assembly/Reveille
24	Au Clair De La Lune
342	Auf Wiedersehn
24	Auld Lang Syne
25	Aura Lee
343	Avalon
25	Ave Maria (Bach/Gounod)
26	Ave Maria (Schubert)
27	Away In A Manger (W.J. Kirkpatrick)
27	Away In A Manger (James R. Murray)
27	Away In A Manger (Spillman)

B

38	Baa! Baa! Black Sheep
343	Baby, Won't You Please Come Home
38	The Banana Boat Song
38	The Band Played On
39	Banks Of The Ohio
39	Barbara Allen
40	Barbara Polka
41	The Barber Of Seville Overture
40	Barcarolle
42	The Barnyard Song (I Had A Rooster)
42	The Battle Cry Of Freedom
43	The Battle Hymn Of The Republic
48	Be Kind To Your Web-Footed Friends
31	Be My Little Baby Bumblebee
344	Beale Street Blues
48	The Bear Went Over The Mountain
43	Beautiful Brown Eyes
44	Beautiful Dreamer
48	Beautiful Isle Of Somewhere

345	Beautiful Ohio
45	Beautiful Savior
33	Because
46	Beethoven's Fifth Symphony (1st Movement Theme)
44	Behold The Savior Of Mankind
45	Believe Me If All Those Endearing Young Charms
345	The Bells Of St. Mary's
46	A Bicycle Built For Two (Daisy Bell)
49	The Big Rock Candy Mountain
52	Bill Bailey, Won't You Please Come Home?
32	The Billboard March
50	Billy Boy
51	Bingo
34	A Bird In A Gilded Cage
44	The Birthday Song
49	Black Is The Color
53	Blessed Assurance
50	Blest Be The Tie That Binds
52	Blood On The Saddle
51	Blow The Man Down
53	The Blue Bells Of Scotland
55	Blue Danube Waltz
54	Bluetail Fly
54	The Boar's Head Carol
56	The Boll Weevil
35	Boola! Boola!
55	The Bowery
57	Brahms' Lullaby
56	Bridal Chorus (From "Lohengrin")
58	Bring A Torch, Jeannette, Isabella
57	Bringing In The Sheaves
58	Buckeye Jim
59	Buffalo Gals
59	Bury Me Not On The Lone Prairie
36	By The Beautiful Sea
36	By The Light Of The Silvery Moon

C

60	The Caissons Go Rolling Along
60	The Campbells Are Coming
63	Camptown Races
62	Can Can
346	Canadian Capers
61	Cantabile
61	Capriccio Italien Theme
65	Careless Love
65	Carnival Of Venice
64	Carol Of The Bells
348	Carolina In The Morning
64	Carry Me Back To Old Virginny
66	Chiapanecas
348	Chicago (That Toddlin' Town)
77	Chinatown, My Chinatown
66	Chopin Ballade No. 1
77	Chopsticks
67	Christ The Lord Is Ris'n Today
65	Christ Was Born On Christmas Day
67	The Church In The Wildwood
68	Cielito Lindo
68	Ciribiribin
69	Clair De Lune
71	Clarinet Polka
69	Clementine
70	Cockles And Mussels (Molly Malone)
347	Cohen Owes Me Ninety-Seven Dollars
349	Colonel Bogey March
72	Columbia, The Gem Of The Ocean
70	Come Back To Sorrento
79	Come, Josephine In My Flying Machine
73	Come To The Sea

73	Come, Thou Almighty King
73	Comin' Through The Rye
78	Concerto Theme (Rachmaninoff) (Concerto No.2, 1st Movement)
78	Concerto Theme (Rachmaninoff) (Concerto No. 2, 3rd Movement)
72	Country Gardens
74	The Coventry Carol
74	The Crawdad Song
75	Cripple Creek
75	Crown Him With Many Crowns
76	The Cruel War Is Raging
77	Cuddle Up A Little Closer, Lovey Mine

D

82	Dance Of The Hours
80	Dance Of The Sugar-Plum Fairy
76	Danny Boy
83	Danube Waves
350	Dardanella
83	Dark Eyes
351	The Darktown Strutters' Ball
81	Deck The Hall
80	Deep River
81	The Desperado
84	Did You Ever See A Lassie?
84	Dixie
351	Do It Again
85	Dog-gone Blues
352	Dolores Waltz
352	Dona Nobis Pacem
354	Down Among The Sheltering Palms
86	Down By The Old Mill Stream
86	Down By The Riverside
84	Down By The Station
87	Down In The Valley
79	Down The Field
353	Down Yonder
87	Drink To Me Only With Thine Eyes
85	The Drunken Sailor
88	Dry Bones
89	Du, Du Liegst Mir Im Herzen

E

88	Eency, Weency Spider
90	Eine Kleine Nachtmusik (Opening Theme)
89	El Capitan
91	Elegie
93	Emilia Polka
92	Emperor Waltz
90	The Entertainer
91	The Erie Canal
356	Estrellita
354	Estudiantina
94	Ev'ry Time I Feel The Spirit
94	Ezekiel Saw The Wheel

F

95	Faith Of Our Fathers
95	Fantasie Impromptu (Chopin)
98	Far Above Cayuga's Waters
96	The Farmer In The Dell
105	Fascination
95	Fight Ye Bulldogs
105	Finlandia
99	The First Noel
97	Fledermaus Waltz
97	Flow Gently, Sweet Afton
98	The Foggy, Foggy Dew

96 For He's A Jolly Good Fellow
356 For Me And My Gal
104 Forty-Five Minutes From Broadway
100 Frankie And Johnny
96 Freight Train
101 Frère Jacques
103 The Friendly Beasts
99 Froggie Went A-Courtin'
102 Funeral March Of A Marionette
102 Funeral March
101 Funiculi, Funicula
103 Für Elise

G

107 Gavotte
111 The Girl I Left Behind
358 The Girl On The Magazine Cover
108 Git Along Home, Cindy
109 Git Along, Little Dogies
108 Give Me That Old Time Religion
106 Give My Regards To Broadway
110 Gladiator March
106 Glow Worm
357 Go Down, Moses
111 Go In And Out The Window
109 Go Tell Aunt Rhody
110 Go, Tell It On The Mountain
107 God Of Our Fathers
111 God Rest Ye Merry, Gentlemen
114 God Save Our King (Queen)
112 Gold And Silver Waltz
115 Goober Peas
113 Good Christian Men, Rejoice
116 Good King Wenceslas
359 A Good Man Is Hard To Find
114 Good Night Ladies
359 Good-bye Broadway, Hello France
114 Goodbye Girls, I'm Through
116 Goodbye, Old Paint
105 Goodbye, My Lady Love
117 Grandfather's Clock
115 The Green Grass Grew All Around
118 Green Grow The Lilacs
119 Greensleeves
117 Grey And Gold Waltz
118 Grieg Piano Concerto (Theme)
119 Gypsy Love Song
120 Gypsy Rondo

H

120 Habañera (From "Carmen")
121 Hail, Columbia
123 Hail To The Chief
124 Hail! Hail! The Gang's All Here
122 Hallelujah Chorus
123 Hand Me Down My Walking Cane
124 The Happy Farmer
126 Hark! The Herald Angels Sing
136 Harrigan
125 Hatikvah
125 Hava Nagilah
360 He Is An Englishman
        (From "H.M.S. Pinafore")
126 He's Got The Whole World In His Hands
126 Hear Them Bells
124 Hearts And Flowers
127 Helena Polka
137 Hello! My Baby
128 Here We Come A-Caroling
127 Hey, Diddle, Diddle

127 Hey, Ho! Nobody Home
129 Hickory, Dickory, Dock
128 High School Cadets
360 Hindustan
361 Hinky Dinky Parley Voo
362 His Eye Is On The Sparrow
129 The Holly And The Ivy
130 Holy God, We Praise Thy Name
131 Holy, Holy, Holy
130 Home On The Range
132 Home Sweet Home
131 Honey, Won't You Come Back To Me?
132 Hopak
129 Hot Cross Buns
133 A Hot Time In The Old Town Tonight
133 House Of The Rising Sun
131 How Dry I Am!
362 How 'Ya Gonna Keep 'Em Down On The
        Farm? (After They've Seen Paree)
134 Humoresque
134 Humpty Dumpty
134 Hungarian Dance No. 5
135 Hush, Little Baby

I

363 I Ain't Got Nobody (And Nobody
        Cares For Me)
135 I Am The Captain Of The Pinafore
144 I Gave My Love A Cherry
        (The Riddle Song)
364 I Have A Song To Sing, O!
        (From "The Yeoman Of The Guard")
144 I Heard The Bells On Christmas Day
364 I Love A Piano
137 I Love You Truly
145 I Love You With All My Heart
145 I Saw Three Ships
366 I Surrender All
136 I Want A Girl
366 I Wish I Could Shimmy Like My Sister Kate
146 I Wish I Were Single Again
138 I Wonder Who's Kissing Her Now
367 I'll Be With You In Apple Blossom Time
367 I'll Build A Stairway to Paradise
146 I'll Take You Home Again, Kathleen
368 I'm Always Chasing Rainbows
368 I'm Forever Blowing Bubbles
369 I'm Just Wild About Harry
147 I've Been Working On The Railroad
138 I've Got Rings On My Fingers
148 Ich Liebe Dich (I Love Thee)
139 Ida, Sweet As Apple Cider
140 If I Had My Way
370 If I Knock The 'L' Out Of Kelly
        (It Would Still Be Kelly To Me)
370 If You Were The Only Girl In The World
145 If You're Happy (And You Know It)
149 Il Bacio (The Kiss)
140 In My Merry Oldsmobile
148 In Old New York
150 In The Evening By The Moonlight
371 In The Garden
141 In The Gloaming
151 In The Good Old Summertime
150 In The Hall Of The Mountain King
142 In The Shade Of The Old Apple Tree
152 In The Sweet Bye And Bye
372 Indian Summer
372 Indiana (Back Home Again In Indiana)
154 Invitation To The Dance

373 Ireland Must Be Heaven
        (For My Mother Came From There)
151 Irish Washerwoman
152 It Came Upon The Midnight Clear
156 It's A Long, Long Way To Tipperary
153 It's Raining, It's Pouring
153 Italian Street Song

J

157 Jack And Jill
373 The Japanese Sandman
374 The Jazz-Me Blues
157 Jeanie With The Light Brown Hair
374 Jelly Roll Blues
158 Jenny Lind Polka
156 Jesu, Joy Of Man's Desiring
158 Jesus Loves Me!
159 Jingle Bells
160 John Brown's Body
161 John Henry
159 John Jacob Jingleheimer Schmidt
160 John Peel
161 Johnny Has Gone For A Soldier
376 Johnson Rag
142 Jolly Coppersmith
163 Jolly Old St. Nicholas
164 Joshua Fought The Battle Of Jericho
162 Joy To The World
162 Juanita
164 Julida Polka
163 Just A Closer Walk With Thee
165 Just A Song At Twilight

K

376 Ka-lu-a
181 Keep The Homefires Burning
165 The Kerry Dance
166 King Cotton
378 A Kiss In The Dark
377 Kiss Me Again
378 Kiss Waltz
380 Kitten On The Keys
379 K-K-K-Katy
163 Kum-Bah-Yah

L

382 La Cinquantaine (Golden Wedding)
383 La Cumparsita
167 La Cucaracha
167 La Donna È Mobile
168 La Golondrina
168 La Marseillaise
169 La Paloma
182 La Sorella
381 Lady Of The Evening
170 Largo (From The "New World Symphony")
171 Las Mañanitas
170 Lavender's Blue
171 Lazy Mary, Will You Get Up?
170 Let Me Call You Sweetheart
385 Let The Rest Of The World Go By
171 Let Us Break Bread Together
385 Li'l Liza Jane
172 The Liberty Bell
174 Liebestraum
173 Light Cavalry Overture
386 Limehouse Blues
172 Listen To The Mocking Bird

175 Little Annie Rooney
174 A Little Bit Of Heaven
175 Little Bo Peep
175 Little Boy Blue
177 Little Brown Jug
176 (I'm Called) Little Buttercup
176 Little Jack Horner
177 Little Miss Muffet
386 Little Sir Echo
177 Little Tommy Tucker
178 Lo, How A Rose E'er Blooming
178 Loch Lomond
178 London Bridge
179 Lonesome Road
179 Lonesome Valley
179 Long, Long Ago
180 Looby Loo
387 Look For The Silver Lining
388 The Love Nest
180 Love's Old Sweet Song
388 Lovesick Blues

M

389 Ma (He's Making Eyes At Me)
390 MacNamara's Band
188 Mademoiselle From Armentiers
187 The Man On The Flying Trapeze
188 A Man Without A Woman
390 Mandy
192 Maori Farewell Song
189 Maple Leaf Rag
190 March Of The Toys
191 March Slav (Tchaikovsky)
191 Marche Militaire
391 Margie
190 Marianne
192 Marine's Hymn
194 Martha Polka
195 Mary Had A Little Lamb
181 Mary's A Grand Old Name
181 Matilda
192 Mattinata
195 Mazel Tov
194 Meditation (From "Thais")
182 Meet Me In St. Louis, Louis
196 Meet Me Tonight In Dreamland
197 Melody In A
197 Melody In F
198 Melody Of Love
391 Memories
196 Merrily We Roll Along
184 Merry Widow Waltz
198 Mexican Hat Dance
196 Michael Finnegan
199 Michael, Row The Boat Ashore
193 Midnight Special
193 A Mighty Fortress Is Our God
199 Mighty Lak' A Rose
199 M-I-N-E
183 Minuet In G (Paderewski)
200 The Missouri Waltz
392 Miya Sama (From "The Mikado")
201 Moment Musicale (Schubert)
185 Moonlight Bay
201 Moonlight Sonata (1st Movement)
202 Morning
393 M-O-T-H-E-R (A Word That Means
    The World To Me)
202 The Mulberry Bush
203 Musetta's Waltz
206 My Bonnie
392 My Buddy

206 My Gal Sal
185 My Heart At Thy Sweet Voice
184 My Hero
393 My Honey's Loving Arms
394 My Isle Of Golden Dreams
394 My Little Girl
395 My Mammy
396 My Man
186 My Melancholy Baby
204 My Old Kentucky Home
204 My Wild Irish Rose

N

207 National Emblem
398 Neapolitan Love Song
219 Nearer My God To Thee
208 'Neath The Old Chestnut Tree
208 Nine Hundred Miles
209 Nobody Knows The Trouble I've Seen
210 Nocturne (Chopin)
207 Noel! Noel!
397 Nola
205 Norwegian Dance
211 Now Thank We All Our God
210 Now The Day Is Over

O

211 O Canada!
213 O Christmas Tree
212 O Come, All Ye Faithful
212 O Come, Little Children
214 O Come, O Come Emmanuel
212 O Holy Night
214 O Little Town Of Bethlehem
398 O Mio Babbino Caro
    (From "Gianni Schicchi")
214 O Sanctissima
215 O Sole Mio
216 Oats, Peas, Beans And Barley Grow
215 Oberek
215 Ode To Joy
217 Oh, Dear! What Can The Matter Be?
400 Oh! How I Hate To Get Up In The Morning
399 Oh Johnny, Oh Johnny, Oh!
216 Oh Marie
218 Oh, Promise Me
217 Oh, Susanna
218 Oh, Them Golden Slippers
216 Oh Where, Oh Where Has My Little
    Dog Gone?
232 Oh! You Beautiful Doll
220 The Old Chisholm Trail
221 Old Dan Tucker
222 Old Folks At Home
209 The Old Gray Mare
220 Old Joe Clark
221 Old King Cole
223 Old MacDonald Had A Farm
223 Old Oaken Bucket
401 The Old Refrain
232 On A Sunday Afternoon
224 On The Banks Of The Wabash
401 On The Beach At Waikiki
224 On Top Of Old Smoky
225 On Wisconsin!
225 Once In Royal David's City
226 Onward Christian Soldiers
228 Orange Marmalade Rag
228 Our Director March
226 Over The River And Through The Woods

227 Over The Waves
402 Over There

P

402 Pack Up Your Troubles In Your Old Kit
    Bag And Smile, Smile, Smile
403 Paper Doll
404 Parade Of The Wooden Soldiers
227 Pat-A-Pan
230 Peg O' My Heart
233 Peggy O'Neil
229 Pizzicato Polka
230 Play A Simple Melody
236 Poet And Peasant Overture
235 Polly Wolly Doodle
237 Polonaise, Opus 53 (Chopin)
234 Polovetzian Dance
235 Pomp and Circumstance
403 Poor Butterfly
238 Pop! Goes The Weasel
237 Praise God From Whom All Blessings Flow
238 Prayer Of Thanksgiving
239 Prelude (From "Carmen")
239 Pretty Baby
405 A Pretty Girl Is Like A Melody
233 Put On Your Old Grey Bonnet
231 Put Your Arms Around Me, Honey

R

234 Ragtime Cowboy Joe
240 Rain-Rain Polka (Prsi-Prsi)
240 Red River Valley
248 Red Wing
241 Reuben And Rachel
241 Reverie
242 Ride Of The Valkyries
243 Ring The Banjo
248 Roamin' In The Gloamin'
242 The Rock Island Line
244 Rock Of Ages
243 Rock-A-Bye, Baby
406 Rock-A-Bye Your Baby With A
    Dixie Melody
244 Romance (Rubenstein)
245 Romeo And Juliet
250 Rondeau (Mouret)
250 Rosalie Schottische
245 The Rose Of Tralee
406 Rose Room
407 Roses Of Picardy
246 Roses From The South
249 Row, Row, Row
247 Row, Row, Row Your Boat
408 Royal Garden Blues
409 Runnin' Wild

S

251 Sailing, Sailing
252 Sailor's Hornpipe
251 Salty Dog
252 Santa Lucia
410 Say It With Music
249 Scarborough Fair
253 Schnitzelbank
263 School Days
251 Scotland The Brave (Tunes Of Glory)
410 Second Hand Rose
256 Semper Fidelis
254 Serenade (Drigo)

254 Serenade (Schubert)
255 Serenade (Toselli)
255 Shall We Gather At The River
257 She Is More To Be Pitied Than Censured
257 She Wore A Yellow Ribbon
258 She'll Be Comin' 'Round The Mountain
409 The Sheik Of Araby
258 Shenandoah
276 Shine On Harvest Moon
275 Shoo, Fly, Don't Bother Me
259 Shortnin' Bread
260 The Sidewalks Of New York
260 Silent Night
259 Silver Threads Among The Gold
261 Simple Simon
273 Sing A Song Of Sixpence
262 Sing We Now Of Christmas
261 The Skaters
262 Skip To My Lou
262 Sleep Holy Babe
264 Sleeping Beauty Waltz (Tchaikovsky)
411 Smiles
412 Somebody Stole My Gal
265 Sometimes I Feel Like A Motherless Child
264 Song Of India
412 Song Of The Islands
265 Song Of The Volga Boatman
266 Sound Off
266 Spring Song (Mendelssohn)
267 St. James Infirmary
276 St. Louis Blues
268 The Star Spangled Banner
268 Stars And Stripes Forever
270 The Streets Of Laredo
413 Stumbling
413 Sugar Blues
270 Surprise Symphony (Theme)
271 Swan Lake (Theme)
278 The Swan
414 Swanee
279 Sweet Adeline
271 Sweet And Low
274 Sweet Betsy From Pike
272 Sweet Genevieve
414 Sweet Little Buttercup
278 Sweet Rosie O'Grady
280 The Sweetheart Of Sigma Chi
272 Sweethearts
273 Swing Low, Sweet Chariot

T

287 Ta-Ra-Ra Boom-Der-É
416 Tain't Nobody's Biz-ness If I Do
282 Take Me Out To The Ball Game
290 Tales From The Vienna Woods
279 Tango (Albeniz)
274 Taps
288 Tarantella
287 Tchaikovsky Piano Concerto
    (1st Movement)
289 Tchaikovsky Symphony No. 6
    (1st Movement)

289 Tell Me Why
288 Ten Little Indians
292 Tenting Tonight
415 That Naughty Waltz
417 That Tumble Down Shack In Athlone
280 That's A Plenty
275 That's Why I Do Like I Do
294 There Is A Tavern In The Town
291 There Was An Old Woman Who Lived
    In A Shoe
282 There's A Long, Long Trail
283 They Didn't Believe Me
292 This Old Man
293 This Train
295 Three Blind Mice
417 Three O'Clock In The Morning
295 Thunder And Blazes
296 Thunderer
418 Tiger Rag (Hold That Tiger)
419 Till The Clouds Roll By
418 Till We Meet Again
384 'Tis The Last Rose Of Summer
298 Tinker Polka
419 Tishomingo Blues
298 Tit-Willow
299 To A Wild Rose
283 Too-Ra-Loo-Ra-Loo-Ral
    (That's An Irish Lullaby)
420 Toot, Toot, Tootsie! (Good-bye!)
297 Toreador Song (Bizet)
302 Tourelay, Tourelay
300 Toyland
286 The Trail Of The Lonesome Pine
297 Tramp! Tramp! Tramp!
300 Traumerei
302 Triumphal March (From "Aida")
301 Trumpet Tune
304 Trumpet Voluntary
301 Turkey In The Straw
304 Turkish March
284 12th Street Rag
305 The Twelve Days Of Christmas
303 Twinkle, Twinkle, Little Star
306 Two Guitars

U

306 Under The Double Eagle
308 The Unfinished Symphony (Theme)
309 University Of Michigan Song
307 Up On The Housetop

V

310 Valse Bleue
308 Venetian Boat Song
309 Vienna Life
312 Vilia
310 Vive L'Amour

W

420 Wabash Blues
311 The Wabash Cannon Ball
312 Wait Till The Sun Shines, Nellie
313 Wait For The Wagon
330 Waiting For The Robert E. Lee
313 Waltz (Brahms)
314 Waltz (Chopin)
314 Waltz Of The Flowers
421 The Wang Wang Blues
332 Washington And Lee Swing
316 Washington Post March
421 'Way Down Yonder In New Orleans
316 Wayfaring Stranger
315 We Three Kings Of Orient Are
318 We Wish You A Merry Christmas
318 The Wearing Of The Green
317 Wedding March
319 Were You There?
320 What A Friend We Have In Jesus
321 What Child Is This?
321 When Irish Eyes Are Smiling
320 When Johnny Comes Marching Home
422 When My Baby Smiles At Me
322 When The Saints Go Marching In
324 When You And I Were Young, Maggie
322 When You Were Sweet Sixteen
331 When You Wore A Tulip
324 When You're Away
422 Where Did Robinson Crusoe Go With
    Friday On Saturday Night?
326 While Shepherds Watched Their Flocks
325 While Strolling Through The
    Park One Day
423 Whispering
323 Whispering Hope
332 The Whistler And His Dog
325 White Coral Bells
327 Who Threw The Overalls In Mrs. Murphy's
    Chowder
326 Will The Circle Be Unbroken
328 William Tell Overture
423 The World Is Waiting For The Sunrise
327 Worried Man Blues

Y

423 Yaaka Hula Hickey Dula
329 Yankee Doodle
334 The Yankee Doodle Boy
336 Yellow Rose Of Texas
335 You Are My True Love
424 You Belong To Me
333 You Made Me Love You
335 You Tell Me Your Dream
334 You're A Grand Old Flag

Z

335 Zum Gali Gali

CLASSIFIED LISTING

CHILDREN'S SONGS

10   A-Hunting We Will Go
10   A-Tisket, A-Tasket
15   All God's Children Got Shoes
14   Alouette
15   The Alphabet Song
19   Animal Fair
24   Au Clair De La Lune
38   Baa! Baa! Black Sheep
42   The Barnyard Song (I Had A Rooster)
48   Be Kind To Your Web-Footed Friends
48   The Bear Went Over The Mountain
50   Billy Boy
51   Bingo
51   Blow The Man Down
57   Brahms' Lullaby
63   Camptown Races
77   Chopsticks
72   Country Gardens
84   Did You Ever See A Lassie?
84   Down By The Station
88   Eency, Weency Spider
96   The Farmer In The Dell
101   Frère Jacques
108   Git Along Home, Cindy
111   Go In And Out The Window
109   Go Tell Aunt Rhody
117   Grandfather's Clock
115   The Green Grass Grew All Around
127   Hey, Diddle, Diddle
127   Hey, Ho! Nobody Home
129   Hickory, Dickory, Dock
129   Hot Cross Buns
134   Humpty Dumpty
135   Hush, Little Baby
147   I've Been Working On The Railroad
145   If You're Happy (And You Know It)
153   It's Raining, It's Pouring
157   Jack And Jill
159   John Jacob Jingleheimer Schmidt
171   Lazy Mary, Will You Get Up?
175   Little Bo Peep
175   Little Boy Blue
176   Little Jack Horner
177   Little Miss Muffet
177   Little Tommy Tucker
178   London Bridge
180   Looby Lou
195   Mary Had A Little Lamb
196   Merrily We Roll Along
196   Michael Finnegan
202   The Mulberry Bush
216   Oats, Peas, Beans And Barley Grow
216   Oh Where, Oh Where Has My Little Dog Gone?
209   The Old Gray Mare
221   Old King Cole
223   Old MacDonald Had A Farm
226   Over The River And Through The Woods
235   Polly Wolly Doodle
238   Pop! Goes The Weasel
241   Reuben And Rachel
243   Rock-A-Bye, Baby
247   Row, Row, Row Your Boat
251   Sailing, Sailing
259   Shortnin' Bread
261   Simple Simon
273   Sing A Song Of Sixpence
262   Skip To My Lou
288   Ten Little Indians
291   There Was An Old Woman Who Lived In A Shoe
292   This Old Man
295   Three Blind Mice
302   Tourelay, Tourelay
303   Twinkle, Twinkle, Little Star
325   White Coral Bells

CHRISTMAS

16   All Through The Night
19   Angels We Have Heard On High
22   As With Gladness Men Of Old
27   Away In A Manger (W.J. Kirkpatrick)
27   Away In A Manger (James R. Murray)
27   Away In A Manger (Spillman)
54   The Boar's Head Carol
58   Bring A Torch, Jeannette, Isabella
64   Carol Of The Bells
65   Christ Was Born On Christmas Day
74   The Coventry Carol

80   Dance Of The Sugar-Plum Fairy
81   Deck The Hall
99   The First Noel
103   The Friendly Beasts
110   Go, Tell It On The Mountain
111   God Rest Ye Merry, Gentlemen
113   Good Christian Men, Rejoice
116   Good King Wenceslas
126   Hark! The Herald Angels Sing
128   Here We Come A-Caroling
129   The Holly And The Ivy
144   I Heard The Bells On Christmas Day
145   I Saw Three Ships
152   It Came Upon The Midnight Clear
159   Jingle Bells
163   Jolly Old St. Nicholas
162   Joy To The World
178   Lo, How A Rose E'er Blooming
190   March Of The Toys
207   Noel! Noel!
213   O Christmas Tree
212   O Come, All Ye Faithful
212   O Come, Little Children
214   O Come, O Come Emmanuel
212   O Holy Night
214   O Little Town Of Bethlehem
214   O Sanctissima
225   Once In Royal David's City
227   Pat-A-Pan
260   Silent Night
262   Sing We Now Of Christmas
262   Sleep Holy Babe
305   The Twelve Days Of Christmas
307   Up On The Housetop
315   We Three Kings Of Orient Are
318   We Wish You A Merry Christmas
321   What Child Is This?
326   While Sheperds Watched Their Flocks

CLASSICS

14   Air (On The G String)
37   Also Sprach Zarathustra
11   Andante Cantabile (Tchaikovsky)
21   Anvil Chorus
25   Ave Maria (Bach/Gounod)
26   Ave Maria (Schubert)
41   The Barber Of Seville Overture
40   Barcarolle
46   Beethoven's 5th Symphony (1st Movement Theme)
55   Blue Danube Waltz
57   Brahms' Lullaby
56   Bridal Chorus (From "Lohengrin")
62   Can Can
61   Cantabile
61   Capriccio Italien Theme
66   Chopin Ballade No. 1
69   Clair De Lune
78   Concerto Theme (Rachmaninoff) (Concerto No. 2, 1st Movement)
78   Concerto Theme (Rachmaninoff) (Concerto No. 2, 3rd Movement)
82   Dance Of The Hours
80   Dance Of The Sugar-Plum Fairy
83   Danube Waves
352   Dona Nobis Pacem
90   Eine Kleine Nachtmusik (Opening Theme)
91   Elegie
95   Fantasie Impromptu (Chopin)
105   Finlandia
102   Funeral March Of A Marionette
102   Funeral March
103   Für Elise
107   Gavotte
112   Gold And Silver Waltz
118   Grieg Piano Concerto (Theme)
120   Gypsy Rondo
122   Hallelujah Chorus
124   The Happy Farmer
132   Hopak
134   Humoresque
134   Hungarian Dance No. 5
135   I Am The Captain Of The Pinafore
364   I Have A Song To Sing, O! (From "The Yeoman Of The Guard")
148   Ich Liebe Dich (I Love Thee)
149   Il Bacio (The Kiss)
150   In The Hall Of The Mountain King
154   Invitation To The Dance
156   Jesu, Joy Of Man's Desiring

167   La Donna È Mobile
170   Largo (From "The New World Symphony")
174   Liebestraum
173   Light Cavalry Overture
176   (I'm Called) Little Buttercup
191   March Slav (Tchaikovsky)
191   Marche Militaire
192   Mattinata
194   Meditation (From "Thais")
197   Melody In F
184   Merry Widow Waltz
183   Minuet in G (Paderewski)
201   Moment Musicale (Schubert)
201   Moonlight Sonata (1st Movement)
202   Morning
203   Musetta's Waltz
185   My Heart At Thy Sweet Voice
210   Nocturne (Chopin)
205   Norwegian Dance
215   Ode To Joy
401   The Old Refrain
398   O Mio Babbino Caro (From "Gianni Schicchi")
229   Pizzicato Polka
236   Poet And Peasant Overture
237   Polonaise, Opus 53 (Chopin)
234   Polovetzian Dance
239   Prelude (From "Carmen")
241   Reverie
242   Ride Of The Valkyries
244   Romance (Rubenstein)
245   Romeo And Juliet
250   Rondeau (Mouret)
254   Serenade (Drigo)
254   Serenade (Schubert)
255   Serenade (Toselli)
261   The Skaters
264   Sleeping Beauty Waltz (Tchaikovsky)
264   Song Of India
266   Spring Song (Mendelssohn)
270   Surprise Symphony (Theme)
271   Swan Lake (Theme)
278   The Swan
290   Tales From The Vienna Woods
279   Tango (Albeniz)
287   Tchaikovsky Piano Concerto (1st Movement)
289   Tchaikovsky Symphony No. 6 (1st Movement)
298   Tit-Willow
299   To A Wild Rose
297   Toreador Song (Bizet)
300   Traumerei
302   Triumphal March (From "Aida")
301   Trumpet Tune
304   Trumpet Voluntary
304   Turkish March
306   Two Guitars
308   The Unfinished Symphony (Theme)
310   Valse Bleue
308   Venetian Boat Song
309   Vienna Life
313   Waltz (Brahms)
314   Waltz (Chopin)
314   Waltz Of The Flowers
317   Wedding March
328   William Tell Overture

COUNTRY/BLUEGRASS

341   Any Time
23   Arkansas Traveler
25   Aura Lee
43   Beautiful Brown Eyes
59   Bury Me Not On The Lone Prairie
65   Careless Love
75   Cripple Creek
87   Down In The Valley
109   Git Along, Little Dogies
116   Goodbye, Old Paint
117   Grandfather's Clock
130   Home On The Range
152   In The Sweet Bye And Bye
388   Lovesick Blues
220   The Old Chisholm Trail
220   Old Joe Clark
224   On Top Of Old Smoky
240   Red River Valley
248   Red Wing
242   The Rock Island Line
251   Salty Dog
301   Turkey In The Straw
326   Will The Circle Be Unbroken

FOLK SONGS

15	All My Trials
16	All Through The Night
14	Alouette
17	Amazing Grace
20	Annabel Lee
22	Annie Laurie
23	Arkansas Traveler
24	Auld Lang Syne
25	Aura Lee
38	The Banana Boat Song
39	Banks Of The Ohio
39	Barbara Allen
43	Beautiful Brown Eyes
45	Believe Me If All Those Endearing Young Charms
49	The Big Rock Candy Mountain
49	Black Is The Color
52	Blood On The Saddle
51	Blow The Man Down
53	The Blue Bells Of Scotland
54	Bluetail Fly
56	The Boll Weevil
58	Buckeye Jim
59	Buffalo Gals
59	Bury Me Not On The Lone Prairie
65	Careless Love
69	Clementine
74	The Crawdad Song
75	Cripple Creek
76	The Cruel War Is Raging
84	Dixie
87	Down In The Valley
87	Drink To Me Only With Thine Eyes
85	The Drunken Sailor
91	The Erie Canal
97	Flow Gently, Sweet Afton
98	The Foggy, Foggy Dew
100	Frankie And Johnny
96	Freight Train
99	Froggie Went A-Courtin'
111	The Girl I Left Behind
108	Git Along Home, Cindy
109	Git Along, Little Dogies
115	Goober Peas
116	Goodbye, Old Paint
118	Green Grow The Lilacs
119	Greensleeves
126	Hear Them Bells
132	Home Sweet Home
133	House Of The Rising Sun
144	I Gave My Love A Cherry (The Riddle Song)
147	I've Been Working On The Railroad
160	John Brown's Body
161	John Henry
161	Johnny Has Gone For A Soldier
170	Lavender's Blue
385	Li'l Liza Jane
177	Little Brown Jug
179	Lonesome Road
190	Marianne
181	Matilda
199	Michael, Row The Boat Ashore
193	Midnight Special
206	My Bonnie
208	Nine Hundred Miles
218	Oh, Them Golden Slippers
220	The Old Chisholm Trail
221	Old Dan Tucker
220	Old Joe Clark
224	On Top Of Old Smoky
240	Red River Valley
242	The Rock Island Line
245	The Rose Of Tralee
252	Sailor's Hornpipe
251	Salty Dog
249	Scarborough Fair
257	She Wore A Yellow Ribbon
258	She'll Be Comin' 'Round The Mountain
258	Shenandoah
275	Shoo, Fly, Don't Bother Me
259	Shortnin' Bread
262	Skip To My Lou
265	Sometimes I Feel Like A Motherless Child
267	St. James Infirmary
270	The Streets Of Laredo
271	Sweet And Low
274	Sweet Betsy From Pike
293	This Train
301	Turkey In The Straw
312	Vilia
313	Wait For The Wagon
316	Wayfaring Stranger
320	When Johnny Comes Marching Home
327	Worried Man Blues
329	Yankee Doodle
336	The Yellow Rose Of Texas

FROM THE MUSICAL STAGE

13	Ah! Sweet Mystery Of Life
342	Auf Wiedersehn
119	Gypsy Love Song
120	Habañera (From "Carmen")
360	He Is An Englishman (From "H.M.S. Pinafore")
135	I Am The Captain Of The Pinafore
364	I Have A Song To Sing, O! (From "The Yeoman Of The Guard")
148	In Old New York
153	Italian Street Song
378	A Kiss In The Dark
377	Kiss Me Again
167	La Donna È Mobile (From "Rigoletto")
176	(I'm Called) Little Buttercup
194	Meditation (From "Thais")
184	Merry Widow Waltz
392	Miya Sama (From "The Mikado")
203	Musetta's Waltz
239	Prelude (From "Carmen")
242	Ride Of The Valkyries
419	Till The Clouds Roll By
298	Tit-Willow
297	Toreador Song (Bizet)
302	Triumphal March (From "Aida")
330	Waiting For The Robert E. Lee

INSPIRATIONAL

10	Abide With Me
15	All God's Children Got Shoes
15	All My Trials
17	Amazing Grace
43	The Battle Hymn Of The Republic
48	Beautiful Isle Of Somewhere
45	Beautiful Savior
44	Behold The Savior Of Mankind
53	Blessed Assurance
50	Blest Be The Tie That Binds
57	Bringing In The Sheaves
67	Christ The Lord Is Ris'n Today
67	The Church In The Wildwood
73	Come, Thou Almighty King
75	Crown Him With Many Crowns
80	Deep River
352	Dona Nobis Pacem
88	Dry Bones
94	Ev'ry Time I Feel The Spirit
94	Ezekiel Saw The Wheel
95	Faith Of Our Fathers
108	Give Me That Old Time Religion
357	Go Down, Moses
107	God Of Our Fathers
122	Hallelujah Chorus
126	He's Got The Whole World In His Hands
362	His Eye Is On The Sparrow
130	Holy God, We Praise Thy Name
131	Holy, Holy, Holy
366	I Surrender All
371	In The Garden
152	In The Sweet Bye And Bye
158	Jesus Loves Me!
164	Joshua Fought The Battle Of Jericho
163	Just A Closer Walk With Thee
163	Kum-Bah-Yah
171	Let Us Break Bread Together
179	Lonesome Valley
199	Michael, Row The Boat Ashore
193	A Mighty Fortress Is Our God
219	Nearer My God To Thee
209	Nobody Knows The Trouble I've Seen
211	Now Thank We All Our God
210	Now The Day Is Over
218	Oh, Promise Me
226	Onward Christian Soldiers
237	Praise God From Whom All Blessings Flow
238	Prayer Of Thanksgiving
244	Rock Of Ages
255	Shall We Gather At The River
273	Swing Low, Sweet Chariot
319	Were You There?
320	What A Friend We Have In Jesus
322	When The Saints Go Marching In
326	Will The Circle Be Unbroken

INTERNATIONAL FAVORITES

11	Ach, Du Lieber Augustin
29	Adios Muchachos
16	Aloha Oe
14	Alouette
22	Annie Laurie
24	Au Clair De La Lune
24	Auld Lang Syne
40	Barbara Polka
53	The Blue Bells Of Scotland
55	Blue Danube Waltz
60	The Campbells Are Coming
62	Can Can
61	Capriccio Italien Theme
65	Carnival Of Venice
66	Chiapanecas
68	Cielito Lindo
68	Ciribiribin
71	Clarinet Polka
70	Cockles And Mussels (Molly Malone)
70	Come Back To Sorrento
73	Come To The Sea
73	Comin' Through The Rye
72	Country Gardens
83	Dark Eyes
89	Du, Du Liegst Mir Im Herzen
93	Emilia Polka
356	Estrellita
354	Estudiantina
105	Finlandia
101	Frère Jacques
101	Funiculi, Funicula
114	God Save Our King (Queen)
125	Hatikvah
125	Hava Nagilah
127	Helena Polka
151	Irish Washerwoman
153	Italian Street Song
158	Jenny Lind Polka
160	John Peel
162	Juanita
164	Julida Polka
165	The Kerry Dance
382	La Cinquantaine (Golden Wedding)
167	La Cucaracha
383	La Cumparsita
168	La Golondrina
168	La Marseillaise
169	La Paloma
171	Las Mañanitas
178	Loch Lomond
192	Maori Farewell Song
194	Martha Polka
195	Mazel Tov
198	Mexican Hat Dance
398	Neapolitan Love Song
205	Norwegian Dance
211	O Canada!
215	O Sole Mio
215	Oberek
216	Oh Marie
229	Pizzicato Polka
240	Rain-Rain Polka (Prsi-Prsi)
250	Rosalie Schottische
252	Santa Lucia
253	Schnitzelbank
265	Song Of The Volga Boatman
288	Tarantella
298	Tinker Polka
384	'Tis The Last Rose Of Summer
306	Two Guitars
310	Vive L'Amour
318	The Wearing Of The Green
335	Zum Gali Gali

MARCHES

23	American Cadets March
18	The American Patrol
28	Anchors Aweigh
48	Be Kind To Your Web-Footed Friends
32	The Billboard March
35	Boola! Boola!
60	The Caissons Go Rolling Along
349	Colonel Bogey March

72 Columbia, The Gem Of The Ocean
79 Down The Field
89 El Capitan
95 Fight Ye Bulldogs
105 Finlandia
110 Gladiator March
123 Hail To The Chief
128 High School Cadets
156 It's A Long, Long Way To Tipperary
142 Jolly Coppersmith
166 King Cotton
168 La Marseillaise
182 La Sorella
172 The Liberty Bell
191 March Slav (Tchaikovsky)
191 Marche Militaire
192 Marine's Hymn
207 National Emblem
225 On Wisconsin!
228 Our Director March
404 Parade Of The Wooden Soldiers
235 Pomp And Circumstance
250 Rondeau (Mouret)
251 Scotland The Brave (Tunes Of Glory)
256 Semper Fidelis
266 Sound Off
268 Stars And Stripes Forever
295 Thunder And Blazes
296 Thunderer
297 Tramp! Tramp! Tramp!
304 Turkish March
306 Under The Double Eagle
309 University Of Michigan Song
332 Washington And Lee Swing
316 Washington Post March
320 When Johnny Comes Marching Home
322 When The Saints Go Marching In
329 Yankee Doodle
336 The Yellow Rose Of Texas
334 You're A Grand Old Flag

PATRIOTIC

17 America (My Country, 'Tis Of Thee)
18 America, The Beautiful
28 Anchors Aweigh
20 Assembly/Reveille
43 The Battle Hymn Of The Republic
60 The Caissons Go Rolling Along
72 Columbia, The Gem Of The Ocean
359 Good-Bye Broadway, Hello France
121 Hail, Columbia
123 Hail To The Chief
172 The Liberty Bell
192 Marine's Hymn
402 Over There
256 Semper Fidelis
268 The Star Spangled Banner
268 Stars And Stripes Forever
274 Taps
329 Yankee Doodle
334 You're A Grand Old Flag

SENTIMENTAL

12 After The Ball
22 Annie Laurie
25 Aura Lee
39 Banks Of The Ohio
39 Barbara Allen
44 Beautiful Dreamer
33 Because
45 Believe Me If All Those Endearing Young Charms
59 Bury Me Not On The Lone Prairie
85 Dog-gone Blues
97 Flow Gently, Sweet Afton
105 Goodbye, My Lady Love
117 Grandfather's Clock
118 Green Grow The Lilacs
119 Greensleeves
119 Gypsy Love Song
124 Hearts And Flowers
132 Home Sweet Home
131 Honey, Won't You Come Back To Me?
144 I Gave My Love A Cherry (The Riddle Song)
137 I Love You Truly
145 I Love You With All My Heart
146 I'll Take You Home Again, Kathleen
148 Ich Liebe Dich (I Love Thee)

141 In The Gloaming
157 Jeanie With The Light Brown Hair
161 Johnny Has Gone For A Soldier
165 Just A Song At Twilight
179 Long, Long Ago
180 Love's Old Sweet Song
208 'Neath The Old Chestnut Tree
218 Oh, Promise Me
414 Sweet Little Buttercup
299 To A Wild Rose

SINGALONGS

28 The Aba Daba Honeymoon
12 After The Ball
30 Alexander's Ragtime Band
24 Auld Lang Syne
38 The Band Played On
48 Be Kind To Your Web-Footed Friends
31 Be My Little Baby Bumblebee
46 A Bicycle Built For Two (Daisy Bell)
52 Bill Bailey, Won't You Please Come Home?
34 A Bird In A Gilded Cage
55 The Bowery
36 By The Beautiful Sea
36 By The Light Of The Silvery Moon
63 Camptown Races
64 Carry Me Back To Old Virginny
77 Chinatown, My Chinatown
79 Come, Josephine In My Flying Machine
81 The Desperado
84 Dixie
86 Down By The Old Mill Stream
86 Down By the Riverside
87 Drink To Me Only With Thine Eyes
105 Fascination
96 For He's A Jolly Good Fellow
104 Forty-Five Minutes From Broadway
106 Give My Regards To Broadway
114 Good Night Ladies
114 Goodbye Girls, I'm Through
105 Goodbye, My Lady Love
115 The Green Grass Grew All Around
124 Hail! Hail! The Gang's All Here
123 Hand Me Down My Walking Cane
136 Harrigan
137 Hello! My Baby
361 Hinky Dinky Parley Voo
130 Home On The Range
131 How Dry I Am!
137 I Love You Truly
136 I Want A Girl
146 I Wish I Were Single Again
138 I Wonder Who's Kissing Her Now
146 I'll Take You Home Again, Kathleen
138 I've Got Rings On My Fingers
139 Ida, Sweet As Apple Cider
140 If I Had My Way
370 If I Knock The 'L' Out Of Kelly
       (It Would Still Be Kelly To Me)
140 In My Merry Oldsmobile
148 In Old New York
150 In The Evening By The Moonlight
151 In The Good Old Summertime
142 In The Shade Of The Old Apple Tree
372 Ireland Must Be Heaven
       (For My Mother Came From There)
156 It's A Long, Long Way To Tipperary
157 Jeanie With The Light Brown Hair
160 John Peel
165 Just A Song At Twilight
379 K-K-K-Katy
181 Keep The Homefires Burning
170 Let Me Call You Sweetheart
385 Let The Rest Of The World Go By
175 Little Annie Rooney
177 Little Brown Jug
180 Love's Old Sweet Song
390 MacNamara's Band
188 Mademoiselle From Armentieres
187 The Man On The Flying Trapeze
188 A Man Without A Woman
190 Marianne
181 Mary's A Grand Old Name
182 Meet Me In St. Louis, Louis
196 Meet Me Tonight In Dreamland
196 Merrily We Roll Along
199 M-I-N-E
200 The Missouri Waltz

185 Moonlight Bay
206 My Bonnie
206 My Gal Sal
184 My Hero
186 My Melancholy Baby
204 My Wild Irish Rose
217 Oh, Susanna
232 Oh! You Beautiful Doll
222 Old Folks At Home
209 The Old Gray Mare
223 Old Oaken Bucket
232 On A Sunday Afternoon
224 On The Banks Of The Wabash
230 Peg O' My Heart
230 Play A Simple Melody
233 Put On Your Old Grey Bonnet
231 Put Your Arms Around Me, Honey
234 Ragtime Cowboy Joe
248 Roamin' In The Gloamin'
249 Row, Row, Row
253 Schnitzelbank
263 School Days
257 She Is More To Be Pitied Than Censured
257 She Wore A Yellow Ribbon
276 Shine On Harvest Moon
260 The Sidewalks Of New York
259 Silver Threads Among The Gold
279 Sweet Adeline
272 Sweet Genevieve
278 Sweet Rosie O'Grady
280 The Sweetheart Of Sigma Chi
287 Ta-Ra-Ra Boom-Der-É
282 Take Me Out To The Ball Game
292 Tenting Tonight
294 There Is A Tavern In The Town
282 There's A Long, Long Trail
283 They Didn't Believe Me
283 Too-Ra-Loo-Ra-Loo-Ral (That's An Irish Lullaby)
286 The Trail Of The Lonesome Pine
284 12th Street Rag
310 Vive L'Amour
311 The Wabash Cannon Ball
312 Wait Till The Sun Shines, Nellie
330 Waiting For The Robert E. Lee
332 Washington And Lee Swing
321 When Irish Eyes Are Smiling
324 When You And I Were Young, Maggie
322 When You Were Sweet Sixteen
331 When You Wore A Tulip
324 When You're Away
325 While Strolling Through The Park One Day
323 Whispering Hope
327 Who Threw The Overalls In Mrs. Murphy's
       Chowder
334 The Yankee Doodle Boy
333 You Made Me Love You
335 You Tell Me Your Dream

SPECIAL OCCASION

24 Auld Lang Syne
25 Ave Maria (Bach/Gounod)
26 Ave Maria (Schubert)
33 Because
44 The Birthday Song
56 Bridal Chorus (From "Lohengrin")
83 Danube Waves
125 Hava Nagilah
137 I Love You Truly
218 Oh, Promise Me
226 Over The River And Through The Woods
235 Pomp And Circumstance
301 Trumpet Tune
304 Trumpet Voluntary
317 Wedding March
335 You Are My True Love

STANDARDS

28 The Aba Daba Honeymoon
12 After The Ball
338 After You've Gone
338 Ain't We Got Fun?
339 Alabama Jubilee
30 Alexander's Ragtime Band
340 All By Myself
16 Aloha Oe
342 April Showers
343 Avalon

24 Auld Lang Syne
343 Baby, Won't You Please Come Home
38 The Band Played On
31 Be My Little Baby Bumblebee
344 Beale Street Blues
33 Because
345 The Bells Of St. Mary's
46 A Bicycle Built For Two (Daisy Bell)
52 Bill Bailey, Won't You Please Come Home?
34 A Bird In A Gilded Cage
55 The Bowery
36 By The Beautiful Sea
36 By The Light Of The Silvery Moon
346 Canadian Capers
64 Carry Me Back To Old Virginny
348 Carolina In The Morning
348 Chicago (That Toddlin' Town)
77 Chinatown, My Chinatown
347 Cohen Owes Me Ninety-Seven Dollars
79 Come, Josephine In My Flying Machine
77 Cuddle Up A Little Closer, Lovey Mine
76 Danny Boy
350 Dardanella
351 The Darktown Strutters' Ball
81 The Desperado
351 Do It Again
354 Down Among The Sheltering Palms
86 Down By The Old Mill Stream
86 Down By The Riverside
353 Down Yonder
90 The Entertainer
98 Far Above Cayuga's Waters
105 Fascination
356 For Me And My Gal
104 Forty-Five Minutes From Broadway
358 The Girl On The Magazine Cover
106 Give My Regards To Broadway
106 Glow Worm
359 A Good Man Is Hard To Find
114 Goodbye Girls, I'm Through
136 Harrigan
137 Hello! My Baby
360 Hindustan
133 A Hot Time In The Old Town Tonight
362 How 'Ya Gonna Keep 'Em Down On The Farm?
   (After They've Seen Paree)
363 I Ain't Got Nobody (And Nobody Cares For Me)
364 I Love A Piano
136 I Want A Girl
366 I Wish I Could Shimmy Like My Sister Kate
138 I Wonder Who's Kissing Her Now
367 I'll Build A Stairway To Paradise
368 I'm Always Chasing Rainbows
369 I'm Just Wild About Harry
138 I've Got Rings On My Fingers
139 Ida, Sweet As Apple Cider
140 If I Had My Way
140 In My Merry Oldsmobile
148 In Old New York
150 In The Evening By The Moonlight
141 In The Gloaming
151 In The Good Old Summertime
142 In The Shade Of The Old Apple Tree
372 Indian Summer
372 Indiana (Back Home Again In Indiana)
373 The Japanese Sandman
374 The Jazz-Me Blues
374 Jelly Roll Blues
376 Johnson Rag
376 Ka-lu-a
379 K-K-K-Katy
181 Keep The Homefires Burning
380 Kitten On The Keys
381 Lady Of The Evening
170 Let Me Call You Sweetheart
386 Limehouse Blues
172 Listen To The Mocking Bird
175 Little Annie Rooney
174 A Little Bit Of Heaven
179 Long, Long Ago
387 Look For The Silver Lining
388 The Love Nest
180 Love's Old Sweet Song
389 Ma (He's Making Eyes At Me)
188 Mademoiselle From Armentiers
187 The Man On The Flying Trapeze
188 A Man Without A Woman

390 Mandy
189 Maple Leaf Rag
391 Margie
181 Mary's A Grand Old Name
182 Meet Me In St. Louis, Louis
196 Meet Me Tonight In Dreamland
197 Melody In A
199 Mighty Lak' A Rose
199 M-I-N-E
200 The Missouri Waltz
185 Moonlight Bay
393 M-O-T-H-E-R (A Word That Means
   The World To Me)
206 My Gal Sal
184 My Hero
393 My Honey's Loving Arms
394 My Little Girl
395 My Mammy
396 My Man
186 My Melancholy Baby
204 My Old Kentucky Home
204 My Wild Irish Rose
397 Nola
400 Oh! How I Hate To Get Up In The Morning
399 Oh Johnny, Oh Johnny, Oh!
217 Oh, Susanna
232 Oh! You Beautiful Doll
222 Old Folks At Home
223 Old Oaken Bucket
232 On A Sunday Afternoon
224 On The Banks Of The Wabash
401 On The Beach At Waikiki
228 Orange Marmalade Rag
402 Pack Up Your Troubles In Your Old Kit Bag And
   Smile, Smile, Smile
403 Paper Doll
230 Peg O' My Heart
230 Play A Simple Melody
403 Poor Butterfly
239 Pretty Baby
405 A Pretty Girl Is Like A Melody
233 Put On Your Old Grey Bonnet
231 Put Your Arms Around Me, Honey
234 Ragtime Cowboy Joe
248 Red Wing
243 Ring The Banjo
248 Roamin' In The Gloamin'
406 Rock-A-Bye Your Baby With A Dixie Melody
406 Rose Room
407 Roses Of Picardy
249 Row, Row, Row
408 Royal Garden Blues
409 Runnin' Wild
410 Say It With Music
263 School Days
410 Second Hand Rose
257 She Is More To Be Pitied Than Censured
409 The Sheik of Araby
276 Shine On Harvest Moon
260 The Sidewalks Of New York
259 Silver Threads Among The Gold
411 Smiles
412 Somebody Stole My Gal
412 Song Of The Islands
276 St. Louis Blues
413 Stumbling
413 Sugar Blues
414 Swanee
279 Sweet Adeline
272 Sweet Genevieve
278 Sweet Rosie O'Grady
280 The Sweetheart Of Sigma Chi
272 Sweethearts
287 Ta-Ra-Ra Boom-Der-É
416 Tain't Nobody's Biz-ness If I Do
282 Take Me Out To The Ball Game
289 Tell Me Why
292 Tenting Tonight
417 That Tumble Down Shack In Athlone
280 That's A Plenty
275 That's Why I Do Like I Do
282 There's A Long, Long Trail
283 They Didn't Believe Me
418 Tiger Rag (Hold That Tiger)
419 Till The Clouds Roll By
419 Tishomingo Blues
283 Too-Ra-Loo-Ra-Loo-Ral (That's An Irish Lullaby)

420 Toot, Toot, Tootsie! (Good-bye!)
300 Toyland
286 The Trail Of The Lonesome Pine
284 12th Street Rag
420 Wabash Blues
311 The Wabash Cannon Ball
330 Waiting For The Robert E. Lee
421 The Wang Wang Blues
332 Washington And Lee Swing
421 'Way Down Yonder In New Orleans
321 When Irish Eyes Are Smiling
422 When My Baby Smiles At Me
324 When You And I Were Young, Maggie
322 When You Were Sweet Sixteen
331 When You Wore A Tulip
324 When You're Away
422 Where Did Robinson Crusoe Go With Friday
   On Saturday Night?
325 While Strolling Through The Park One Day
423 Whispering
323 Whispering Hope
332 The Whistler And His Dog
327 Who Threw The Overalls In Mrs. Murphy's
   Chowder
423 The World Is Waiting For The Sunrise
423 Yaaka Hula Hickey Dula
333 You Made Me Love You
335 You Tell Me Your Dream

WALTZES

11 Ach, Du Lieber Augustin
12 After The Ball
340 Alice Blue Gown
345 Beautiful Ohio
55 Blue Danube Waltz
68 Cielito Lindo
79 Come, Josephine In My Flying Machine
352 Dolores Waltz
92 Emperor Waltz
354 Estudiantina
105 Fascination
97 Fledermaus Waltz
104 Forty-Five Minutes From Broadway
112 Gold And Silver Waltz
118 Green Grow The Lilacs
117 Grey And Gold Waltz
137 I Love You Truly
138 I Wonder Who's Kissing Her Now
367 I'll Be With You In Apple Blossom Time
368 I'm Forever Blowing Bubbles
370 If You Were The Only Girl In The World
149 Il Bacio (The Kiss)
140 In My Merry Oldsmobile
151 In The Good Old Summertime
378 Kiss Waltz
377 Kiss Me Again
168 La Golondrina
385 Let The Rest Of The World Go By
386 Little Sir Echo
198 Melody Of Love
391 Memories
184 Merry Widow Waltz
200 The Missouri Waltz
392 My Buddy
184 My Hero
394 My Isle Of Golden Dreams
216 Oh Marie
232 On A Sunday Afternoon
227 Over The Waves
233 Peggy O'Neil
246 Roses From The South
252 Santa Lucia
278 Sweet Rosie O'Grady
272 Sweethearts
290 Tales From The Vienna Woods
289 Tell Me Why
415 That Naughty Waltz
417 Three O'Clock In The Morning
418 Till We Meet Again
310 Valse Bleue
309 Vienna Life
313 Waltz (Brahms)
314 Waltz (Chopin)
314 Waltz Of The Flowers
424 You Belong To Me

A-HUNTING WE WILL GO

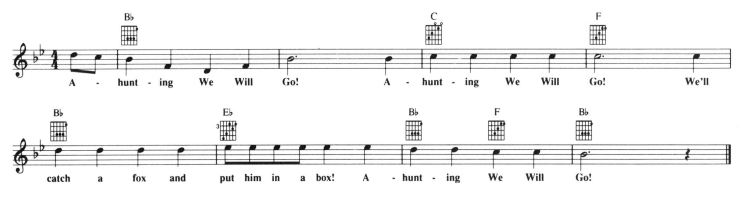

A - hunt - ing We Will Go! A - hunt - ing We Will Go! We'll catch a fox and put him in a box! A - hunt - ing We Will Go!

A-TISKET, A-TASKET

A Tis - kit, A Tas - ket, a green and yel - low bas - ket, I wrote a let - ter to my love and on the way I dropped it, I dropped it, I dropped it, and on the way I dropped it, A lit - tle boy picked it up and put it in his poc - ket.
(girl)   (her)

ABIDE WITH ME

Words by Henry F. Lyte; Music by William H. Monk

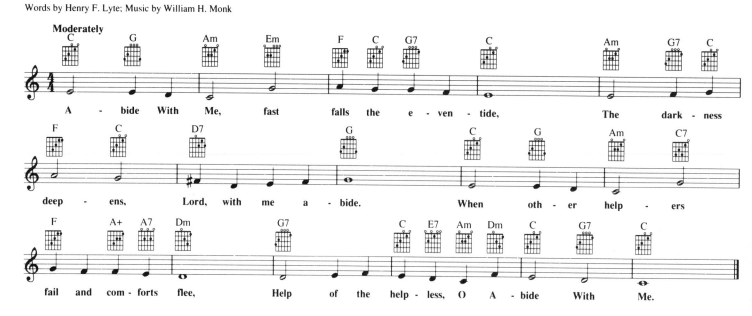

A - bide With Me, fast falls the e - ven - tide, The dark - ness deep - ens, Lord, with me a - bide. When oth - er help - ers fail and com - forts flee, Help of the help - less, O A - bide With Me.

ACH, DU LIEBER AUGUSTIN

Ach, Du Lie - ber Au - gus - tin, Au - gus - tin, Au - gus - tin,

Ach, Du Lie - ber Au - gus - tin, al - les ist weg:

Bock ist weg, stock ist weg, Auch ich bin in dem dreck

Ach, Du Lie - ber Au - gus - tin, al - les ist weg.

ANDANTE CANTABILE
(Tchaikovsky)

P.I. Tchaikovsky

AFTER THE BALL

Words and Music by Charles K. Harris

1. A little maiden climbed an old man's knee, Begged for a story, "Do, uncle, please! Why are you single; why live alone? Have you no babies, have you no home?" "I had a sweetheart, years, years ago; Where she is now, pet, you will soon know. List to the story, I'll tell it all, I believed her faithless, after The Ball."

2. "Bright lights were flashing in the grand ballroom, Softly the music, playing sweet tunes, There came my sweetheart, my love, my own, "I wish some water; leave me alone." When I returned, dear, there stood a man, Kissing my sweetheart, as lovers can. Down fell the glass, pet, broken that's all, Just as my heart was, after The Ball."

3. (See additional lyrics)

Chorus

After The Ball is over, After the break of morn, After the dancers' leaving; After the stars are

gone; _____ Man - y a heart is ach - ing, If you could read them all; _____
_____ Man - y the hopes that have van - ish'd Af - ter The Ball. _____

Additional Lyrics

3. Long years have passed, child. I've never wed,
True to my lost love, though she is dead.
She tried to tell me, tried to explain;
I would not listen, pleadings were vain.
One day a letter came from that man;
He was her brother, the letter ran.
That's why I'm lonely, no home at all;
I broke her heart After The Ball.

AH! SWEET MYSTERY OF LIFE

Lyric by Rida Johnson Young
Music by Victor Herbert

Ah! Sweet Mys - ter - y Of Life, at last I've found thee, Ah! I know at last the sec - ret of it

all; All the long - ing, seek - ing, striv - ing, wait - ing, yearn - ing, The burn - ing hopes, the joy and i - dle tears that

fall! _____ For 'tis love, and love a - lone, the world is seek - ing; And 'tis
love, and love a - lone, the world is seek - ing; For 'tis

love, and love a - lone, that can re - pay! 'Tis the an - swer, 'tis the end and all of
love, and love a - lone, that can re - pay! 'Tis the an - swer, 'tis the end and all of

liv - ing, _____ For it is love a - lone that rules for aye! For 'tis
liv - ing, _____ For it is love a - lone that rules for aye! _____

AIR
(On The G String)

J.S. Bach

ALOUETTE

A - lou - et - te, gen - tille A - lou - et - te, A - lou - et - te, je te plu - me - rai.

Je te plu - me - rai la tete, Je te plu - me - rai la tete, Et la tete, et la tete, Et la tete, et la tete, O!

A - lou - et - te, gen - tille A - lou - et - te, A - lou - et - te, je te plu - me - rai.

ALL GOD'S CHILDREN GOT SHOES

ALL MY TRIALS

THE ALPHABET SONG

ALL THROUGH THE NIGHT

Moderately

Sleep, my Child and peace at-tend Thee, All Through The Night; Guard-ian an-gels
While the moon her watch is keep-ing, All Through The Night; While the wear-y
You, my God, a Babe of won-der, All Through The Night; Dreams you dream can't

God will send Thee, All Through The Night. Soft the drow-sy hours are creep-ing, Hill and vale in
world is sleep-ing, All Through The Night, Through your dreams you're swift-ly steal-ing, Vis-ions of de-
break from thun-der, All Through The Night. Chil-dren's dreams can not be brok-en; Life is but a

slum-ber sleep-ing, God His lov-ing vig-il keep-ing, All Through The Night.
light re-veal-ing. Christ-mas time is so ap-peal-ing, All Through The Night.
love-ly tok-en. Christ-mas should be soft-ly spok-en All Through The Night.

ALOHA OE

Words and Music by Queen Liliuokalani

Slowly

Proud-ly swept the rain cloud by the cliff As on it glid-ed through the trees. Still __

fol-low-ing with grief the li-ko, The a-mi-mi-le-mua of the vale. Fare-

well to thee, fare-well to thee, Thou charm-ing one who dwells a-mong the bow-ers. One

fond em-brace be-fore I now de-part, Un-til we meet __ a-gain.

AMAZING GRACE

1. A - maz - ing___ Grace! How sweet the sound That saved a ___
2 - 5. *(See additional lyrics)*

wretch like me!___ I once ___ was lost but now ___ am

found; Was blind, but ___ now I see. ___ 'Twas me. ___

Additional Lyrics

2. 'Twas grace that taught my heart to fear,
   And grace my fears relieved;
   How precious did that grace appear
   The hour I first believed.

3. Thro' many dangers, toils and snares,
   I have already come;
   'Tis grace hath bro't me safe thus far,
   And grace will lead me home.

4. How sweet the name of Jesus sounds
   In a believer's ear.
   It soothes his sorrows, heals his wounds,
   And drives away his fear.

5. Must Jesus bear the cross alone
   And all the world go free?
   No, there's a cross for ev'ry one
   And there's a cross for me.

AMERICA
(My Country, 'Tis Of Thee)

Lyrics by Samuel F. Smith
Music by Henry Carey

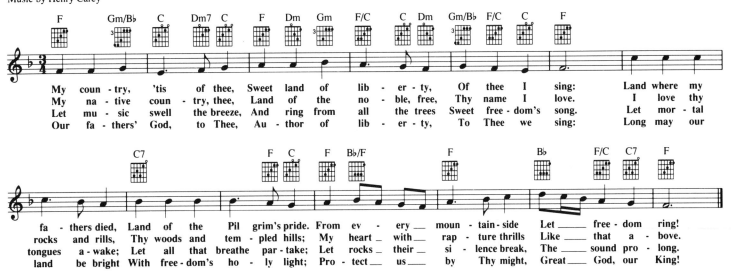

My coun - try, 'tis of thee, Sweet land of lib - er - ty, Of thee I sing: Land where my
My na - tive coun - try, thee, Land of the no - ble, free, Thy name I love. I love thy
Let mu - sic swell the breeze, And ring from all the trees Sweet free - dom's song. Let mor - tal
Our fa - thers' God, to Thee, Au - thor of lib - er - ty, To Thee we sing: Long may our

fa - thers died, Land of the Pil grim's pride. From ev - ery ___ moun - tain-side Let ___ free - dom ring!
rocks and rills, Thy woods and tem - pled hills; My heart ___ with rap - ture thrills Like ___ that a - bove.
tongues a - wake; Let all that breathe par - take; Let rocks ___ their si - lence break, The ___ sound pro - long.
land be bright With free - dom's ho - ly light; Pro - tect ___ us by Thy might, Great ___ God, our King!

AMERICA, THE BEAUTIFUL

Lyrics by Katherine Lee Bates
Music by Samuel A. Ward

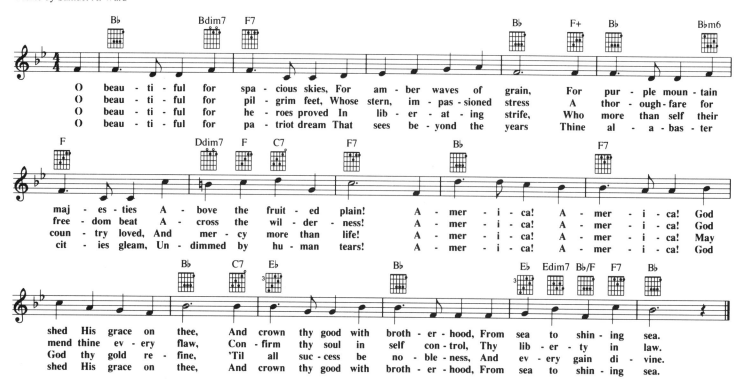

O beau-ti-ful for spa-cious skies, For am-ber waves of grain, For pur-ple moun-tain
O beau-ti-ful for pil-grim feet, Whose stern, im-pas-sioned stress A thor-ough-fare for
O beau-ti-ful for he-roes proved In lib-er-at-ing strife, Who more than self their
O beau-ti-ful for pa-triot dream That sees be-yond the years Thine al-a-bas-ter

maj-es-ties A-bove the fruit-ed plain! A-mer-i-ca! A-mer-i-ca! God
free-dom beat A-cross the wil-der-ness! A-mer-i-ca! A-mer-i-ca! God
coun-try loved, And mer-cy more than life! A-mer-i-ca! A-mer-i-ca! May
cit-ies gleam, Un-dimmed by hu-man tears! A-mer-i-ca! A-mer-i-ca! God

shed His grace on thee, And crown thy good with broth-er-hood, From sea to shin-ing sea.
mend thine ev-ery flaw, Con-firm thy soul in self con-trol, Thy lib-er-ty in law.
God thy gold re-fine, 'Til all suc-cess be no-ble-ness, And ev-ery gain di-vine.
shed His grace on thee, And crown thy good with broth-er-hood, From sea to shin-ing sea.

THE AMERICAN PATROL

F. W. Meacham

ANGELS WE HAVE HEARD ON HIGH

1. An - gels We Have Heard On High Sweet - ly sing - ing o'er the plains, And the moun - tains
2. Shep - herds, why this ju - bi - lee? Why your joy - ous strains pro - long? What the glad - some
3 - 4. *(See additional lyrics)*

in re - ply Ech - o - ing their joy - ous strains. } Glo -
ti - dings be Which in - spire your heaven - ly song? }

Refrain

- - ri - a in ex - cel - sis De - o, Glo -

- - ri - a. in ex - cel - sis De - o.

Additional Lyrics

3. Come to Bethlehem and see
   Him whose birth the angels sing;
   Come, adore on bended knee
   Christ the Lord, the newborn King.
   (Refrain)

4. See within a manger laid
   Jesus, Lord of heaven and earth!
   Mary, Joseph, lend your aid,
   with us sing our Savior's birth.
   (Refrain)

ANIMAL FAIR

Moderately

I went to the An - i - mal Fair, _____ The birds and beasts were there, _____ The

big ba - boon, by the light of the moon Was comb - ing his au - burn hair. _____ The

mon - key, he got drunk, _____ And sat on the el - e - phant's trunk, _____ The el - e - phant sneezed, And

fell on his knees, And what be - came of the monk, the monk, the monk, the monk?

ANNABEL LEE

ASSEMBLY/REVEILLE

ANVIL CHORUS

Giuseppe Verdi

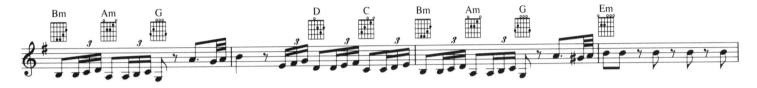

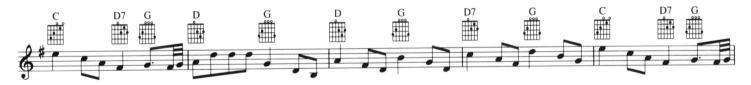

ANNIE LAURIE

By William Douglas and Lady John Scott

1. Max - wel - ton's braes are bon - nie, Where ear - ly fa's the____ dew, And it's
   there that An - nie Lau - rie Gave
   2-3. *(See additional lyrics)*

me her prom - ise true. Gave me her prom - ise true, Which ne'er for - got will

be. And for bon - nie An - nie____ Lau - rie____ I'd____ lay____ me doon and dee.

Additional Lyrics

2. Her brow is like the snawdrift,
   Her neck is like the swan,
   Her face it is the fairest
   That e'er the sun shone on,
   That e'er the sun shone on,
   An' dark blue is her ee . . .

3. Like dew on the gowan lying
   Is the fa' o' her fairy feet;
   An' like winds in summer sighing,
   Her voice is low an' sweet,
   Her voice is low an' sweet,
   An' she's a' the world to me . . .

AS WITH GLADNESS MEN OF OLD

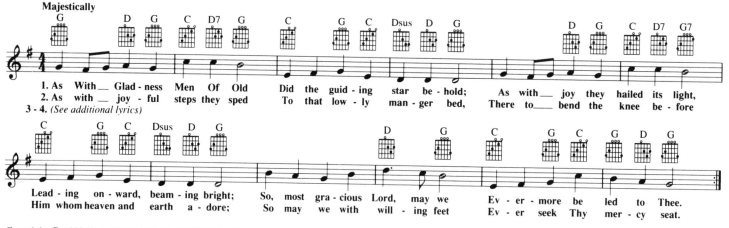

1. As With____ Glad - ness Men Of Old Did the guid - ing star be - hold; As with____ joy they hailed its light,
2. As with____ joy - ful steps they sped To that low - ly man - ger bed, There to____ bend the knee be - fore
   3 - 4. *(See additional lyrics)*

Lead - ing on - ward, beam - ing bright; So, most gra - cious Lord, may we Ev - er - more be led to Thee.
Him whom heaven and earth a - dore; So may we with will - ing feet Ev - er seek Thy mer - cy seat.

Additional Lyrics

3. As they offered gifts most rare
   At that manger rude and bare,
   So may we with holy joy,
   Pure and free from sin's alloy,
   All our costliest treasures bring.
   Christ, to thee, our heavenly King.

4. Holy Jesus, every day
   Keep us in the narrow way;
   And, when earthly things are past,
   Bring our ransomed souls at last
   Where they need no star to guide,
   Where no clouds Thy glory hide.

ARKANSAS TRAVELER

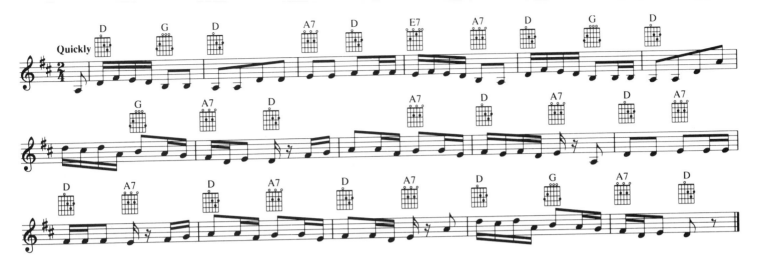

AMERICAN CADETS MARCH

AU CLAIR DE LA LUNE

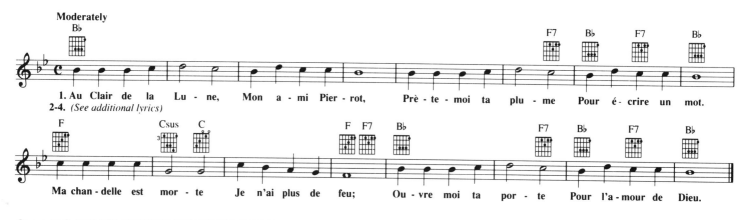

1. Au Clair de la Lu - ne, Mon a - mi Pier - rot, Prè - te - moi ta plu - me Pour é - crire un mot.
2-4. *(See additional lyrics)*

Ma chan - delle est mor - te Je n'ai plus de feu; Ou - vre moi ta por - te Pour l'a - mour de Dieu.

Additional Lyrics

2. Au Clair De La Lune Pierrot répondit,
"Je n'ai pas de plume, je suis dans mon lit.
Va chez la voisine, je crois qu'elle y est.
Car dans sa cuisine on bat le briquet."

3. Au clair De La Lune s'en fût Arlequin,
Frapper chez la brune, ell' répond soudain:
"Qui frapp' de la sorte?" Il dit à son tour:
"Ouvrez votre porte, pour le dieu d'amour!"

4. Au Clair De La Lune, on n'y voit qu'un peu.
On chercha la plume, on chercha du feu.
En cherchant d'la sorte, je n'sais c'qu'on trouva;
Mais je sais qu'la porte sur eux se ferma.

Singable Translation

1. "At thy door I'm knocking, by the pale moonlight,
Lend a pen, I pray thee, I've a word to write;
Guttered is my candle, my fire burns no more;
For the love of heaven, open up the door!"

2. Pierrot cried in answer by the pale moonlight,
"In my bed I'm lying, late and chill the night;
Yonder at my neighbor's, someone is astir;
Fire is freshly kindled, get a light from her."

3. To the neighbor's house then, by the pale moonlight,
Goes our gentle Lubin to beg a pen to write;
"Who knocks there so softly?" calls a voice above.
"Open wide your door now for the God of Love!"

4. Seek they pen and candle by the pale moonlight,
They can see so little since dark is now the night;
What they find while seeking, that is not revealed;
All behind her door is carefully concealed.

AULD LANG SYNE

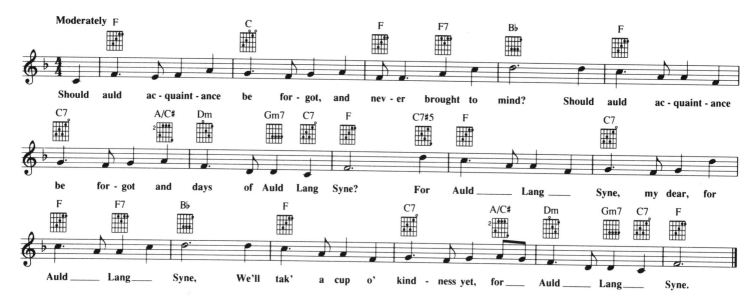

Should auld ac - quaint - ance be for - got, and nev - er brought to mind? Should auld ac - quaint - ance

be for - got and days of Auld Lang Syne? For Auld ____ Lang ____ Syne, my dear, for

Auld ____ Lang ____ Syne, We'll tak' a cup o' kind - ness yet, for ____ Auld ____ Lang ____ Syne.

AURA LEE

By W.W. Fosdick and George R. Poulton

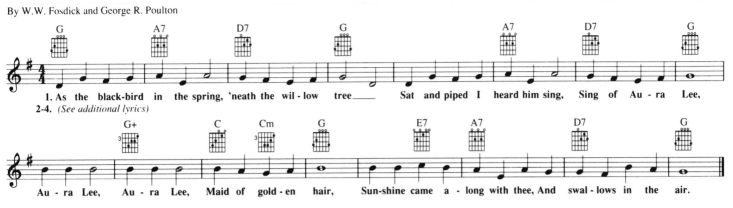

1. As the black-bird in the spring, 'neath the wil-low tree____ Sat and piped I heard him sing, Sing of Au-ra Lee,
2-4. *(See additional lyrics)*

Au-ra Lee, Au-ra Lee, Maid of gold-en hair, Sun-shine came a-long with thee, And swal-lows in the air.

Additional Lyrics

2. In thy blush the rose was born;
   Music when you spake.
   Through thine azure eyes the moon
   Sparkling seemed to break.
   Aura Lee, Aura Lee,
   Birds of crimson wing
   Never song have sung to me
   As in that bright, sweet spring.

3. Aura Lee, the bird may flee,
   The willow's golden hair
   Swing through winter fitfully,
   On the stormy air.
   Yet if thy blue eyes I see,
   Gloom will soon depart.
   For to me, sweet Aura Lee
   Is sunshine through the heart.

4. When the mistletoe was green
   'Midst the winter's snows,
   Sunshine in thy face was seen,
   Kissing lips of rose.
   Aura Lee, Aura Lee,
   Take my golden ring.
   Love and light return with thee,
   And swallows with the spring.

AVE MARIA
(Bach/Gounod)

J.S. Bach
Charles Gounod

Reverently

A - ve, Ma - ri - a! Gra - ti - a ple - na. Do - mi - nus Te - cum

be - ne - dic - ta tu in mu - li - e - ri - bus et ____ be - ne - dic - tus

fruc - tus ____ ven ____ tris ____ tu - i Je - sus. Sanc - ta ____ Ma - ri - a Sanc - ta ____ Ma -

ri - a ____ Ma - ri - a, O - ra - pro no - bis, no - bis pec - ca - to - ri - bus nunc ____ et in ____

Ho - ra, in ho - ra ____ mor - tis ____ nos - trae. ____ A - men. A - men.

AVE MARIA
(Schubert)

Music by Franz Schubert

Very slowly

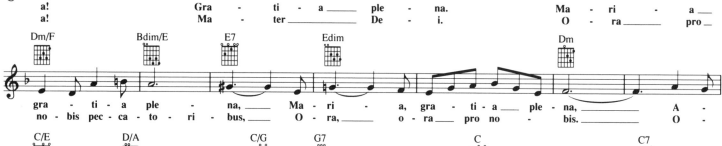

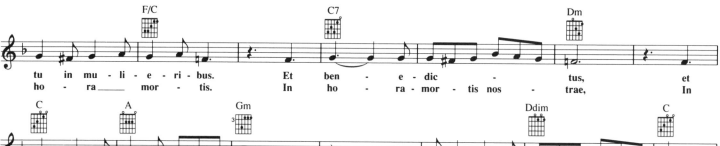

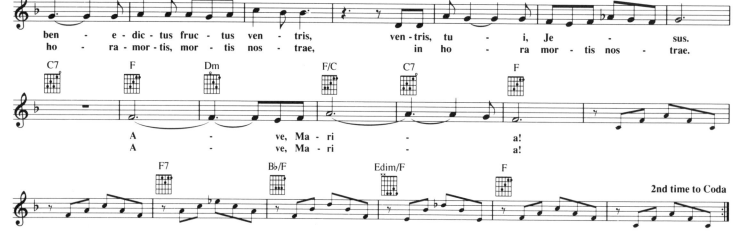

2nd time to Coda

CODA

AWAY IN A MANGER
(Spillman)

Music by Jonathan E. Spillman

Moderately

A - way In A ___ Man - ger, no crib for His bed, The lit - tle Lord Je - sus lay down his sweet head; The

stars in the ___ heav - ens look'd down where He lay, The lit - tle Lord Je - sus, a - sleep in the hay. The ___

cat - tle are low - ing, the poor ba - by wakes, But ___ lit - tle Lord Je - sus no cry - ing ___ He makes; I

love Thee, Lord ___ Je - sus look down from the sky, And stay by my cra - dle to watch lul - la - by.

AWAY IN A MANGER
(James R. Murray)

Music by James R. Murray

Slowly

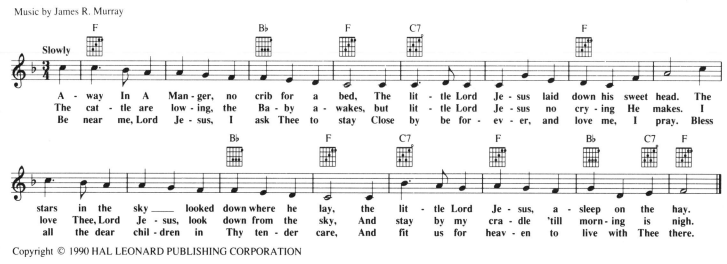

A - way In A Man - ger, no crib for a bed, The lit - tle Lord Je - sus laid down his sweet head. The

The cat - tle are low - ing, the Ba - by a - wakes, but lit - tle Lord Je - sus no cry - ing He makes. I

Be near me, Lord Je - sus, I ask Thee to stay Close by be for - ev - er, and love me, I pray. Bless

stars in the sky ___ looked down where he lay, the lit - tle Lord Je - sus, a - sleep on the hay.

love Thee, Lord Je - sus, look down from the sky, And stay by my cra - dle 'till morn - ing is nigh.

all the dear chil - dren in Thy ten - der care, And fit us for heav - en to live with Thee there.

AWAY IN A MANGER
(W.J. Kirkpatrick)

Music by W.J. Kirkpatrick

Simply

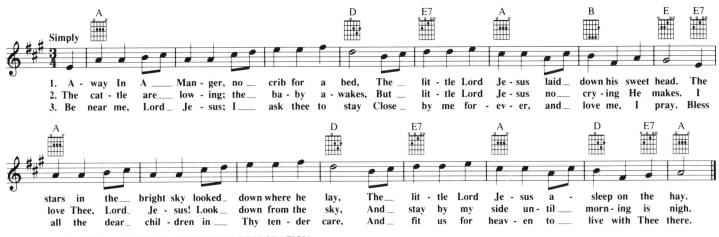

1. A - way In A ___ Man - ger, no crib for a bed, The ___ lit - tle Lord Je - sus laid ___ down his sweet head. The
2. The cat - tle are ___ low - ing; the ___ ba - by a - wakes, But ___ lit - tle Lord Je - sus no ___ cry - ing He makes. I
3. Be near me, Lord ___ Je - sus; I ___ ask thee to stay Close ___ by me for - ev - er, and ___ love me, I pray. Bless

stars in the ___ bright sky looked ___ down where he lay, The ___ lit - tle Lord Je - sus a - sleep on the hay.

love Thee, Lord ___ Je - sus! Look ___ down from the sky, And ___ stay by my side un - til ___ morn - ing is nigh.

all the dear ___ chil - dren in ___ Thy ten - der care, And ___ fit us for heav - en to ___ live with Thee there.

THE ABA DABA HONEYMOON

Words and Music by Arthur Fields and Walter Donovan

"Ab - a, dab - a, da - ba, da - ba, dab - a, dab - a, dab," said the Chim - pie to the Monk,

"bab - a, dab - a, dab - a, dab - a, dab - a, dab - a, dab," said the Mon - key to the Chimp.

All night long they'd chat - ter a - way,__ all day long they're hap - py and gay, __ swing - ing and

sing - ing in their hun - key, ton - key way. "Ab - a, dab - a, dab - a, dab - a,

dab - a, dab - a, dab," means __ "Monk, I love but you," "bab - a, dab - a, dab," in mon - key talk means

"Chimp, I love you too," then the big ba - boon, one night in June, he mar - ried them, and

ver - y soon they went up - on __ their ab - a, dab - a hon - ey - moon.__

ANCHORS AWEIGH

Words and Music by Capt. Alfred H. Miles (Ret.),
and Chas. A. Zimmerman

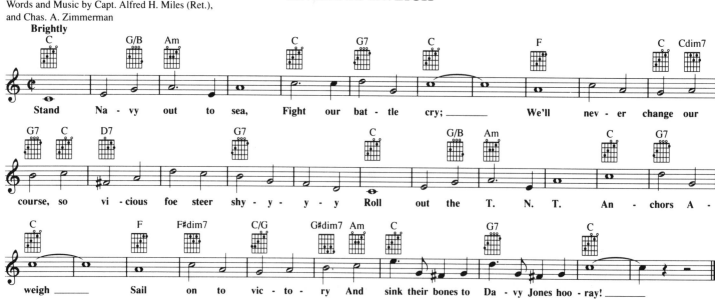

Stand Na - vy out to sea, Fight our bat - tle cry; _____ We'll nev - er change our

course, so vi - cious foe steer shy - y - y - y - y Roll out the T. N. T. An - chors A -

weigh _____ Sail on to vic - to - ry And sink their bones to Da - vy Jones hoo - ray! _____

ADIOS MUCHACHOS

Julio Sanders

ALEXANDER'S RAGTIME BAND

By Irving Berlin

BE MY LITTLE BABY BUMBLEBEE

Lyric by Stanley Murphy
Music by Henry I. Marshall

THE BILLBOARD MARCH

John N. Klohr

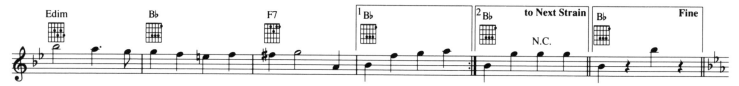

BECURE

Words by Edward Teschemacher
Music by Guy d'Hardelot

BECAUSE

A BIRD IN A GILDED CAGE

Arthur J. Lamb and Harry von Tilzer

wast - ed life, For youth can - not mate with age,_____ And her beau - ty was

sold For an old man's gold, She's A Bird In A Gild - ed Cage."_____

A.M. Hirsch

BOOLA! BOOLA!

BY THE BEAUTIFUL SEA

Words by Harold R. Atteridge
Music by Harry Carroll

Bright Tempo

By the sea, by the sea By The Beau-ti-ful Sea____ You and I, you and
I Oh how hap-py we'll be____ When each wave comes a-roll-ing in We will
duck or swim And we'll float and fool a-round the wa-ter O-ver and
un-der and then up for air____ Pa is rich, Ma is rich so now what do we care?___
___ I love to be be-side your side, Be-side the sea, be-side the sea-side ___
___ By The Beau-ti-ful Sea. By the Sea.____

BY THE LIGHT OF THE SILVERY MOON

Lyric by Ed Madden
Music by Gus Edwards

Moderately

By The Light____ Of The Sil-ver-y Moon.____ I want to
spoon,____ To my hon-ey I'll croon love's tune,____ Hon-ey moon ____
___ keep a shin-ing in June,____ Your sil-v'ry beams will bring love
dreams We'll be cud-dling soon,____ By the sil-ver-y moon.____

ALSO SPRACH ZARATHUSTRA

R. Strauss

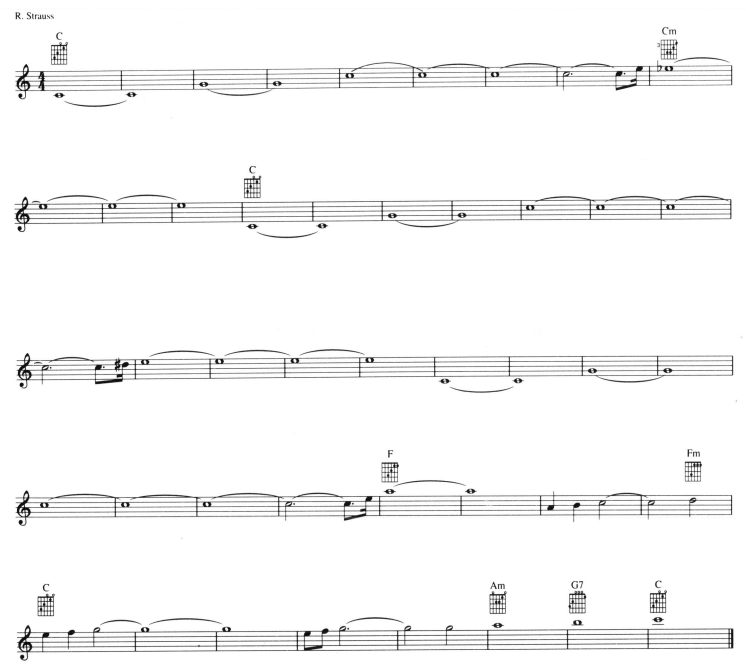

BAA! BAA! BLACK SHEEP

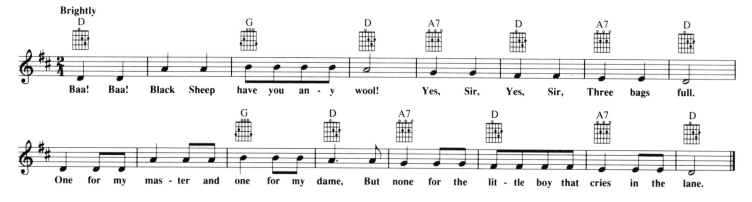

Baa! Baa! Black Sheep have you an - y wool! Yes, Sir, Yes, Sir, Three bags full.

One for my mas - ter and one for my dame, But none for the lit - tle boy that cries in the lane.

THE BANANA BOAT SONG

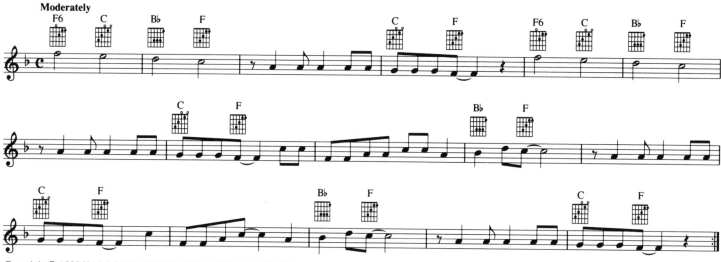

THE BAND PLAYED ON

By John E. Palmer

Cas - ey would waltz with a straw - ber - ry blonde, And The Band Played On,_____ He'd glide 'cross the

floor with the girl he a - dor'd and The Band Played On._____ But his brain was so load - ed it

near - ly ex - plod - ed. The poor girl would shake with a - larm. _____ He'd ne'er leave the girl with the

straw - ber - ry curls, And The Band Played On. _____ On. _____

BANKS OF THE OHIO

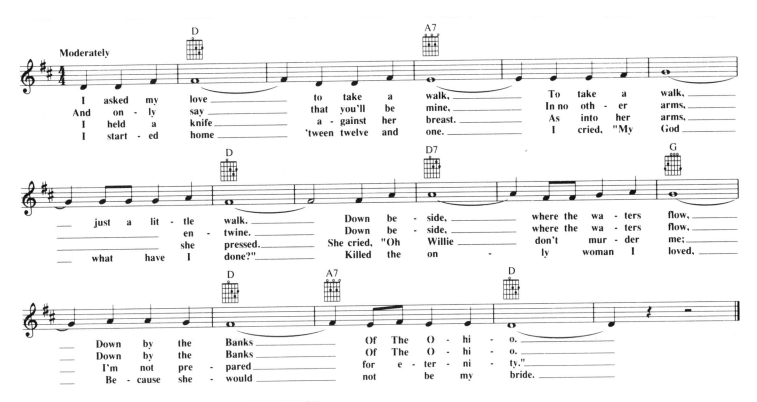

I asked my love to take a walk, To take a walk, In no oth - er arms,
And on - ly say that you'll be mine, As into her arms,
I held a knife a - gainst her breast. I cried, "My God

just a lit - tle walk. Down be - side, where the wa - ters flow,
en - twine. Down be - side, where the wa - ters flow,
she pressed. She cried, "Oh Willie don't mur - der me;
what have I done?" Killed the on - ly woman I loved,

Down by the Banks Of The O - hi - o.
Down by the Banks Of The O - hi - o.
I'm not pre - pared for e - ter - ni - ty."
Be - cause she - would not be my bride.

BARBARA ALLEN

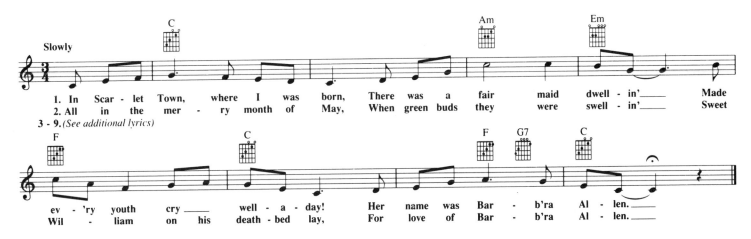

1. In Scar - let Town, where I was born, There was a fair maid dwell - in' Made
2. All in the mer - ry month of May, When green buds they were swell - in' Sweet

3 - 9. *(See additional lyrics)*

ev - 'ry youth cry well - a - day! Her name was Bar - b'ra Al - len.
Wil - liam on his death - bed lay, For love of Bar - b'ra Al - len.

Additional Lyrics

3. He sent his servant to the town,
   He sent him to her dwelling,
   Sayin', "Master's sick, he's very sick,
   For the love of Barbara Allen."

4. Then slowly, slowly she got up,
   And slowly she came nigh to him;
   And all she said when she got there,
   "Young man, I think you're dyin'."

5. When he was dead and in his grave,
   Her heart was filled with sorrow,
   "Oh mother dear, go make my bed,
   For I shall die tomorrow."

6. And as she on her death-bed lay,
   Begged to be buried by him,
   And she repented of the day
   That she did e'er deny him.

7. "Farewell, farewell, ye maidens all,
   And shun the fault I fell in;
   So now rake warning by the fall
   Of cruel Barbara Allen."

8. They buried her in the churchyard,
   And William's buried by her.
   A red rose grew from William's breast,
   And from her feet there grew a briar.

9. They grew as high as the church top,
   They could not grow any higher;
   There they tied in a lover's knot,
   For all true lovers to admire.

BARBARA POLKA

BARCAROLLE

Jacques Offenbach

THE BARBER OF SEVILLE OVERTURE

Gioacchino Rossini

THE BARNYARD SONG
(I Had A Rooster)

1. I had a roost-er and the roost-er pleased me. I fed ___ my roost-er on a green ber-ry
2. I had a cat and the cat pleased me. I fed ___ my cat on a green ber-ry

3-5. *(See additional lyrics)*

1st time omit these 4 measures for verses 2-5 repeat as needed.

tree. The lit-tle cat ___ went "meow, meow," the lit-tle roost-er went
tree. The

"cock - a - doo-dle doo dee doo-dle-dee doo-dle-dee doo-dle-dee do."

D.C. for verses 2-5

Additional Lyrics

3. I had a pig and the pig pleased me.
I fed my pig on a green berry tree.
The little pig went "oink oink."
The little cat went "meow meow."
Chorus:

4. I had a cow and the cow pleased me.
I fed my cow on a green berry tree.
The little cow went "moo moo."
The little pig went "oink oink."
The little cat went "meow meow."
Chorus:

5. I had a baby and the baby pleased me.
I fed my baby on a green berry tree.
The little baby went "waah waah."
The little cow went "moo moo."
The little pig went "oink oink."
The little cat went "meow meow."
Chorus:

THE BATTLE CRY OF FREEDOM

George F. Root

Yes, we'll ral-ly 'round the flag boys, we'll ral-ly once a-gain, Shout-ing The Bat-tle Cry Of Free-dom; We will
We are spring-ing to the call of our broth-ers gone be-fore, Shout-ing The Bat-tle Cry Of Free-dom; And we'll

ral-ly from the hill-side, we'll gath-er from the plain, Shout-ing The Bat-tle Cry Of Free-dom.
fill the va-cant ranks with a mil-lion free-men more, Shout-ing The Bat-tle Cry Of Free-dom.

The

Un-ion for-ev-er, hur-rah, boys, hur-rah! Down with the trai-tor, Up with the star; While we

ral-ly 'round the flag, boys, ral-ly once a-gain, Shout-ing The Bat-tle Cry Of Free-dom.

THE BATTLE HYMN OF THE REPUBLIC

Lyrics by Julia Ward Howe
Music by William Steffe

BEAUTIFUL BROWN EYES

Additional Lyrics

1. Willie, my darling, I love you,
   Love you with all of my heart;
   Tomorrow we were to be married,
   But liquor has kept us apart.
   Refrain

2. I staggered into the barroom,
   I fell down on the floor,
   And the very last words that I uttered,
   "I'll never get drunk any more."
   Refrain

3. Seven long years I've been married,
   I wish I was single again,
   A woman don't know half her troubles
   Until she has married a man.
   Refrain

Steven Foster

BEAUTIFUL DREAMER

Beau - ti - ful Dream - er, wake un - to me, Star - light and dew - drops are
Sounds of the rude world heard in the day, Lulled by the moon - light have
Gone are the cares of life's bus - y throng, Beau - ti - ful Dream - er a -

wait - ing for thee.
all passed a way. Beau - ti - ful Dream -
wake un - to

er, queen of my song, List while I woo thee with soft mel - o - dy.

CODA

me. Beau - ti - ful Dream - er, a - wake un - to me.

BEHOLD THE SAVIOR OF MANKIND

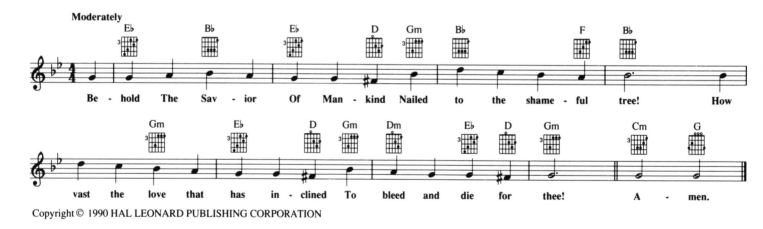

Be - hold The Sav - ior Of Man - kind Nailed to the shame - ful tree! How

vast the love that has in - clined To bleed and die for thee! A - men.

THE BIRTHDAY SONG

BEAUTIFUL SAVIOR

Beau - ti - ful Sav - iour, King of Cre - a - tion, Son of _____
Fair are the mead - ows, Fair are the wood - lands, Robed in _____

God and _____ Son of Man; Tru - ly I'd love _____ Thee,
flowers of _____ bloom - ing spring; Je - sus is fair - er,

Tru - ly I'd serve _____ Thee, Light of my soul, my joy, my crown.
Je - sus is pur - er, He makes our sor - rowing spir - it sing.

BELIEVE ME IF ALL THOSE ENDEARING YOUNG CHARMS

Be - lieve Me, If All Those En - dear - ing Young Charms which I gaze on so fond - ly to -

day, _____ Were to change by to - mor - row and flee from my arms, Like _ fai - ry gifts fad - ing a -

way. _____ Thou woulds't still be a - dored as this mo - ment thou art: Let thy

love - li - ness fade as it will, _____ And a - round the dear ru - in, each

wish of my heart, Would en - twine it - self ver - dant - ly still. _____

BEETHOVEN'S FIFTH SYMPHONY
(1st Movement Theme)

A BICYCLE BUILT FOR TWO
(Daisy Bell)

Words and Music by Harry Dacre

1. There is a flow - er with - in my heart, Dai - sy,
2. We will go "tan - dem" as man and wife, Dai - sy,
3. (See additional lyrics)

Dai - sy! Plant - ed one day by a glanc - ing dart,
Dai - sy! "Ped - dling" a - way down the road of life,

Additional Lyrics

3. I will stand by you in "wheel" or woe,
Daisy, Daisy!
You'll be the belle which I'll ring, you know!
Sweet little Daisy Bell!
You'll take the "lead" in each "trip" we take,
Then, if I don't do well,
I will permit you to use the brake,
My beautiful Daisy Bell!

BE KIND TO YOUR WEB-FOOTED FRIENDS

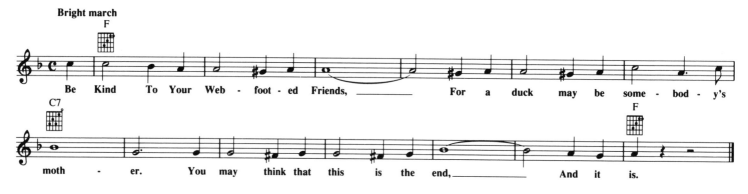

Be Kind To Your Web-foot-ed Friends, _____ For a duck may be some-bod-y's moth-er. You may think that this is the end, _____ And it is.

THE BEAR WENT OVER THE MOUNTAIN

The Bear Went O-ver The Mount-tain, The Bear Went O-ver The
saw an-oth-er moun-tain, he saw an-oth-er

Moun-tain, The Bear Went O-ver The Moun-tain to
moun-tain, He saw an-oth-er moun-tain and

see what he could see. _____ He
that's what he could see. _____

Words by Jessie Brown Pounds
Music by J.S. Fearis

BEAUTIFUL ISLE OF SOMEWHERE

Some-where the sun is shin-ing, Some-where the song-birds dwell; _____ Hush, then thy sad re-pin-ing;
Some-where the day is long-er, Some-where the task is done; _____ Some-where the heart is strong-er,
Some-where the load is lift-ed, Close by an o-pen gate; _____ Some-where the clouds are rift-ed,

God lives, and all _____ is well. _____ Some-where, Some-where, Beau-ti-ful Isle _____ Of
Some-where the guer-don won. _____ }
Some-where the an-gels wait. _____

Some-where! Land of the true, where we live a-new, Beau-ti-ful Isle _____ Of Some-where!

BIG ROAD BLUES

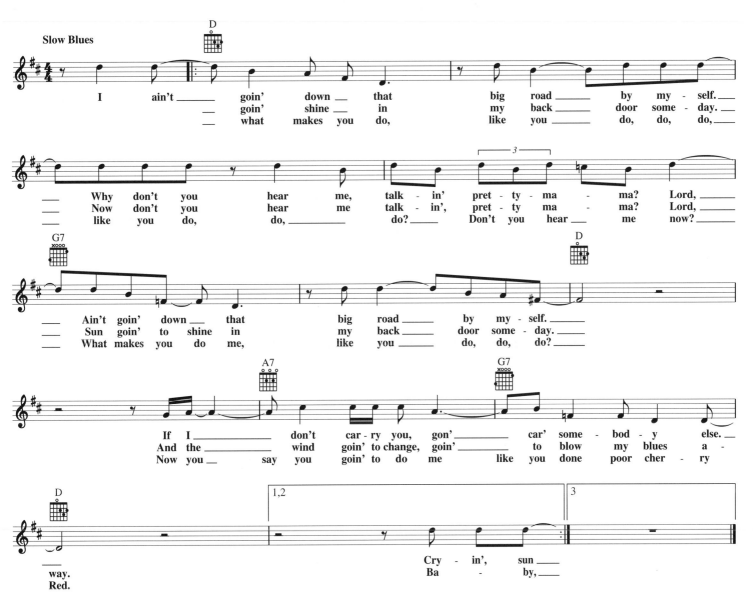

Slow Blues

I ain't goin' down that big road by my self.
goin' shine in my back door some day.
what makes you do, like you do, do, do,

Why don't you hear me, talk-in' pret-ty-ma - ma? Lord,
Now don't you hear me talk - in', pret-ty ma - ma? Lord,
like you do, do, do? Don't you hear me now?

Ain't goin' down that big road by my self.
Sun goin' to shine in my back door some day.
What makes you do me, like you do, do, do?

If I don't car-ry you, gon' car' some - bod - y else.
And the wind goin' to change, goin' to blow my blues a -
Now you say you goin' to do me like you done poor cher - ry

1,2
3

Cry - in', sun
Ba - by,

way.
Red.

Copyright © 1999 by HAL LEONARD CORPORATION

BLACK IS THE COLOR

Freely

Black, black, Black Is The Col - or of my true love's hair. Those
How I love my love and well she knows, I

lips are like some ros - y fair; The pur - est eyes and the
love the grass where - on she goes: When she on earth no

neat - est hands, I love the grass where - on she stands.
more I see, My life will quick - ly o - ver be.

Copyright © 1990 by HAL LEONARD PUBLISHING CORPORATION

BILLY BOY

1. Oh_____ where have you been, Bil - ly Boy, Bil - ly Boy, Oh_____
2. Did she bid you come in, Bil - ly Boy, Bil - ly Boy, Did she
3 - 7. *(See additional lyrics)*

where have you been, charm - ing Bil - ly? _____ I have
bid you come in, charm - ing Bil - ly? _____ Yes, she

been to seek a wife, she's the joy _____ of my life.⎱ She's a
bade me to come in, let me kiss her on the chin.⎰

young thing and can - not leave her moth - er.

Additional Lyrics

3. Did she set for you a chair, Billy Boy, Billy Boy,
   Did she set for you a chair, charming Billy?
   Yes, she set for me a chair,
   And the bottom wasn't there,
   She's a young thing and cannot leave her mother.

4. Can she bake a cherry pie, Billy Boy, Billy Boy,
   Can she bake a cherry pie, charming Billy?
   She can bake a cherry pie,
   Quick as a cat can wink her eye,
   She's a young thing and cannot leave her mother.

5. How old is she, Billy Boy, Billy Boy,
   How old is she, charming Billy?
   She's three times six and four times seven,
   Twenty-eight and eleven,
   She's a young thing and cannot leave her mother.

6. Can she sing a pretty song, Billy Boy, Billy Boy,
   Can she sing a pretty song, charming Billy?
   She can sing a pretty song,
   But she gets the words all wrong,
   She's a mother and cannot leave her young thing.

7. Are her eyes very bright, Billy Boy, Billy Boy,
   Are her eyes very bright, charming Billy?
   Yes, her eyes are very bright
   But unfortunately lack sight
   And she can't describe me to her mother.

BLEST BE THE TIE THAT BINDS

Words by John Fawcett
Music by Hans Georg Nageli

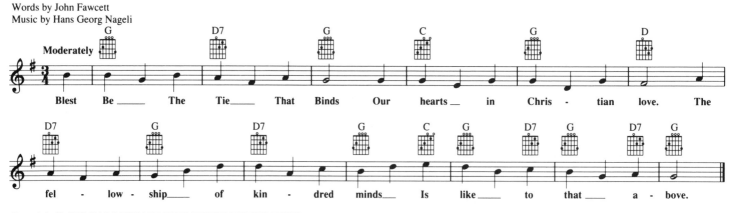

Blest Be _____ The Tie_____ That Binds Our hearts ___ in Chris - tian love. The

fel - low - ship_____ of kin - dred minds___ Is like ___ to that ___ a - bove.

BINGO

NOTE: Each time a letter of BINGO is deleted in the lyric, clap your hands in place of singing the letter.

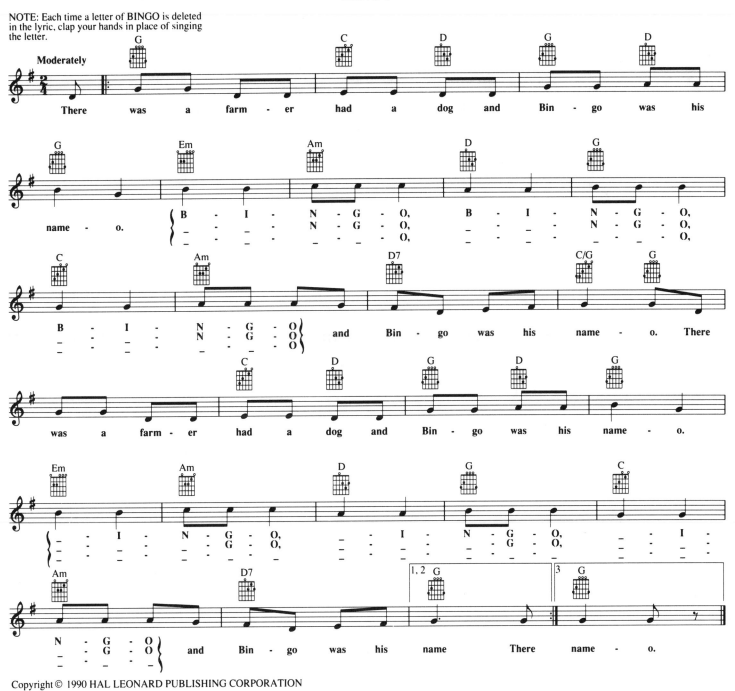

Moderately

There was a farm-er had a dog and Bin-go was his name-o. B-I-N-G-O, B-I-N-G-O, B-I-N-G-O, and Bin-go was his name-o. There was a farm-er had a dog and Bin-go was his name-o. and Bin-go was his name There name-o.

BLOW THE MAN DOWN

Fast Waltz

Oh, Blow The Man Down, bul-lies, Blow The Man Down. To me way, hey, Blow The Man Down. Oh___ Blow The Man Down, bul-lies, Blow him a-way, Give me some time to Blow The Man Down.

BILL BAILEY, WON'T YOU PLEASE COME HOME?

Words and Music by Hughie Cannon

Won't you come home, Bill Bai - ley, won't you come home? She moans the whole day long; _____ I'll do the cook - ing, dar - ling I'll pay the rent, I know I've done you wrong. _____ "Mem- ber that rain - y eve that I drove you out, With noth - in' but a fine tooth comb? _____ I know I'm to blame, well, ain't that a shame? Bill Bai - ley, Won't You Please Come Home? _____ Home? _____

Copyright © 1990 MILWIN MUSIC

BLOOD ON THE SADDLE

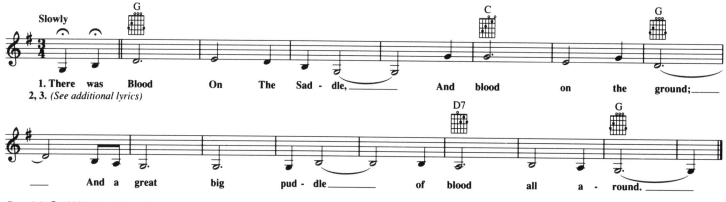

1. There was Blood On The Sad - dle, _____ And blood on the ground; _____
2, 3. (See additional lyrics)
____ And a great big pud - dle _____ of blood all a - round. _____

Copyright © 1990 HAL LEONARD PUBLISHING CORPORATION

Additional Lyrics

2. The cowboy lay in it,
   All covered with gore,
   And he won't go riding
   No broncos no more.

3. Oh, pity the cowboy,
   All bloody and red,
   For his bronco fell on him
   And mashed in his head.

BLESSED ASSURANCE

Lyrics by Fanny Crosby, Van Alstyne
Music by Phoebe P. Knapp

Bless-ed As-sur-ance Je-sus is mine ___ Oh, what a fore-taste of glo-ry di-vine. ___ Heir of sal-
Per-fect sub-mis-sion all is at rest I in my Sav-ior am hap-py and blest. ___ Watch-ing and

va-tion pur-chase of God ___ Born of His Spir-it washed in His blood. ___ This is my
wait-ing look-ing a-bove Filled with His good-ness lost in His love. ___ } This is my

sto-ry this is my song ___ Prais-ing my Sav-ior all the day long ___ This is my

sto-ry this is my song ___ Prais-ing my Sav-ior all the day long. ___

THE BLUE BELLS OF SCOTLAND

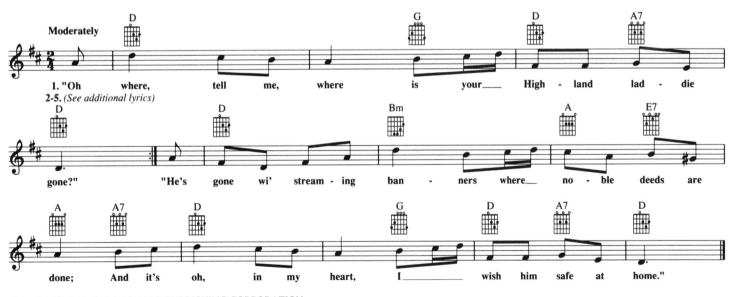

Moderately

1. "Oh where, tell me, where is your ___ High-land lad-die
2-5. (See additional lyrics)

gone?" "He's gone wi' stream-ing ban-ners where ___ no-ble deeds are

done; And it's oh, in my heart, I ___ wish him safe at home."

Additional Lyrics

2. "Oh what, lassie, what does your Highland laddie wear?"
(repeat)
"A scarlet coat and bonnet wi' bonnie yellow hair,
And there's nane in the world can wi' my love compare."

3. "Oh where, tell me, does your Highland laddie dwell?"
(repeat)
"He dwells in merry Scotland at the sign of the Blue Bell,
And it's oh! in my heart that I love my laddie well."

4. "Suppose, just suppose, that your Highland lad should die?"
(repeat)
"The bagpipes should play o'er him, and I'd lay me down and cry;
But it's oh! in my heart that I wish he may not die."

5. "Oh what will you claim for your constancy to him?"
(repeat)
"I'll claim a priest to wed us, and a clerk to say amen!
And I'll ne'er part from my bonnie Highland man."

BLUETAIL FLY

1. When I was young I used to wait on Mas-ter and hand him his plate, And
2. And when he'd ride in the af-ter-noon, I'd fol-low after with a hick-o-ry broom; The
3 - 5. *(See additional lyrics)*

pass the bot-tle when he got dry, And brush a-way the Blue-tail Fly!
po-ny be-ing ver-y shy, When bit-ten by the Blue-tail Fly!

Refrain:
Jim-my crack corn, and I don't care, Jim-my crack corn, and I don't care,

Jim-my crack corn, and I don't care, My Mas-ter's gone a-way.

Additional Lyrics

3. One day while riding round the farm,
   The flies so numerous they did swarm;
   One changed to bite him on the thigh,
   The devil take the Bluetail Fly!
   Refrain

4. The pony run, he jump, he kick.
   He threw my Master in the ditch;
   He died and the jury wondered why,
   The verdict was the Bluetail Fly!
   Refrain

5. They laid him under a 'simmon tree,
   His epitaph is there to see:
   "Beneath this stone Jim forced to lie,
   A victim of the Bluetail Fly!"
   Refrain

THE BOAR'S HEAD CAROL

The boar's head in hand bear I, Be-decked with bays and rose-ma-ry; And I
The boar's head as I un-der-stand, Is the rar-est dish in all this land, Which
Our stew-ard hath pro-vid-ed this, In hon-or of the King of bliss, Which

pray you, my mas-ters, be mer-ry, *Quot es-tis in con-vi-vi-o.*
thus be-decked with a gay gar-land, *Let us ser-vi-re can-ti-co.*
on this day to be serv-ed is, *In Re-gi-nen-si a-tri-o.*

Ca-put a-pri de-fe-ro, Red-dens lau-des Do-mi-no.

BLUE DANUBE WALTZ

Johann Strauss

THE BOWERY

Words by Charles H. Hoyt
Music by Percy Gaunt

The Bow - 'ry The Bow - 'ry They say such things and they do strange things. On The

Bow - 'ry The Bow - 'ry I'll nev-er go there an-y more.

THE BOLL WEEVIL

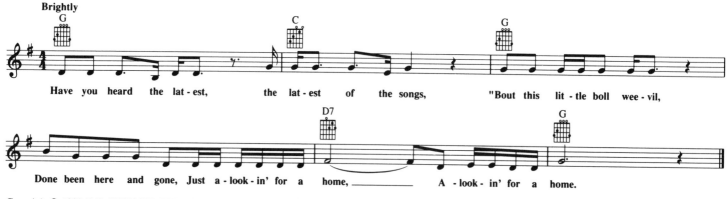

Brightly

Have you heard the lat-est, the lat-est of the songs, "Bout this lit-tle boll wee-vil,

Done been here and gone, Just a-look-in' for a home, _____ A-look-in' for a home.

BRIDAL CHORUS
(From "LOHENGRIN")

Richard Wagner

Moderately

BRAHMS' LULLABY

Johannes Brahms

BRINGING IN THE SHEAVES

Lyrics by Knowles Shaw
Music by George A. Minor

Sow - ing in the morn - ing, sow - ing seeds of kind - ness, Sow - ing in the noon - tide
Sow - ing in the sun - shine, sow - ing in the shad - ows, Fear - ing nei - ther clouds nor
Go - ing forth with weep - ing, sow - ing for the Mas - ter, Tho' the loss sus - tained our

and the dew - y eve, Wait - ing for the har - vest and the time of reap - ing,
win - ter's chill - ing breeze, By and by the har - vest and the la - bor end - ed,
spir - it of - ten grieves, When our weep - ing's o - ver he will bid us wel - come,

We shall come re - joic - ing, Bring - ing In The Sheaves. Bring - ing In The Sheaves, Bring - ing In The Sheaves,

We shall come re - joic - ing, Bring - ing In The Sheaves. Bring - ing In The Sheaves, Bring - ing In The Sheaves,

We shall come re - joic - ing, Bring - ing In The Sheaves. Bring - ing In The Sheaves.

BRING A TORCH, JEANNETTE, ISABELLA

Bring A Torch,__ Jean-nette, Is-a-bel-la, Bring a torch,__ come swift-ly and run. Christ is
Has-ten now,__ good folk of the vil-lage, Has-ten now,__ the Christ Child to see. You wi

born, tell the folk of the vil-lage, Je-sus is sleep-ing in His cra-dle, Ah, ah,
find Him a-sleep in a man-ger, Qui-et-ly come and whis-per soft-ly, Hush, hush,

Beau-ti-ful is the Moth-er, Ah, ah, Beau-ti-ful is her Son.__
Peace-ful-ly now He slum-bers, Hush, hush, Peace-ful-ly now He sleeps.__

BUCKEYE JIM

1. 'Way up yon-der a-bove the sky, A blue-bird lived in a jay-bird's eye.__
2-4. (See additional lyrics)

Buck-eye Jim, you can't go, Go weave and spin, you can't go, Buck-eye Jim.

Additional Lyrics

2. 'Way up yonder above the moon,
   A blue-jay nests in a silver spoon.

3. 'Way down yonder in a wooden trough,
   An old *wo*-man died of the whoopin' cough.

4. 'Way down yonder on a hollow log,
   A red bird danced with a green bullfrog.

BUFFALO GALS

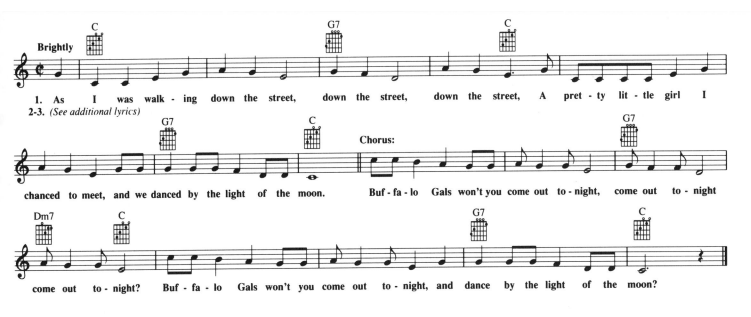

1. As I was walk-ing down the street, down the street, down the street, A pret-ty lit-tle girl I
2-3. *(See additional lyrics)*

chanced to meet, and we danced by the light of the moon. Buf-fa-lo Gals won't you come out to-night, come out to-night

come out to-night? Buf-fa-lo Gals won't you come out to-night, and dance by the light of the moon?

Additional Lyrics

2. I asked her if she'd stop and talk, stop and talk, stop and talk,
Her feet took up the whole sidewalk, and left no room for me.

3. I asked her if she'd be my wife, be my wife, be my wife,
Then I'd be happy all my life, if she'd marry me.

BURY ME NOT ON THE LONE PRAIRIE

1. "Oh, Bu-ry Me Not On The Lone Prai-rie," These words came low
2. "Oh, Bu-ry Me Not On The Lone Prai-rie," Where the wild coy-otes
3-6. *(See additional lyrics)*

and mourn-ful-ly From the pal-lid lips of a youth who
will howl o'er me, In a nar-row grave, just six by

lay On his dy-ing bed at the close of day.
three. Oh, Bu-ry Me Not On The Lone Prai-rie."

Additional Lyrics

3. "I've always wished to be laid when I died
In the little churchyard on the green hillside;
By my father's grave there let mine be,
And Bury Me Not On The Lone Prairie."

4. "Oh, bury me not"– and his voice failed there,
But we took no heed of his dying prayer.
In a narrow grave, just six by three,
We buried him on the lone prairie.

5. And the cowboys now, as they roam the plain,
(For they marked the spot where his bones were lain)
Fling a handful of roses over the grave,
With a prayer to Him who his soul will save.

6. "Oh, Bury Me Not On The Lone Prairie,
Where the wolves can howl and growl o'er me.
Fling a handful of roses over my grave,
With a prayer to Him who my soul will save."

THE CAISSONS GO ROLLING ALONG

Words and Music by Edmund L. Gruber

THE CAMPBELLS ARE COMING

CANTABILE

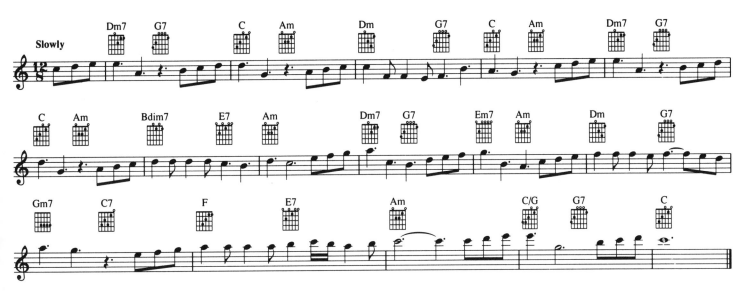

CAPRICCIO ITALIEN THEME

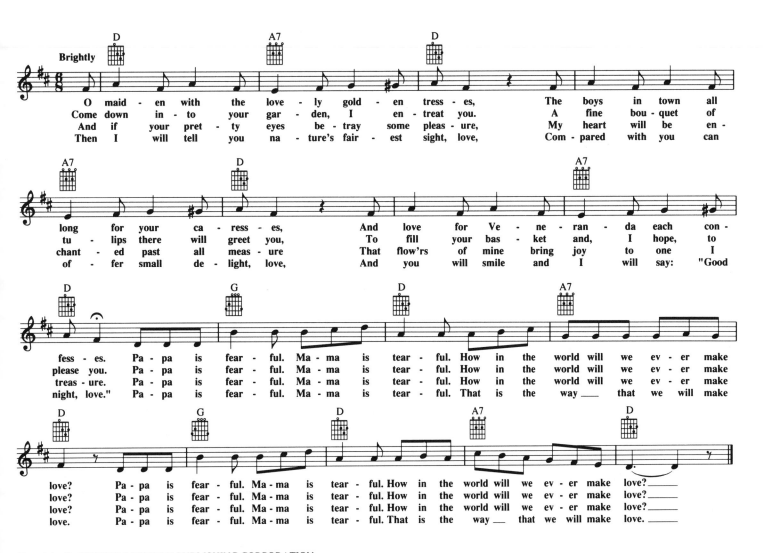

CAN CAN

Jacques Offenbach

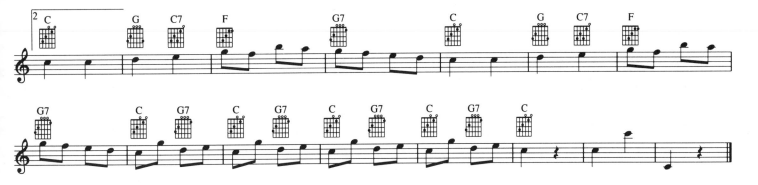

CAMPTOWN RACES

By Stephen Foster

Fast, at a gallop

1. Camp - town la - dies sing this song, Doo - dah, doo - dah.
2-4. *(See additional lyrics)*

Camp - town race - track five miles long, Oh doo - dah - day.

Come down there with my hat caved in, Doo - dah, doo - dah,

Go back home with my pock - et full of tin, Oh doo - dah - day.

Chorus

Goin' to run all night, Goin' to run all day, I

bet my mon - ey on the bob - tail nag, Some - bod - y bet on the bay.

Additional Lyrics

2. The long-tail filly and the big black hoss . . .
   They fly the track and they both cut across . . .
   The blind hoss sticken in a big mud hole . . .
   Can't touch bottom with a ten-foot pole . . .
   Chorus

3. Old muley cow come onto the track . . .
   The bobtail fling her over his back . . .
   Then fly along like a railroad car . . .
   Running a race with a shooting star . . .
   Chorus

4. See them flying on a ten-mile heat . . .
   'Round the race track, then repeat . . .
   I win my money on the bobtail nag . . .
   I keep my money in an old towbag . . .
   Chorus

CAROL OF THE BELLS

P. Leontovich

CARRY ME BACK TO OLD VIRGINNY

Words and Music by James A. Bland

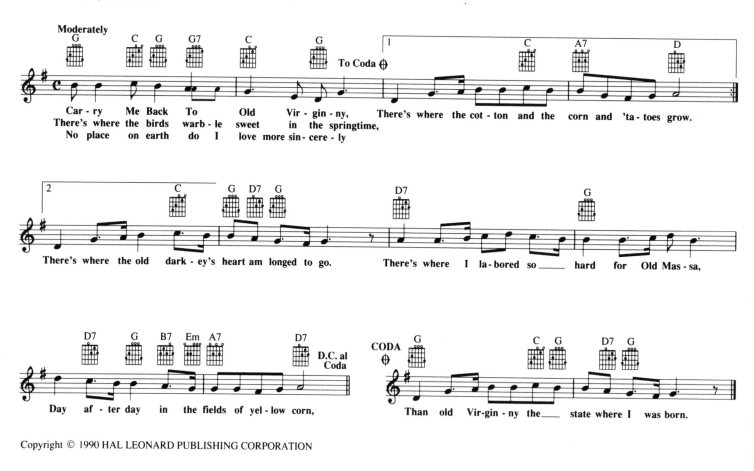

CARELESS LOVE

Love, oh love, oh Care - less Love,
cried last night and the night before.
Love, oh love, oh Care - less Love,
Tonight I'll cry, then cry no more.
Love, oh

love, oh Care - less Love, Oh, see what love has done to me. ___ I me. ___

CARNIVAL OF VENICE

Julius Benedict

CHRIST WAS BORN ON CHRISTMAS DAY

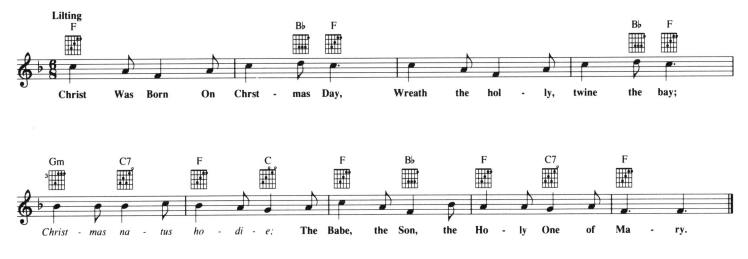

Christ Was Born On Chrst - mas Day, Wreath the hol - ly, twine the bay;

Christ - mas na - tus ho - di - e; The Babe, the Son, the Ho - ly One of Ma - ry.

CHIAPANECAS

CHOPIN BALLADE NO. 1

CHRIST THE LORD IS RIS'N TODAY

Christ The Lord Is Ris'n To - day, _____ Al - le - lu - ia! Our tri - umph - ant
Hymns of praise then let us sing, _____ Un - to Christ, our
But the pains which He en - dured, _____ Our sal - va - tion

ho - ly day, _____ Al - le - lu - ia. Who died once up - on the Cross, Al - le -
heav'n - ly King, _____ Who en - dured the Cross and grave, }
have pro - cured, _____ Now a - bove the sky He's King,

lu - ia. Suf - fer _____ to re - deem our loss. _____ Al - le - lu - ia.
Sin - ners _____ to re - deem and save. _____ }
Where _____ the _____ an - gels ev - er sing. _____

THE CHURCH IN THE WILDWOOD

By Wm. S. Pitts

1. There's a church in the val - ley by the wild - wood, No _____ love - li - er spot in the dale; No _____ place is so dear to my
2. Oh _____ come to The Church In The Wild - wood, to the tress where the wild flow - ers bloom; Where the part - ing _____ hymn will be
3. (See additional lyrics)

child - hood As the lit - tle brown church in the vale. } Oh, _____ come, come, come, come, Come to The Church In The Wild - wood, Oh,
chant - ed We will weep _____ by the side of the tomb.

come to the church in the vale. No _____ spot is so dear to my child - hood As the lit - tle brown _____ church in the vale.

Additional Lyrics
3. From the church in the valley by the wildwood,
When day fades away into night;
I would fain from this spot of my childhood
Wing my way to the mansions of light.

68

CIELITO LINDO

By C. Fernandez

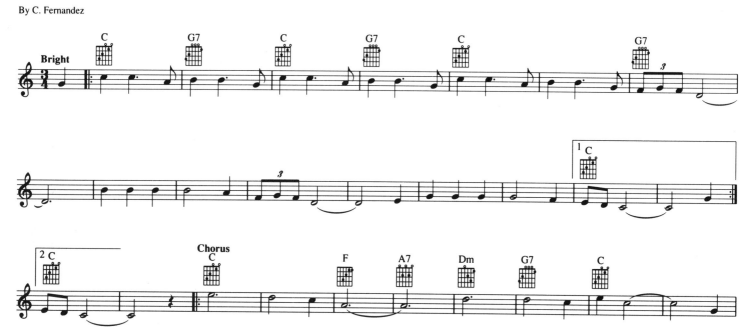

CIRIBIRIBIN

Music by A. Pestalozza

CLAIR DE LUNE

CLEMENTINE

Additional Lyrics

2. Light she was and, like a fairy,
And her shoes were number nine,
Herring boxes, without topses,
Sandals were for Clementine.
Chorus

3. Drove she ducklings to the water,
Every morning just at nine,
Stubbed her toe upon a splinter,
Fell into the foaming brine.
Chorus

4. Ruby lips above the water
Blowing bubbles soft and fine,
But alas I was no swimmer,
So I lost my Clementine.
Chorus

5. There's a churchyard, on the hillside,
Where the flowers grow and twine,
There grow roses, 'mongst the posies,
Fertilized by Clementine.
Chorus

COCKLES AND MUSSELS
(Molly Malone)

In Dub-lin's fair cit-y, Where girls are so pret-ty, 'Twas there I first met with sweet
She was a fish-mon-ger, But sure 'twas no won-der, For so were her moth-er and
She died of a fe-ver, And noth-ing could save her, And that was the end of sweet

Mol-ly Ma-lone. She drove a wheel-bar-row Through streets broad and nar-row,
fa-ther be-fore. They drove their wheel-bar-rows Through streets broad and nar-row, } Cry-ing,
Mol-ly Ma-lone. Her ghost wheels a bar-row Through streets broad and nar-row,

"Cock-les And Mus-sels, a-live, a-live-o. A-live, a-live-o,_____ A-

live, a-live-o."_____ Cry-ing, "Cock-les And Mus-sels, A-live, a-live-o."

COME BACK TO SORRENTO

By Ernesto Di Curtis
Slowly

CLARINET POLKA

THE COVENTRY CAROL

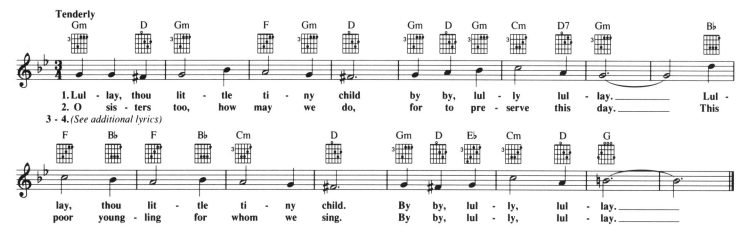

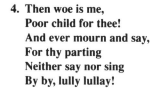

Tenderly

1. Lul - lay, thou lit - tle ti - ny child by by, lul - ly lul - lay. _____ Lul-
2. O sis - ters too, how may we do, for to pre - serve this day. _____ This
3 - 4. *(See additional lyrics)*

lay, thou lit - tle ti - ny child. By by, lul - ly, lul - lay. _____
poor young - ling for whom we sing. By by, lul - ly, lul - lay. _____

Additional Lyrics

3. Herod the king,
   In his raging,
   Charged he hath this day.
   His men of might,
   In his own sight,
   All young children to slay.

4. Then woe is me,
   Poor child for thee!
   And ever mourn and say,
   For thy parting
   Neither say nor sing
   By by, lully lullay!

THE CRAWDAD SONG

Brightly

1. You get a line and I'll get a pole, hon - ey, You get a line and
2 - 5. *(See additional lyrics)*

I'll get a pole, ba - by; You get a line and I'll get a pole and

we'll go fish - in' at the craw - dad hole. Hon - ey, ba - by mine. _____

Additional Lyrics

2. Get up old man, you slept too late, honey, (twice)
   Get up old man, you slept too late,
   Last piece of crawdad's on your plate,
   Honey, sugar baby mine.

3. Get up old woman, you slept too late, honey, (twice)
   Get up old woman, you slept too late,
   Crawdad man done passed your gate,
   Honey, sugar baby mine.

4. What you gonna do when the lake goes dry, (twice)
   What you gonna do when the lake goes dry,
   Sit on the bank and watch the crawdads die,
   Honey, sugar baby mine.

5. What you gonna do when the crawdads die, honey? (twice)
   What you gonna do when the crawdads die,
   Sit on the bank until I cry,
   Honey, sugar baby mine.

CRIPPLE CREEK

1. I ___ got a gal at the head ___ of the creek, Go up to see her 'bout the
Kiss her on the mouth, just as sweet as an - y wine,

2 - 3. *(See additional lyrics)*

mid - dle of the week, Wraps her - self a - round me like a sweet per - ta - ter vine.

Chorus

Go - in' up Crip - ple Creek, go - in' in a run, Go - in' up Crip - ple Creek to have a lit - tle fun.
Go - in' up Crip - ple Creek, go - in' in a whirl, Go - in' up Crip - ple Creek to see ___ my ___ girl.

Additional Lyrics

2. Girls on the Cripple Creek 'bout half grown,
Jump on a boy like a dog on a bone.
Roll my britches up to my knees,
I'll wade old Cripple Creek when I please.

3. Cripple Creek's wide and Cripple Creek's deep,
I'll wade old Cripple Creek afore I sleep,
Roads are rocky and the hillside's muddy
And I'm so drunk that I can't stand study.*

*steady

CROWN HIM WITH MANY CROWNS

M. Bridges

Crown Him With Ma - ny Crowns, The Lamb up - on His throne. Hark! how the heaven - ly
Crown Him the Lord of love! Be - hold His hands and side, Those wounds, yet vis - i -
Crown Him the Lord of peace! Whose power a scep - tre sways In heaven and earth, that

an - them ___ drowns All mu - sic but its own! A - wake, my soul, and sing of Him who died for
ble a - bove, In beau - ty glo - ri - fied: No an - gel in the sky can ful - ly bear that
war may ___ cease, And all be prayer and praise. His reign shall know no end; And round His pier - ced

thee; and hail Him as thy match - less King through all e - ter - ni - ty.
sight, But down - ward bends his wond - 'ring eye at mys - ter - ies so bright.
feet, Fair flowers of Par - a - dise ex - tend their fra - grance ev - er sweet.

THE CRUEL WAR IS RAGING

1. The Cruel War Is Rag - ing and John - ny has to fight, I
2 - 11. *(See additional lyrics)*

want to be with him from morn - ing till night.

Additional Lyrics

2. I'll go to your captain, get down upon my knees,
   Ten thousand gold guineas I'd give for your release.

3. Ten thousand gold guineas, it grieves my heart so;
   Won't you let me go with you? - Oh, no, my love, no.

4. Tomorrow is Sunday and Monday is the day
   Your captain calls for you, and you must obey.

5. Your captain calls for you, it grieves my heart so,
   Won't you let me go with you? - Oh, no, my love, no.

6. Your waist is too slender, your fingers are too small,
   Your cheeks are too rosy to face the cannonball.

7. Your cheeks are too rosy, it grieves my heart so,
   Won't you let me go with you? - Oh, no, my love, no.

8. Johnny, oh Johnny, I think you are unkind,
   I love you far better than all other mankind.

9. I love you far better than tongue can express,
   Won't you let me go with you? - Oh, yes, my love, yes.

10. I'll pull back my hair, men's clothes I'll put on,
    I'll pass for your comrade as we march along.

11. I'll pass for your comrade and none will ever guess,
    Won't you let me go with you? - Yes, my love, yes.

DANNY BOY

Melody Traditional
Lyrics by Fred Weatherly

Slowly

1. Oh Dan - ny Boy the pipes the pipes are call - ing ____ from glen to glen and
2. *(See additional lyrics)*

down the moun - tain side ____ The sum - mer's gone and all the ros - es fall - ing 'tis you, 'tis

you must go and I must bide. But come ye back when Sum - mer's in the mea - dow,

or when the val - ley's hushed and white with snow. 'Tis I'll be there in sun - shine or in

sha - dow Oh Dan - ny Boy, Oh Dan - ny Boy I love you so. ____

Additional Lyrics

2. And when ye come and all the flowers are dying
   If I am dead, as dead I well may be
   You'll come and find the place where I am lying
   And kneel and say an Ave there for me.

3. And I shall hear tho' soft you tread above me
   And all my grave will warmer sweeter be
   If you will bend and tell me that you love me
   Then I shall sleep in peace until you come to me.

CHINATOWN, MY CHINATOWN

Words by William Jerome,
Music by Jean Schwartz

Allegro Moderato

Chi - na - town, My Chi - na - town, ___ Where the lights are low, ___ Hearts that know no oth - er land, ___

Drift - ing to and fro, ___ Dream - y, dream - y Chi - na - town, ___ Al - mond eyes of brown, ___

Hearts seem light and life seems bright ___ in dream - y Chi - na - town town. ___

CHOPSTICKS

Playfully

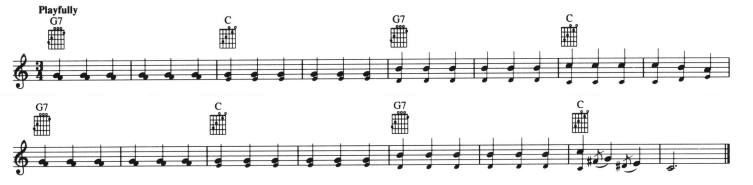

CUDDLE UP A LITTLE CLOSER, LOVEY MINE

Words by Otto Hauerbach
Music by Karl Hoschna

Slowly

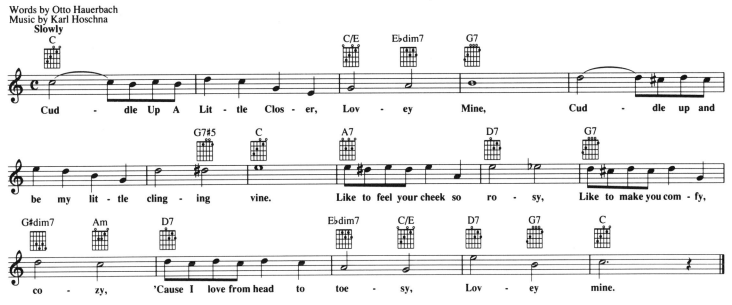

Cud - dle Up A Lit - tle Clos - er, Lov - ey Mine, Cud - dle up and

be my lit - tle cling - ing vine. Like to feel your cheek so ro - sy, Like to make you com - fy,

co - zy, 'Cause I love from head to toe - sy, Lov - ey mine.

CONCERTO THEME
(Rachmaninoff) - (Concerto No. 2, 1st Movement)

Rachmaninoff

CONCERTO THEME
(Rachmaninoff) - (Concerto No. 2, 3rd Movement)

Rachmaninoff

Moderately, with expression

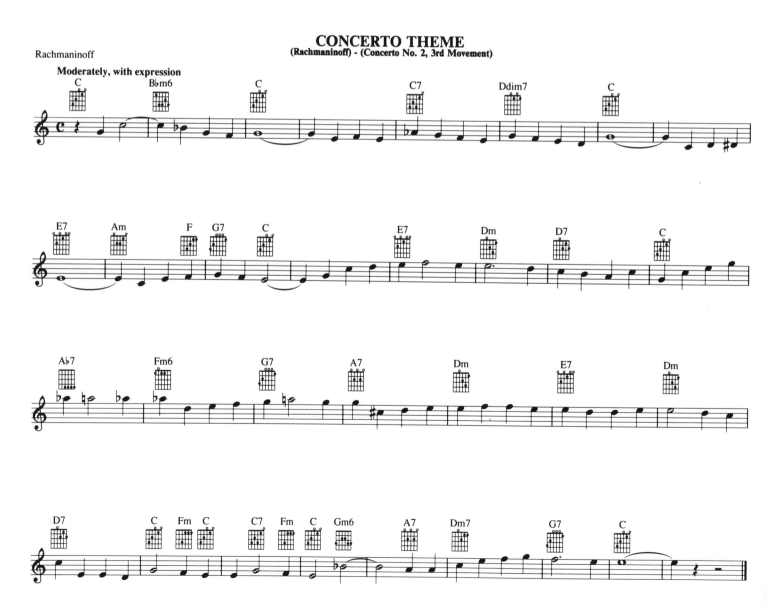

COME, JOSEPHINE IN MY FLYING MACHINE

Words by Alfred Bryan
Music by Fred Fisher

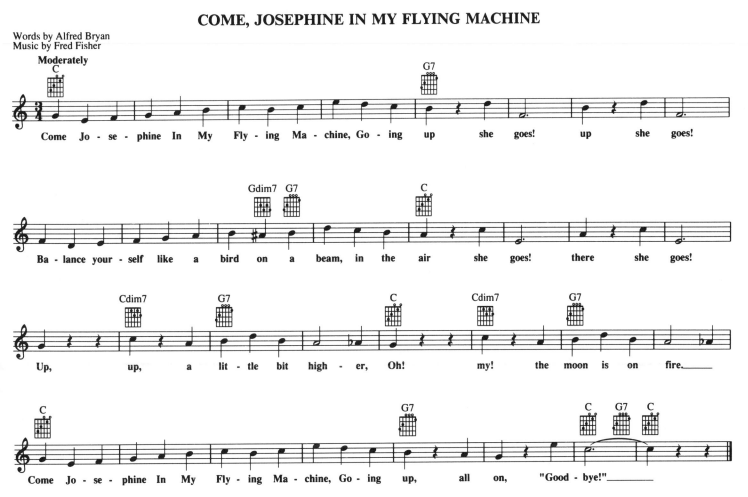

Come Jo-se-phine In My Fly-ing Ma-chine, Go-ing up she goes! up she goes!

Ba-lance your-self like a bird on a beam, in the air she goes! there she goes!

Up, up, a lit-tle bit high-er, Oh! my! the moon is on fire.___

Come Jo-se-phine In My Fly-ing Ma-chine, Go-ing up, all on, "Good - bye!"___

DOWN THE FIELD

Words by C. W. O'Connor
Music by Stanleigh P. Friedman

March, march on Down The Field, fight-ing for E - li, Break thru the crim-son

line, their strength to de-fy, ___ We'll give a long cheer for E - li's men, we're

here to win a-gain, Har-vard's team can fight to the end, but Yale will win. ___

DANCE OF THE SUGAR-PLUM FAIRY

Peter Tchaikovsky
Slowly

DEEP RIVER

Deep_____ Riv - er, my home is o - ver Jor - dan._____ Deep_____ Riv - er, Lord, I

want to cross o - ver in - to camp ground. Oh, don't you want to go to that Gos - pel feast, That prom - ised land where
go in - to heav - en and take my seat. I'll cast my crown at
when I get to heav'n I'll walk all a - bout. There's no one there to

all is peace? Lord, I want to cross o - ver in - to camp ground. Oh,
Je - sus' feet. Lord, I want to cross o - ver in - to camp ground. Oh, } Deep_____ Riv - er, my home is o - ver
turn me out. Lord, I want to cross o - ver in - to camp ground. Oh, }

Jor - dan._____ Deep_____ Riv - er, Lord, I want to cross o - ver in - to camp ground. { I'll camp ground.
Oh,

DECK THE HALL

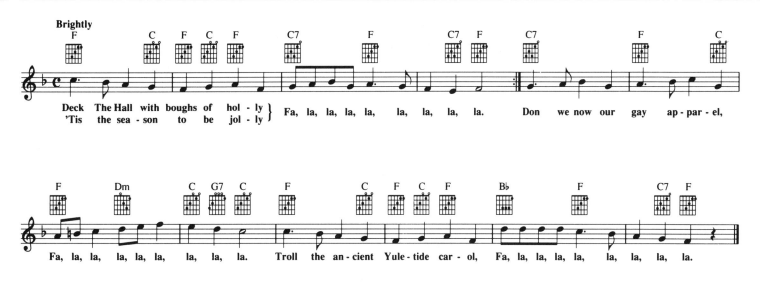

Deck The Hall with boughs of hol - ly
'Tis the sea - son to be jol - ly } Fa, la, la, la, la, la, la, la, la. Don we now our gay ap - par - el,

Fa, la, la, la, la, la, la, la, la. Troll the an - cient Yule - tide car - ol, Fa, la, la, la, la, la, la, la, la.

Copyright © 1990 HAL LEONARD PUBLISHING CORPORATION

THE DESPERADO

1. He was a des - pe - ra - do from the wild and wool - ly west, He came in to Chi - ca - go just to give the west a
2 - 3. *(See additional lyrics)*

rest. He wore a big som - brer - o and a gun be - neath his vest, And ev - 'ry - where he went he gave his war

Chorus

whoop. He was a big brave man and a des - pe - ra - do, From Crip - ple Creek way down in Col - o - ra - do, and he

walked a - round like a big tor - na - do, And ev - 'ry - where he went he gave his war whoop.

Copyright © 1990 HAL LEONARD PUBLISHING CORPORATION

Additional Lyrics

2. He went to Coney Island just to take in all the sights,
   He saw the hootchie-kootchie and the girls dressed up in tights,
   He got so darned excited that he shot out all the lights,
   And everywhere he went he gave his war whoop.
   Chorus

3. A great big fat policeman was a-walking down his beat,
   He saw the desperado come a-walking down the street.
   He grabbed him by the whiskers, and he grabbed him by the seat,
   And threw him where he couldn't give his war whoop.
   Chorus

DANCE OF THE HOURS

A. Ponchielli

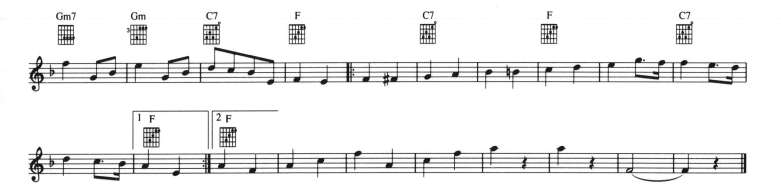

DANUBE WAVES

By Ion Ivanovici

Moderate, graceful waltz

DARK EYES

Fast

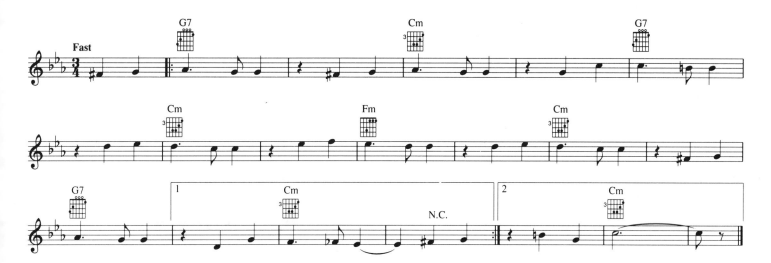

DID YOU EVER SEE A LASSIE?

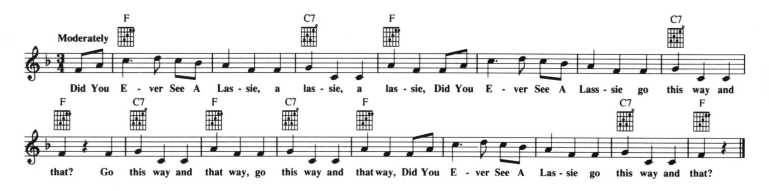

DIXIE

By Dan Emmett

DOWN BY THE STATION

DOG-GONE BLUES

Dog-gone Blues. _ Yes, I'm sing-ing those Dog-gone Blues. _ Life is bring-ing me all bad news_ and
bro-ken dreams. _ E-ven the milk-man brou... Dog-gone Blues. _ What on earth am I
gon-na do?_ I feel ...og-gone _ Blues. _____

Th

With spirit

1. What shall we do with The Drunk-en Sail-or? What shall we do with The Drunk-en Sail-or?
2. Put him in the long boat till he's so-ber, Put him in the long boat till he's so-ber,
3-5. *(See additional lyrics)*

What shall we do with The Drunk-en Sail-or? } Ear-lye in the morn-ing. Hoo-ray and up she ris-es,
Put him in the long boat till he's so-ber,

Hoo-ray and up she ris-es, Hoo-ray and up she ris-es, Ear-lye in the morn-ing.

Additional Lyrics

3. Pull out the plug and wet him all over,
   Pull out the plug and wet him all over,
   Pull out the plug and wet him all over,
   Earlye in the morning.
   Chorus

4. Tie him to the top mast when she's under,
   Tie him to the top mast when she's under,
   Tie him to the top mast when she's under,
   Earlye in the morning.
   Chorus

5. Put him in the scuppers with the hosepipe on him,
   Put him in the scuppers with the hosepipe on him,
   Put him in the scuppers with the hosepipe on him,
   Earlye in the morning.
   Chorus

DOWN BY THE OLD MILL STREAM

Music by Tell Taylor

Copyright © 1990 MILWIN MUSIC

DOWN BY THE RIVERSIDE

Copyright © 1990 HAL LEONARD PUBLISHING CORPORATION

Additional Lyrics

2. I'm gonna join hands with everyone,
   Down By The Riverside, Down By The Riverside,
   Down By The Riverside,
   I'm gonna join hands with everyone,
   Down By The Riverside,
   And study war no more.

3. I'm gonna put on my long white robe . . .

4. I'm gonna walk with the Prince of Peace . .

DOWN IN THE VALLEY

1. Down In The Val - ley, ____ Val - ley so low, ____
2 - 5. *(See additional lyrics)*

Hang your head o - ver, ____ Hear the wind blow. ____

Copyright © 1990 HAL LEONARD PUBLISHING CORPORATION

Additional Lyrics

2. Roses love sunshine, violets love dew
   Angels in heaven, know I love you.
   Know I love you dear, know I love you.
   Angels in heaven, know I love you.

3. If you don't love me, love whom you please
   Throw your arms round me, give my heart ease.
   Give my heart ease love, give my heart ease.
   Throw your arms round me, give my heart ease.

4. Build me a castle forty feet high
   So I can see him as he rides by
   As he rides by love, as he rides by
   So I can see him as he rides by.

5. Write me a letter, send it by mail
   Send it in care of Birmingham jail.
   Birmingham jail love, Birmingham jail
   Send it in care of Birmingham jail.

DRINK TO ME ONLY WITH THINE EYES

1. Drink To Me On - ly With ____ Thine Eyes, ____ And I ____ will pledge with mine; ____
2 - 3. *(See additional lyrics)*

Or leave a kiss with - in ____ the cup ____ and I'll ____ not ask for wine. ____ The

thirst ____ that from the soul ____ doth rise, Doth ask a drink di - vine, ____

But might I of Jove's nec - tar sip, ____ I would ____ not ask for wine.

Copyright © 1990 HAL LEONARD PUBLISHING CORPORATION

Additional Lyrics

2. I sent thee late a rosy wreath,
   Not so much honoring thee,
   As giving it a hope that there
   It could not withered be.

3. But thou thereon didst only breathe,
   And sent'st it back to me,
   Since when it grows and smells, I swear,
   Not of itself, but thee.

DRY BONES

EENCY, WEENCY SPIDER

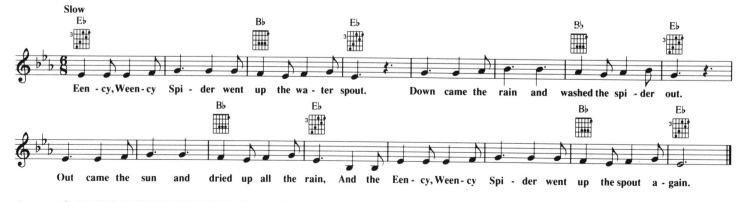

DU, DU LIEGST MIR IM HERZEN

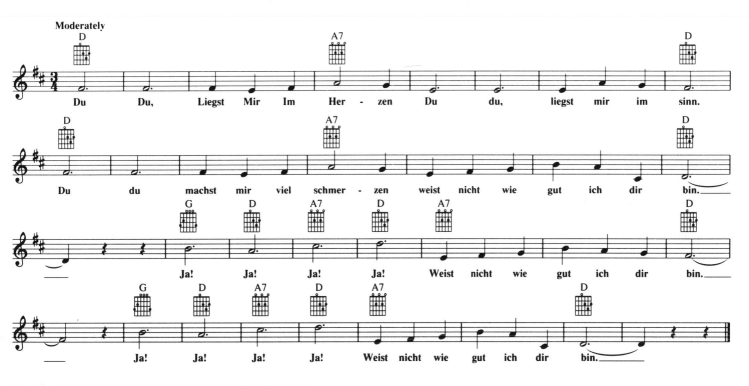

Du Du, Liegst Mir Im Her - zen Du du, liegst mir im sinn.

Du du machst mir viel schmer - zen weist nicht wie gut ich dir bin.

Ja! Ja! Ja! Ja! Weist nicht wie gut ich dir bin.

Ja! Ja! Ja! Ja! Weist nicht wie gut ich dir bin.

EL CAPITAN

John Philip Sousa

EINE KLEINE NACHTMUSIK
(Opening Theme)

Wolfgang Amadeus Mozart

THE ENTERTAINER

Scott Joplin

ELEGIE

Jules Massenet

THE ERIE CANAL

I've got a mule, her name is Sal,
We'd bet-ter get a-long our way
Fif-teen miles on The E-rie Can-al.
She's a good old work-er and a
'Cause you bet your life I nev-er

good old pal,
part with Sal,
Fif-teen miles on The E-rie Can-al.
We've hauled some barg-es in our day,
Get up there, mule, here comes a lock,

filled with lum-ber, coal and hay, And we know ev-'ry inch of the way From Al-ba-ny to
we'll make Rome 'bout six o'-clock. One more trip and back we'll go, Right back home to

Buf-fa-lo.
Buf-fa-lo.
Low bridge ev-'ry-bod-y down! Low bridge, for we're go-ing thru a town; And you'll

al-ways know your neigh-bor, you'll al-ways know your pal, If you've ev-er nav-ig-at-ed on The E-rie Can-al.

EMPEROR WALTZ

Johann Strauss

EMILIA POLKA

EV'RY TIME I FEEL THE SPIRIT

Moderately, very steady

Ev - 'ry Time I ___ Feel The Spir - it, ___ Mov - in' in my heart, ___ I will pray. _____ Ev - 'ry Time I ___ Feel The

Spir - it, ___ Mov - in' in my heart, ___ I will pray. ___ Up - on the moun - tain ___ when my Lord spoke, ___ Out of his mouth came ___ fire and

Oh, I have sor - rows ___ and I have woe, ___ And I have heart - ache ___ here be -

smoke. ___ Look'd all a - round me, ___ It look'd so fine, ___ 'Till I asked my Lord ___ if all were mine. ___ Ev - 'ry

low; ___ But while God leads me, ___ I'll nev - er fear, ___ For I am shel - tered ___ by His care. ___ Ev - 'ry

EZEKIEL SAW THE WHEEL

E - ze - kiel Saw The Wheel, ___ 'way ___ up in the mid - dle of the air, E - ze - kiel Saw The Wheel,

lit - tle wheel run by faith, And the big wheel run by the grace ___ of ___ God, There's a wheel ___ in a wheel,

'way in the mid - dle of the air. And the

'way in the mid - dle of the air.

1. Some go to church for to sing ___ and ___ shout, 'way in the mid - dle of the

2. Nev - er can tell what a hyp - o - crite 'll do, 'way in the mid - dle of the

3. Don't pray for things that ___ you ___ don't ___ need, 'way in the mid - dle of the

air, Be - fore ___ six months they're ___ all ___ turned out, 'way in the mid - dle of the air.

air, He'll lie a - bout me and he'll lie a - bout you, 'way in the mid - dle of the air.

air, The Lord ___ don't like no ___ sin ___ and greed, 'way in the mid - dle of the air

Additional Lyrics

4. There's one thing sure that you can't do,
'way in the middle of the air,
You can't serve God and Satan, too,
'way in the middle of the air.
Chorus

5. One of these days about twelve o'clock,
'way in the middle of the air,
This old world's gonna reel and rock,
'way in the middle of the air.
Chorus

FAITH OF OUR FATHERS

Words and Music by Fredrick W. Faber
Henry F. Hemy and J. G. Walton

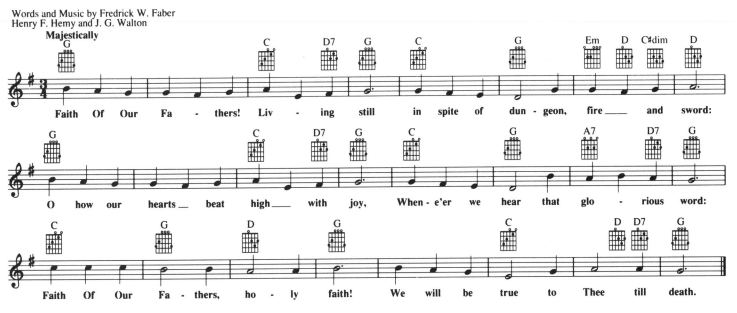

Faith Of Our Fa - thers! Liv - ing still in spite of dun - geon, fire ___ and sword:

O how our hearts ___ beat high ___ with joy, When - e'er we hear that glo - rious word:

Faith Of Our Fa - thers, ho - ly faith! We will be true to Thee till death.

FANTASIE IMPROMPTU
(Chopin)

Frederic Chopin

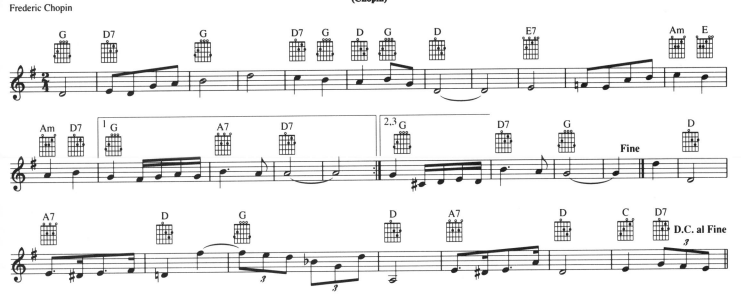

FIGHT YE BULLDOGS

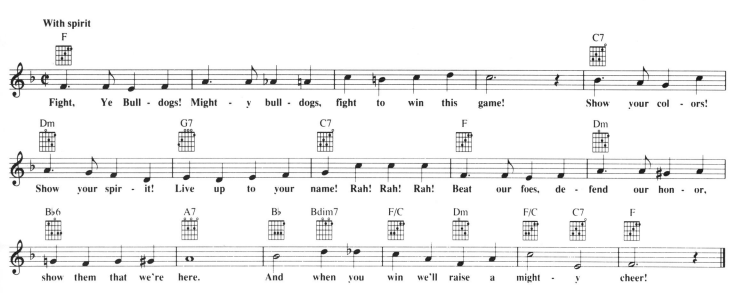

Fight, Ye Bull - dogs! Might - y bull - dogs, fight to win this game! Show your col - ors!

Show your spir - it! Live up to your name! Rah! Rah! Rah! Beat our foes, de - fend our hon - or,

show them that we're here. And when you win we'll raise a might - y cheer!

THE FARMER IN THE DELL

1. The Farm-er In The Dell,_____ The Farm-er In The Dell,
2. The farm-er takes a wife,_____ The farm-er takes a wife,
3. (See additional lyrics)

Heigh - ho, the der-ry O! { The Farm-er In The Dell.
{ The farm-er takes a wife.

Additional Lyrics

3. The wife takes the child,
The wife takes the child,
Heigh-ho, the derry o!
The wife takes the child.

4. The child takes the nurse,
The child takes the nurse,
Heigh-ho, the derry o!
The child takes the nurse.

5. The nurse takes the dog,
The nurse takes the dog,
Heigh-ho, the derry o!
The nurse takes the dog.

6. The dog takes the cat,
The dog takes the cat,
Heigh-ho, the derry o!
The dog takes the cat.

7. The cat takes the rat,
The cat takes the rat,
Heigh-ho, the derry o!
The cat takes the rat.

8. The rat takes the cheese,
The rat takes the cheese,
Heigh-ho, the derry o!
The rat takes the cheese.

9. The cheese stands alone,
The cheese stands alone,
Heigh-ho, the derry o!
The cheese stands alone.

FOR HE'S A JOLLY GOOD FELLOW

For He's A Jol-ly Good Fel-low, For He's A Jol-ly Good Fel-low, For____

He's A Jol-ly Good Fel-low, Which no-bod-y can de-ny,_____

Which no-bod-y can de-ny,_____ Which no-bod-y can de-ny. _____ For

FREIGHT TRAIN

FLEDERMAUS WALTZ

Johann Strauss

FLOW GENTLY, SWEET AFTON

Music by Alexander Hume
Words by Robert Burns

Additional Lyrics

2. How lofty sweet Afton, thy neighboring hills,
   Far marked with the courses of clear winding rills.
   There daily I wander as morn rises high,
   My flocks and my Mary's sweet cot in my eye.
   How pleasant thy banks and green valleys below,
   Where wild in the woodlands the primroses blow.
   There oft as mild evening creeps over the lea,
   The sweet-scented birk shades my Mary and me.

3. Thy crystal stream Afton, how lovely it glides,
   And winds by the cot where my Mary resides.
   How wanton thy waters her snowy feet lave,
   As gath'ring sweet flow'rets, she stems thy clear wave.
   Flow Gently, Sweet Afton, among thy green braes,
   Flow gently, sweet river, the theme of my lays.
   My Mary's asleep by the murmuring stream,
   Flow Gently, Sweet Afton, disturb not her dreams.

FAR ABOVE CAYUGA'S WATERS

Lyrics by A.C. Weekes and W. M. Smith
Music by H. S. Thompson

Far A - bove Cay - u - ga's Wa - ters, With its waves of blue;_____
Far a - bove the bus - y hum - ming of the bustl - ing town._____

Stands our no - ble Al - ma Ma - ter, Glo - ri - ous to view._____
Reared a - gainst the arch of Heav - en looks she proud - ly down._____

Raise the cho - rus, speed it on - ward, Loud her prais - es tell;_____

Hail to thee, our Al - ma Ma - ter! Hail! All hail! Cor - nell!_____

THE FOGGY, FOGGY DEW

1. When I was a bach - e - lor, I lived all a - lone, I worked at the weav - er's trade,__ And the on - ly, on - ly thing that I
2 - 3. (See additional lyrics)

did__ that was wrong Was to woo a fair young maid. I wooed her in the win - ter time, and part of the sum - mer,

too, And the on - ly, on - ly thing that I did__ that was wrong Was to keep her from The Fog - gy, Fog - gy Dew.

Additional Lyrics

2. One night she came to my bedside,
When I was fast asleep,
She flung her arms around my neck
And then began to weep.
She wept, she cried, she tore her hair,
Ah me, what could I do?
So all night long I held her in my arms,
Just to keep her from the foggy, foggy dew.

3. Still I am a bachelor, I live with my son,
We work at the weaver's trade.
And every time I look into his eyes
He reminds me of that fair young maid.
He reminds me of the winter time,
And part of the summer, too,
And of the many, many times I held her in my arms,
Just to keep her from the foggy, foggy dew.

THE FIRST NOEL

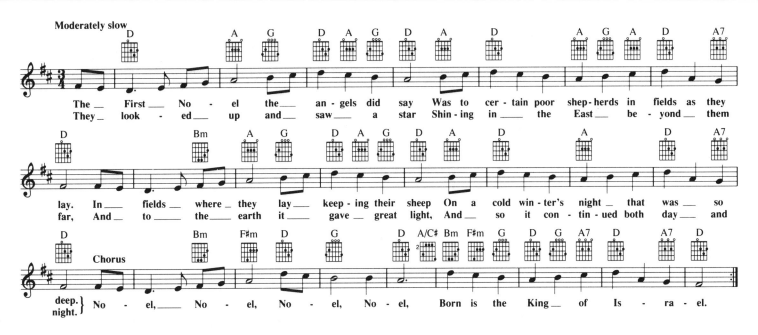

The __ First __ No - el the __ an - gels did say Was to cer - tain poor shep - herds in fields as they
They __ look - ed __ up and __ saw a star Shin - ing in __ the East __ be - yond __ them

lay. In __ fields __ where __ they lay __ keep - ing their sheep On a cold win - ter's night __ that was __ so
far, And __ to __ the __ earth it __ gave __ great light, And __ so it con - tin - ued both day __ and

Chorus

deep.}
night.} No - el, __ No - el, No - el, No - el, Born is the King __ of Is - ra - el.

FROGGIE WENT A-COURTIN'

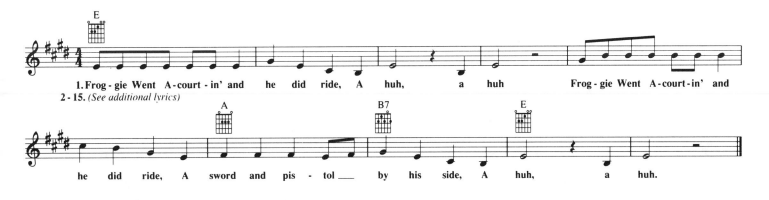

1. Frog - gie Went A - court - in' and he did ride, A huh, a huh Frog - gie Went A - court - in' and
2 - 15. *(See additional lyrics)*

he did ride, A sword and pis - tol __ by his side, A huh, a huh.

Additional Lyrics

2. Well, he rode down to Miss Mouses's door, a-huh, a-huh,
   Well, he rode down to Miss Mouses's door,
   Where he had ofter been before, a-huh, a-huh.

3. He took Miss Mousie on his knee, a-huh, a-huh,
   He took Miss Mousie on his knee,
   Said, "Miss Mousie will you marry me?" A-huh, a-huh.

4. "I'll have to ask my Uncle Rat, etc.
   See what he will say to that.", etc.

5. "Without my Uncle Rat's consent,
   I would not marry the President."

6. Well, Uncle Rat laughed and shook his fat sides,
   To think his niece would be a bride.

7. Well, Uncle Rat rode off to town
   To buy his niece a wedding gown.

8. "Where will the wedding supper be?"
   "Way down yonder in a hollow tree."

9. "What will the wedding supper be?"
   "A fried mosquito and a roasted flea."

10. First to come in were two little ants,
    Fixing around to have a dance.

11. Next to come in was a bumble bee,
    Bouncing a fiddle on his knee.

12. Next to come in was a fat sassy lad,
    Thinks himself as big as his dad.

13. Thinks himself a man indeed,
    Because he chews the tobacco weed.

14. And next to come in was a big tomcat,
    He swallowed the frog and the mouse and the rat.

15. Next to come in was a big old snake,
    He chased the party into the lake.

FRANKIE AND JOHNNY

1. Frank-ie And John-nie were lov-ers! Oh, Lord-y how __ they could love! They swore to be true __ to each
2-13. *(See additional lyrics)*

oth-er, Just as true as the stars a-bove, __ He was her man, _____ But he done her wrong. _____

Additional Lyrics

2. Frankie she was a good woman
   As everybody know,
   Spent a hundred dollars
   Just to buy her man some clothes.
   He was her man, but he was doing her wrong.

3. Frankie went down to the corner
   Just for a bucket of beer,
   Said: "Mr. bartender
   Has my loving Johnny been here?
   "He was my man, but he's a-doing me wrong."

4. "Now I don't want ot tell you no stories
   And I don't want to tell you no lies
   I was your man about an hour ago
   With a gal named Nellie Bligh
   He was your man, but he's a-doing you wrong."

5. Frankie she went down to the hotel
   Didn't go there for fun,
   Underneath her kimona
   She carried a forty-four gun.
   He was her man, but he was doing her wrong.

6. Frankie looked over the transom
   To see what she could spy,
   There sat Johnny on the sofa
   Just loving up Nellie Bligh.
   He was her man, but he was doing her wrong.

7. Frankie got down from that high stool
   She didn't want to see no more;
   Rooty-toot-toot three times she shot
   Right through that hardwood door.
   He was her man, but he was doing her wrong.

8. Now the first time that Frankie shot Johnny
   He let out an awful yell,
   Second time she shot him
   There was a new man's face in hell.
   He was her man, but he was doing her wrong.

9. "Oh roll me over easy
   Roll me over slow
   Roll me over on the right side
   For the left side hurts me so."
   He was her man, but he was doing her wrong.

10. Sixteen rubber-tired carriages
    Sixteen rubber-tired hacks
    They take poor Johnny to the graveyard
    They ain't gonna bring him back.
    He was her man, but he was doing her wrong.

11. Frankie looked out of the jailhouse
    To see what she could see,
    All she could hear was a two-string bow
    Crying nearer my God to thee.
    He was her man, but he was doing her wrong.

12. Frankie she said to the sheriff
    "What do you reckon they'll do?"
    Sheriff he said "Frankie,
    "It's the electric chair for you."
    He was her man, but he was doing her wrong.

13. This story has no moral
    This story has no end
    This story only goes to show
    That there ain't no good in men!
    He was her man, but he was doing her wrong.

FRÈRE JACQUES

Frè - re Jac - ques, Frè - re Jac - ques, Dor - mez vous, dor - mez vous?
Are you sleep - ing, are you sleep - ing, Broth - er John, broth - er John?

Son - nez les ma - ti - nes, son - nez les ma - ti - nes } Ding, ding, dong, ding, ding, dong.
Morn - ing bells are ring - ing, morn - ing bells are ring - ing } Ding, ding, dong, ding, ding, dong.

FUNICULI, FUNICULA

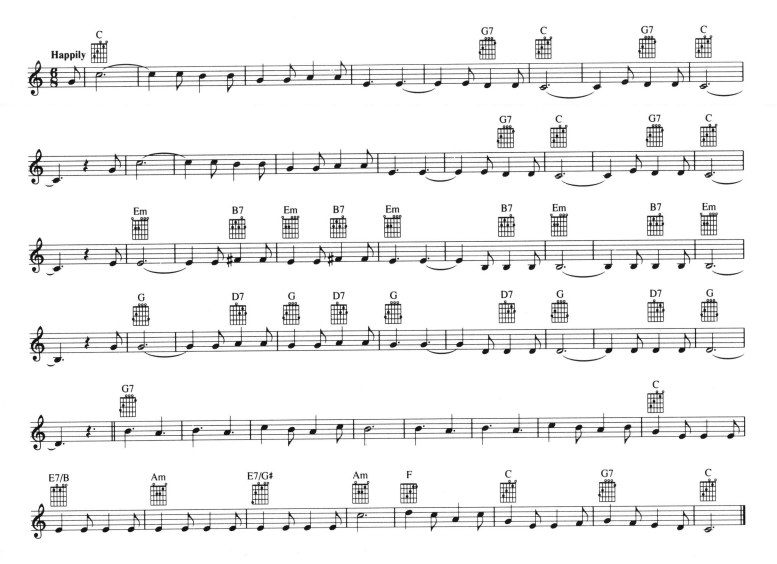

FUNERAL MARCH

Frédéric Chopin

Very Slow

FUNERAL MARCH OF A MARIONETTE

Charles Gounod

Mysteriously

THE FRIENDLY BEASTS

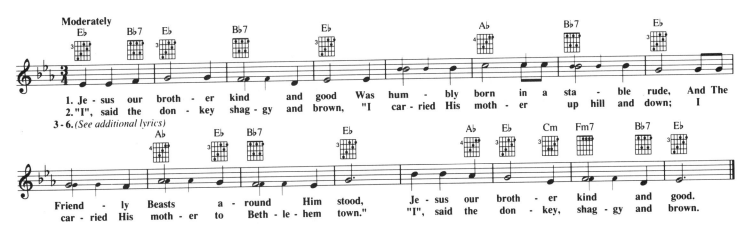

Moderately

1. Je - sus our broth - er kind and good Was hum - bly born in a sta - ble rude, And The
2. "I", said the don - key shag - gy and brown, "I car - ried His moth - er up hill and down; I

3 - 6. *(See additional lyrics)*

Friend - ly Beasts a - round Him stood, Je - sus our broth - er kind and good.
car - ried His moth - er to Beth - le - hem town." "I", said the don - key, shag - gy and brown.

Additional Lyrics

3. "I," said the cow all white and red,
   "I gave Him my manger for His bed;
   I gave Him my hay to pillow His head."
   "I," said the cow all white and red.

4. "I," said the sheep with the curly horn,
   "I gave Him my wool for His blanket warm;
   He wore my coat on Christmas morn."
   "I," said the sheep with curly horn.

5. "I," said the dove from the rafters high,
   "I cooed Him to sleep that He would not cry;
   We cooed Him to sleep, my mate and I."
   "I," said the dove from the rafters high.

6. Thus every beast by some good spell,
   In the stable dark was glad to tell
   Of the gift he gave Emanuel,
   The gift he gave Emanuel.

FÜR ELISE

Ludwig Van Beethoven

Brightly
N.C.

FORTY-FIVE MINUTES FROM BROADWAY

George M. Cohan

FASCINATION

F. D. Marchetti

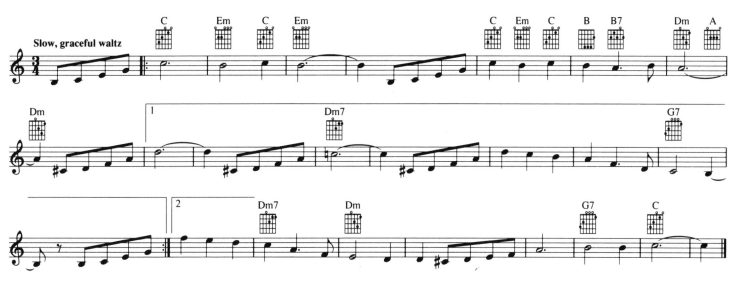

FINLANDIA

J. Sibelius

GOODBYE, MY LADY LOVE

Joseph E. Howard

Good - bye, My La - dy Love, Fare - well, my tur - tle dove, You are the

i - dol and dar - ling of my heart, But some day you will come back to me,

and love me ten - der - ly, so Good - bye, My La - dy Love, good - bye.

GIVE MY REGARDS TO BROADWAY

George M. Cohan

Give My Re - gards To Broad - way, Re - mem - ber me to Her - ald Square;

Tell all the gang, at For - ty Sec - ond Street that I will soon be there.

Whis - per of how I'm yearn - ing to min - gle with the old time throng;

Give my re - gards to old Broad - way and say that I'll be there, ere long. long._____

GLOW WORM

Paul Lincke

GAVOTTE

Francois J. Gossec

Moderately fast

GOD OF OUR FATHERS

Daniel C. Roberts
George Warren

With majesty

God Of Our Fa - thers, Whose al - might - y hand, heads forth in
Re - fresh Thy peo - ple on their toil - some way, Lead us from

beau - ty, all the star - ry band of shin - ning worlds in
night to nev - er end - ing day; Fill all our lives with

splen - dor through the skies, our grate - ful songs, be - fore Thy throne a - rise.
love and grace di - vine And glor - y, laud and praise be ev - er Thine.

GIT ALONG HOME, CINDY

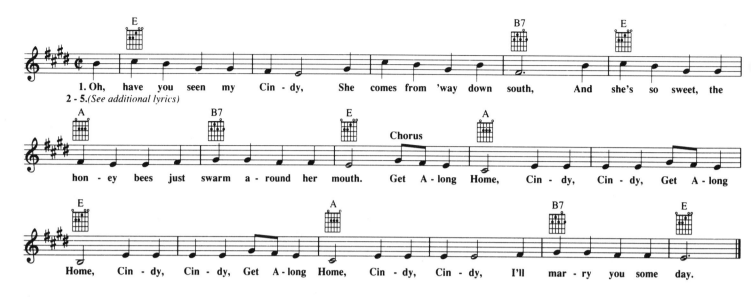

1. Oh, have you seen my Cin - dy, She comes from 'way down south, And she's so sweet, the
2 - 5. (See additional lyrics)

hon - ey bees just swarm a - round her mouth. Get A - long Home, Cin - dy, Cin - dy, Get A - long

Chorus

Home, Cin - dy, Cin - dy, Get A - long Home, Cin - dy, Cin - dy, I'll mar - ry you some day.

Copyright © 1990 HAL LEONARD PUBLISHING CORPORATION

Additional Lyrics

2. I wish I was an apple,
   A-hangin' in a tree,
   And ev'ry time my sweetheart passed,
   She'd take a bite of me.

3. She told me that she loved me,
   She called me sugar plum,
   She throwed 'er arms around me,
   I thought my time had come.

4. She took me to the parlor,
   She cooled me with her fan.
   She swore I was the purtiest thing
   In the shape of mortal man.

5. I wish I had a needle,
   As fine as I could sew;
   I'd sew the girls to my coat tail,
   And down the road I'd go.

GIVE ME THAT OLD TIME RELIGION

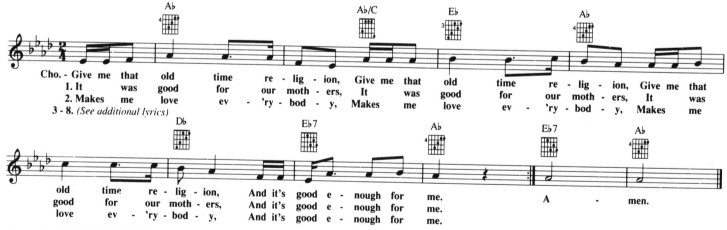

Cho. - Give me that old time re - lig - ion, Give me that old time re - lig - ion, Give me that
1. It was good for our moth - ers, It was good for our moth - ers, It was
2. Makes me love ev - 'ry - bod - y, Makes me love ev - 'ry - bod - y, Makes me
3 - 8. (See additional lyrics)

old time re - lig - ion, And it's good e - nough for me. A - men.
good for our moth - ers, And it's good e - nough for me.
love ev - 'ry - bod - y, And it's good e - nough for me.

Copyright © 1990 MILWIN MUSIC

Additional Lyrics

3. It has saved our fathers,
   And it's good enough for me.

4. It was good for the prophet Daniel,
   And it's good enough for me.

5. It was good for the Hebrew children,
   And it's good enough for me.

6. It was tried in the fiery furnace,
   And it's good enough for me.

7. It was good for Paul and Silas,
   And it's good enough for me.

8. It will do when I am dying,
   And it's good enough for me.

GIT ALONG, LITTLE DOGIES

1. As I was a-walk-in' one morn-ing for pleas-ure, I spied a cow-punch-er a-stroll-in' a-long. His
2-7. *(See additional lyrics)*

hat was thrown back and his spurs were a-jin-glin', And as he ap-proached he was sing-ing this song. Whoop-ee

ti - yi - yo, Git A - long Lit - tle Do - gies, It's your___ mis-for-tune, and none of my own, Whoop-ee

ti - yi - yo, Git A - long Lit - tle Do - gies, you know that Wy - o - ming will be your new home.

Additional Lyrics

2. Early in the springtime we'll round up the dogies,
   Slap on their brands and bob off their tails;
   Round up our horses, load up the chuck wagon,
   Then throw those dogies upon the trail.

4. Some of the boys goes up the trail for pleasure,
   But that's where they git it most awfully wrong;
   For you haven't any idea the trouble they give us,
   When we go driving them dogies along.

6. Your mother she was raised way down in Texas,
   Where the jimson weed and sandburs grow;
   Now we'll fill you up on prickly pear and cholla,
   Till you are ready for the trail to Idaho.

3. It's whooping and yelling and driving the dogies,
   Oh, how I wish you would go on,
   It's whooping and punching and go on, little dogies,
   For you know Wyoming will be your new home.

5. When the night comes on and we hold them on the bed-ground,
   These little dogies that roll on so slow;
   Roll up the herd and cut out the strays,
   And roll the little dogies that never rolled before.

7. Oh, you'll be soup for Uncle Sam's Injuns,
   "It's beef, heap beef," I hear them cry.
   Git along, git along, git along, little dogies,
   You're going to be beef steers by and by.

GO TELL AUNT RHODY

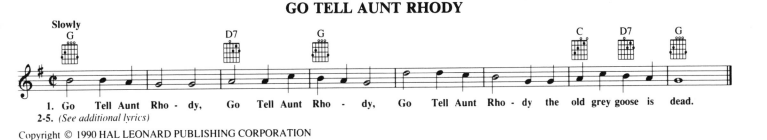

1. Go Tell Aunt Rho - dy, Go Tell Aunt Rho - dy, Go Tell Aunt Rho - dy the old grey goose is dead.
2-5. *(See additional lyrics)*

Additional Lyrics

2. The one she was saving, *(three times)*
   To make a feather bed.

4. The goslings are crying, *(three times)*
   Because their mama's dead.

3. The gander is weeping, *(three times)*
   Because his wife is dead.

5. She died in the water, *(three times)*
   With her heels above her head.

GLADIATOR MARCH

John Philip Sousa

GO, TELL IT ON THE MOUNTAIN

While shep - herds kept their watch - ing O'er si - lent flocks by night, Be - hold through - out the
shep - herds feared and trem - bled When lo! a - bove the earth rang out the an - gel

heav - ens There shone a ho - ly light.____ Go, Tell It On The Moun - tain O - ver the hills and
cho - rus that hailed our Sav - ior's birth.____ }

ev - 'ry - where, Go, Tell It On The Moun - tain that Je - sus Christ__ is born. The born.

GO IN AND OUT THE WINDOW

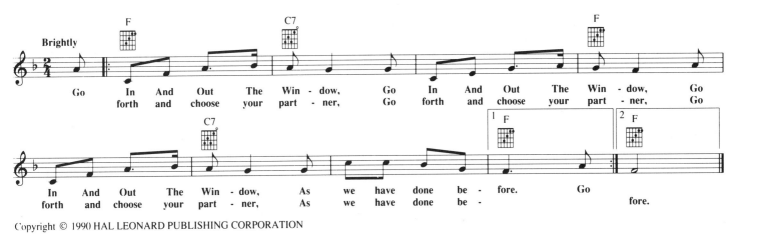

Go In And Out The Win - dow, Go In And Out The Win - dow, Go
Go forth and choose your part - ner, Go forth and choose your part - ner, Go

In And Out The Win - dow, As we have done be - fore. Go
forth and choose your part - ner, As we have done be - fore. fore.

THE GIRL I LEFT BEHIND

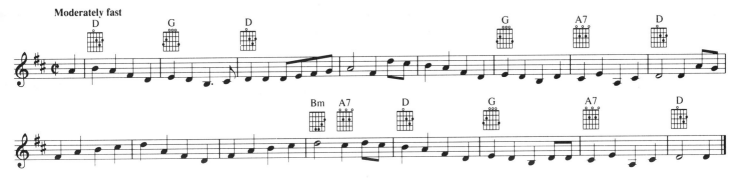

GOD REST YE MERRY, GENTLEMEN

God Rest Ye Mer - ry Gen - tle - men, let noth - ing you dis - may. Re - mem - ber Christ our
In Beth - le - hem, in Jew - ry. This bless - ed Babe was born. And laid with - in a
From God our Heav'n - ly Fa - ther, a bless - ed An - gel came; And un - to cer - tain

Sa - vi - our was born on Christ - mas Day. To save us all from Sa - tan's pow'r. When
man - ger, up on this bless - ed morn; That which His Moth - er Ma - ry, did
Shep - herds, brought ti - dings of the same; How that in Beth - le - hem was born the

we were gone a - stray; } O____ ti - dings of com - fort and joy, com - fort and
noth - ing take in scorn. }
Son of God by Name.

joy. O____ ti - dings of com - fort and joy.

GOLD AND SILVER WALTZ

Franz Lehar

Waltz tempo

GOOD CHRISTIAN MEN, REJOICE

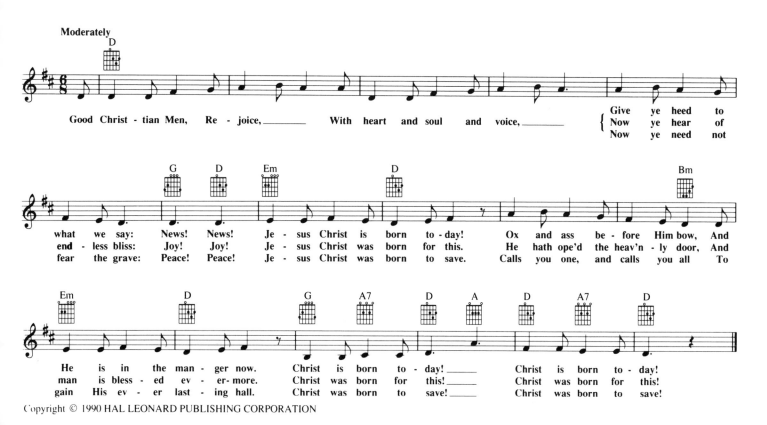

Good Christ - tian Men, Re - joice,_____ With heart and soul and voice,_____ { Give ye heed to
Now ye hear of
Now ye need not

what we say: News! News! Je - sus Christ is born to - day! Ox and ass be - fore Him bow, And
end - less bliss: Joy! Joy! Je - sus Christ was born for this. He hath ope'd the heav'n - ly door, And
fear the grave: Peace! Peace! Je - sus Christ was born to save. Calls you one, and calls you all To

He is in the man - ger now. Christ is born to - day!_____ Christ is born to - day!
man is bless - ed ev - er - more. Christ was born for this!_____ Christ was born for this!
gain His ev - er last - ing hall. Christ was born to save!_____ Christ was born to save!

GOD SAVE OUR KING (QUEEN)

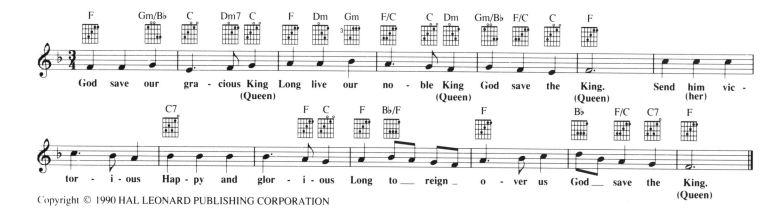

God save our gra-cious King (Queen) Long live our no-ble King (Queen) God save the King. (Queen) Send him vic-(her) tor-i-ous Hap-py and glor-i-ous Long to __ reign __ o-ver us God __ save the King. (Queen)

GOOD NIGHT LADIES

Brightly

Good Night, La - dies, __ Good Night, La - dies! __ Good Night La - dies, __ We're going to leave you now.

Mer - ri - ly we roll a - long, roll a - long, roll a - long, Mer - ri - ly we roll a - long, O'er the deep blue sea.

GOODBYE GIRLS, I'M THROUGH

Words by John Golden
Music by Ivan Caryll

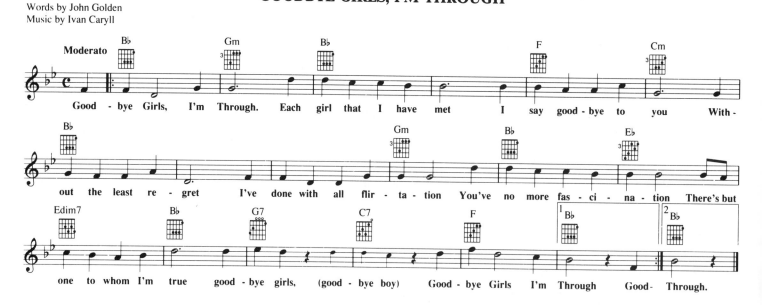

Moderato

Good - bye Girls, I'm Through. Each girl that I have met I say good-bye to you With -

out the least re - gret I've done with all flir - ta - tion You've no more fas - ci - na - tion There's but

one to whom I'm true good - bye girls, (good - bye boy) Good - bye Girls I'm Through Good- Through.

GOOBER PEAS

Moderately

1. Sit - ting by the road - side on a sum-mer day, Chat - ting with my mess - mates, pass-ing time a - way,
2-4. *(See additional lyrics)*

Ly - ing in the shad - ow un - der-neath the trees, Good-ness, how de - li - cious, eat - ing Goo - ber Peas!

Peas! peas! peas! peas! eat - ing Goo - ber Peas! Good-ness how de - li - cious, eat - ing Goo - ber Peas!

Additional Lyrics

2. When a horseman passes, the soldiers have a rule,
   To cry out at their loudest, "Mister, here's your mule!"
   But another pleasure enchantinger than these,
   Is wearing out your grinders, eating Goober Peas!

3. Just before the battle the Gen'ral hears a row,
   He says, "The Yanks are coming, I hear their rifles now."
   He turns around in wonder, and what do you think he sees?
   The Georgia Militia - eating Goober Peas!

4. I think my song has lasted almost long enough,
   The subject's interesting, but rhymes are mighty rough,
   I wish this war was over, when free from rags and fleas,
   We'd kiss our wives and sweethearts and gobble Goober Peas!

THE GREEN GRASS GREW ALL AROUND

Lively

Once there was a tree, was the pret - ti - est lit - tle tree, and the tree grew in the ground.

And on that tree there grew a limb,
And on that limb there grew a branch, } and The Green Grass Grew All A - round. And the
And on that branch there grew a leaf,

tree in the ground, { and the limb on the tree,
and the branch on the limb, } and The Green Grass Grew All A - round.
and the leaf on the branch,

Oh, The Green Grass Grew All A - round, all a - round, and The Green Grass Grew All A - round. round.

GOOD KING WENCESLAS

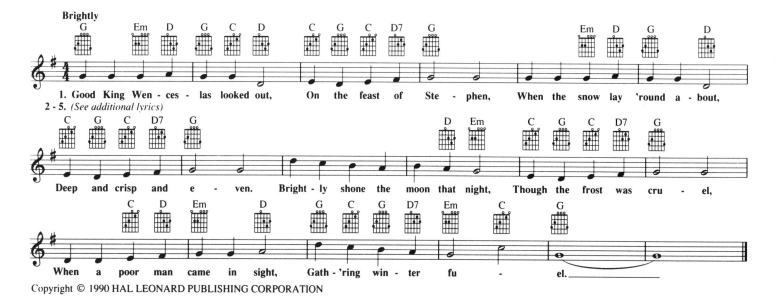

Brightly

1. Good King Wen-ces-las looked out, On the feast of Ste-phen, When the snow lay 'round a-bout,

2 - 5. (See additional lyrics)

Deep and crisp and e-ven. Bright-ly shone the moon that night, Though the frost was cru-el,

When a poor man came in sight, Gath-'ring win-ter fu-el. _____

Additional Lyrics

2. "Hither page, and stand by me,
   If thou know'st it, telling,
   Yonder peasant, who is he?
   Where and what his dwelling?"
   "Sire, he lives a good league hence,
   Underneath the mountain;
   Right against the forest fence,
   By Saint Agnes' fountain."

3. "Bring me flesh, and bring me wine,
   Bring me pine-logs hither;
   Thou and I will see him dine,
   When we bear them thither."
   Page and monarch forth they went,
   Forth they went together;
   Through the rude winds wild lament:
   And the bitter weather.

4. "Sire, the night is darker now,
   And the wind blows stronger;
   Fails my heart, I know not how,
   I can go not longer."
   "Mark my footsteps, my good page,
   Tread thou in them boldly:
   Thou shalt find the winter's rage
   Freeze thy blood less coldly."

5. In his master's steps he trod,
   Where the snow lay dinted;
   Heat was in the very sod
   Which the saint had printed.
   Therefore, Christain men, be sure
   Wealth or rank possessing,
   Ye who now will bless the poor,
   Shall yourselves find blessing.

GOODBYE, OLD PAINT

Gently and flowing

Good-bye, Old Paint, I'm a-leav-in' Chey-enne.

1. I'm a-leav-in' Chey-
2. My foot in the
3. Old Paint's a good

enne, I'm off to Mon-tan', ____ Good-Bye, Old Paint, I'm a leav-in' Chey-enne.

stir-rup, my po-ny won't stand, ____ Good-Bye, Old Paint, I'm a leav-in' Chey-enne.

po-ny, he pac-es when he can, ____ Good-bye lit-tle An-nie, I'm off to Mon-tan'.

GRANDFATHER'S CLOCK

Henry C. Work

Moderately slow

1. My grand-fath-er's clock was too large for the shelf so it stood nine-ty years on the floor. It was
   tall - er by half than the old man him - self tho' it weighed not a pen-ny-weight

2- 4. (See additional lyrics)

more. It was bought on the morn of the day that he was born and was al - ways his trea - sure and

pride; But it stopped short nev - er to go a - gain when the old man____

died. Nine - ty years with - out slum-ber - ing, tick, tock, tick, tock, his life sec-onds num-ber - ing, tick, tock, tick, tock. It

stopped short nev - er to go a - gain when the old man died.

Additional Lyrics

2. In watching its pendulum swing to and fro,
   Many hours had he spent while a boy;
   And in childhood and manhood the clock
       seemed to know,
   And to share both his grief and his joy.
   For it struck twenty-four when he entered
       at the door,
   With a blooming and beautiful bride.

3. My grandfather said that of those he could hire,
   Not a servant so faithful he found;
   For it wasted no time, and had but one desire,
   At the close of each week to be wound.
   And it kept in its place, not a frown upon its face,
   And its hands never hung by its side.

4. It rang an alarm in the dead of the night,
   An alarm that for years had been dumb;
   And we knew that his spirit was pluming
       its flight,
   That his hour of departure had come.
   Still the clock kept the time, with a soft and
       muffled chime,
   As we silently stood by his side.

GREY AND GOLD WALTZ

Brightly

GREEN GROW THE LILACS

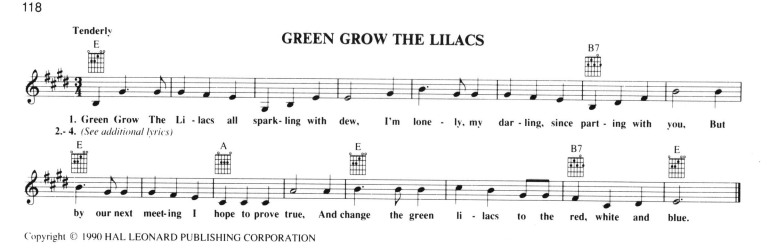

Tenderly

1. Green Grow The Li-lacs all spark-ling with dew, I'm lone-ly, my dar-ling, since part-ing with you, But
2.- 4. *(See additional lyrics)*

by our next meet-ing I hope to prove true, And change the green li-lacs to the red, white and blue.

Additional Lyrics

2. I used to have a sweetheart, but now I have none,
   Since she's gone and left me, I care not for one.
   Since she's gone and left me, contented I'll be,
   For she loves another one better than me.

3. I passed my love's window, both early and late,
   The look that she gave me, it made my heart ache.
   Oh, the look that she gave me was painful to see,
   For she loves another one better than me.

4. I wrote my love letters in rosy red lines,
   She sent me an answer all twisted in twines,
   Saying, "Keep your love letters and don't waste your time,
   Just you write to your love and I'll write to mine."

GRIEG PIANO CONCERTO
(Theme)

Edvard Grieg
Moderately

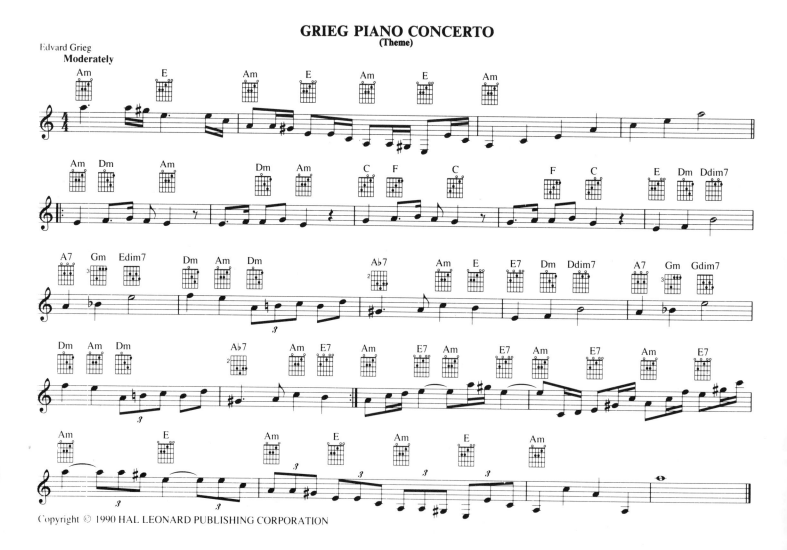

GREENSLEEVES

1. Alas, my love, ____ you do me wrong, ____ To cast me off ____ dis - cour - teous - ly, And
I have loved ____ you oh, so long, ____ De -
2- 4. *(See additional lyrics)*

light - ing in ____ your com - pa - ny. Green - sleeves ____ was all my joy, ____
Green - sleeves was my heart of gold, ____ And

Green - sleeves ____ was my de - light. who but my la - dy Green - sleeves.

Additional Lyrics

2. I have been ready at your hand,
To grant whatever you would crave;
I have both wagered life and land,
Your love and good-will for to have.
If you intend thus to disdain,
It does the more enrapture me,
And even so, I still remain
A lover in captivity.

3. My men were clothed all in green,
And they did ever wait on thee;
All this was gallant to be seen;
And yet thou wouldst not love me.
Thou couldst desire no earthly thing
But still thou hadst it readily.
Thy music still to play and sing;
And yet thou wouldst not love me.

4. Well, I will pray to God on high,
That thou my constancy mayst see,
And that yet once before I die,
Thou wilt vouchsafe to love me.
Ah, Greensleeves, now farewell, adieu,
To God I pray to prosper thee,
For I am still thy lover true,
Come once again and love me.

GYPSY LOVE SONG

Harry B. Smith
Victor Herbert

Slum - ber on, my lit - tle gyp - sy sweet - heart, Dream of the field and the
Can you hear me, hear me in that dream - land,
Can you hear the song ____ that ____ tells you,

grove. ____ Where your fan - cies rove? ____

Slum - ber on, my lit - tle gyp - sy sweet - heart, Wild lit - tle wood - land

dove. ____ All my ____ heart's true love? ____

GYPSY RONDO

Joseph Haydn

HABAÑERA
(From "CARMEN")

Georges Bizet

HAIL, COLUMBIA

Words by Joseph Hopkinson
Music by Philip Phile

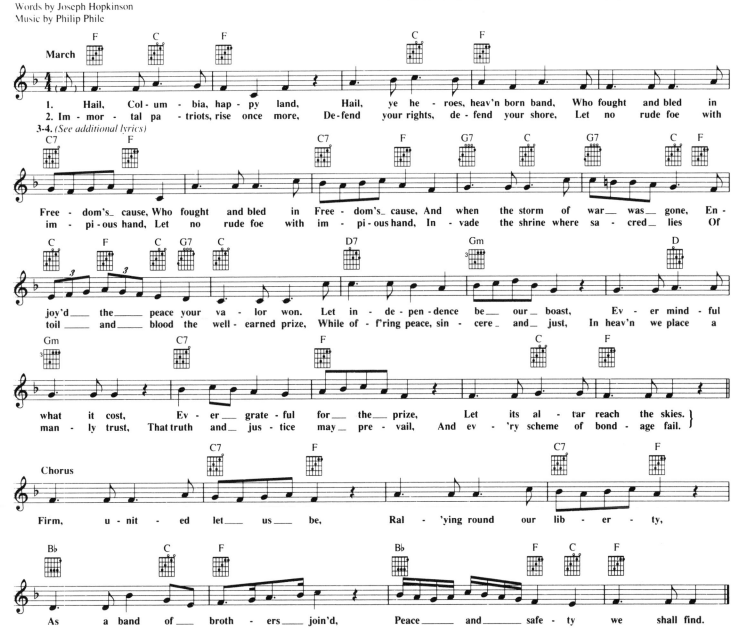

Additional Lyrics

3. Sound, sound the trump of fame,
   Let Washington's great fame
   Ring through the world with loud applause,
   Ring through the world with loud applause,
   Let ev'ry chime to freedom dear,
   Listen with a joyful ear,
   With equal skill, with God-like pow'r
   He governs in the fearful hour
   Of horrid war, or guides with ease
   The happier time of honest peace.
   Chorus

4. Beloved the chief who now commands,
   Once more to serve his country stands,
   The rock on which the storm will beat,
   The rock on which the storm will beat.
   But arm'd in virtue firm and true,
   His hopes are fixed on Heav'n and you,
   When hope was sinking in dismay,
   When glooms obscured Columbia's day,
   His steady mind from changes free
   Resolv'd on Death or Liberty.
   Chorus

HALLELUJAH CHORUS

G. F. Handel

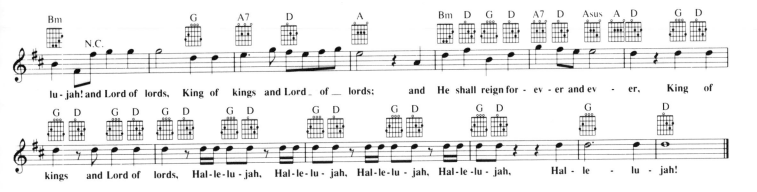

lu-jah! and Lord of lords, King of kings and Lord of lords; and He shall reign for-ev-er and ev-er, King of
kings and Lord of lords, Hal-le-lu-jah, Hal-le-lu-jah, Hal-le-lu-jah, Hal-le-lu-jah, Hal-le-lu-jah!

HAIL TO THE CHIEF

James Sanderson

Slowly

HAND ME DOWN MY WALKING CANE

James A. Bland

Moderately

Hand Me Down____ My Walk-ing Cane,____ Hand Me Down____ My Walk-ing
down____ my bot-tle of corn,____ Hand me down____ my bot-tle of

Cane,____ Oh, Hand Me Down My Walk-ing Cane, I'm a goin' to leave on that
corn,____ Oh, hand me down my bot-tle of corn, I'm a goin' to leave Drunk as

mid-night train, 'Cause all of my sins are tak-en a-way.____ Hand me
sure as you're born, 'Cause all of my sins are tak-en a-way.____

HAIL! HAIL! THE GANG'S ALL HERE

Hail! Hail! The Gang's All Here, What the heck do we care, what the heck do we care,

Hail! Hail! The Gang's All Here, What the heck do we care now!

THE HAPPY FARMER

Robert Schumann

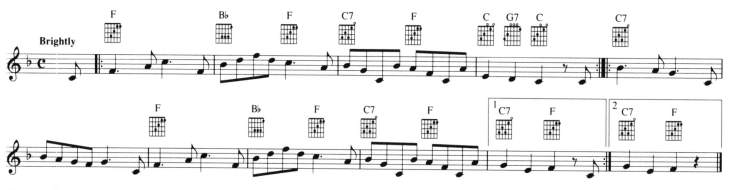

HEARTS AND FLOWERS

Theo. M. Tobani

HATIKVAH

HAVA NAGILAH

HARK! THE HERALD ANGELS SING

Words by Charles Wesley
Music by Felix Mendelssohn-Bartholdy

HE'S GOT THE WHOLE WORLD IN HIS HANDS

HEAR THEM BELLS

HELENA POLKA

HEY, DIDDLE, DIDDLE

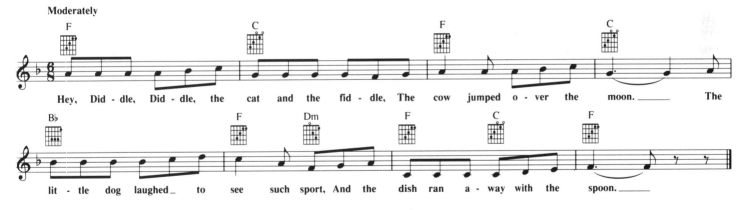

Hey, Did - dle, Did - dle, the cat and the fid - dle, The cow jumped o - ver the moon. _____ The lit - tle dog laughed _ to see such sport, And the dish ran a - way with the spoon. _____

HEY, HO! NOBODY HOME

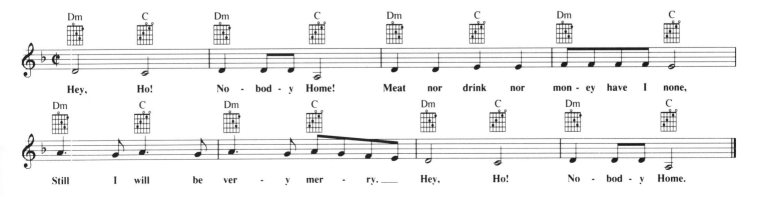

Hey, Ho! No - bod - y Home! Meat nor drink nor mon - ey have I none, Still I will be ver - y mer - ry. _____ Hey, Ho! No - bod - y Home.

HERE WE COME A-CAROLING

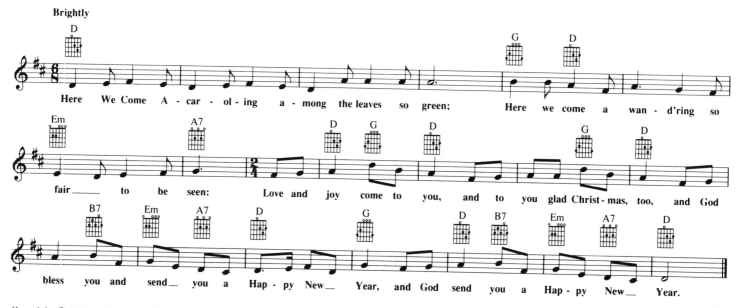

Here We Come A - car - ol - ing a - mong the leaves so green; Here we come a wan - d'ring so

fair ___ to be seen: Love and joy come to you, and to you glad Christ - mas, too, and God

bless you and send ___ you a Hap - py New ___ Year, and God send you a Hap - py New ___ Year.

HIGH SCHOOL CADETS

John Philip Sousa
Brightly

HICKORY, DICKORY, DOCK

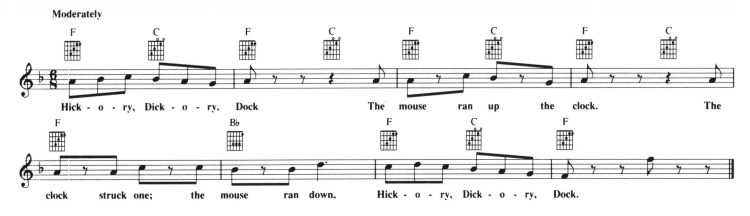

Moderately

Hick - o - ry, Dick - o - ry, Dock The mouse ran up the clock. The

clock struck one; the mouse ran down, Hick - o - ry, Dick - o - ry, Dock.

THE HOLLY AND THE IVY

Slowly

1,6. The Hol - ly And The I - vy, when they are both full grown, Of ___ all the trees that are
2. The hol - ly bears a blos - som, as white as the li - ly flower, and ___ Ma - ry bore sweet _
3. The hol - ly bears a ber - ry, as red as a - ny blood, and ___ Ma - ry bore sweet _
4- 5. *(See additional lyrics)*

in the wood, the ___ hol - ly bears the crown.
Je - sus Christ, to ___ be our sweet Sa - vior. } The ris - ing of the sun ___ and the run - ning of the
Je - sus Christ, to ___ do poor sin - ners good.

deer, the ___ play - ing of the mer - ry or - gan, sweet sing - ing in the choir.

Additional Lyrics

4. The holly bears a prickle,
   As sharp as any thorn
   And Mary bore sweet Jesus Christ
   On Christmas Day in the morn.
   (Refrain)

5. The holly bears a bark,
   As bitter as any gall,
   And Mary bore sweet Jesus Christ
   For to redeem us all.
   (Refrain)

HOT CROSS BUNS

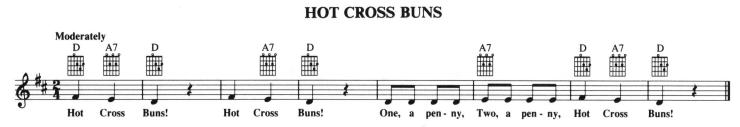

Moderately

Hot Cross Buns! Hot Cross Buns! One, a pen - ny, Two, a pen - ny, Hot Cross Buns!

HOLY GOD, WE PRAISE THEY NAME

Words based on a translation by Clarence Walworth

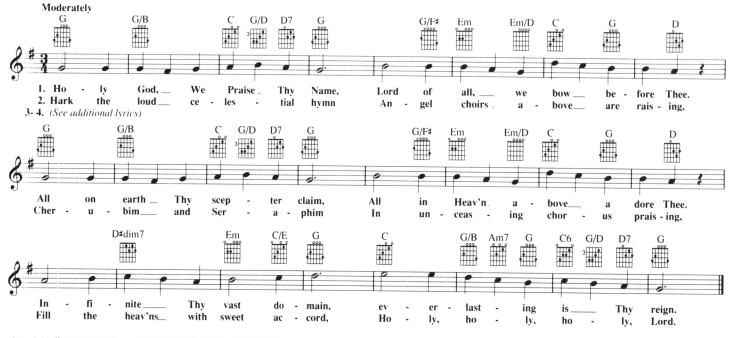

1. Ho - ly God, __ We Praise Thy Name, Lord of all, __ we bow __ be - fore Thee.
2. Hark the loud __ ce - les - tial hymn An - gel choirs __ a - bove __ are rais - ing,
3-4. *(See additional lyrics)*

All on earth __ Thy scep - ter claim, All in Heav'n a - bove __ a dore Thee.
Cher - u - bim __ and Ser - a - phim In un - ceas - ing chor - us prais - ing,

In - fi - nite ___ Thy vast do - main, ev - er - last - ing is ___ Thy reign.
Fill the heav'ns __ with sweet ac - cord, Ho - ly, ho - ly, ho - ly, Lord.

Additional Lyrics

3. Lo, the apostolic train
   Joins Thy sacred name to hallow.
   Prophets swell the gald refrain
   And the white-robed martyrs follow.
   And from morn to set of sun
   Thru the church the song goes on.

4. Holy Father, Holy Son,
   Holy Spirit, Three we name Thee.
   While in essence only one,
   Undivided God we claim Thee.
   And adoring bend the knee,
   While we sing our praise to Thee.

HOME ON THE RANGE

Dr. Brewster Higley
Daniel E. Kelley

1. Oh, give me a home where the buf - fa - lo roam Where the deer and the an - te - lope play; __ Where sel - dom is heard a dis -
2. How of - ten at night when the heav - ens are bright, From the light of the glit - ter - ing stars, __ Have I stood there, a - mazed and
3. Where the air is so pure and the zeph - yrs so free; And the breez - es so balm - y and light, __ Oh, I would not ex - change, my
4. Oh, give me a land where the bright dia - mond sand Flows lei - sure - ly down with the stream, __ Where the grace - ful white swan glides

cour - ag - ing word, And the skies are not cloud - y all day. ___
asked as I gazed, If their glo - ry ex - ceeds that of ours. ___
home on the range, For the glit - ter - ing cit - ies so bright. ___
slow - ly a - long, Like a maid in a heav - en - ly dream. ___

Refrain:
Home, Home On The Range, _ Where the deer and the an - te - lope

play; ___ Where sel - dom is heard a dis - cour - ag - ing word, And the skies are not cloud - y all day. ___

HOLY, HOLY, HOLY

Words by Reginald Heber
Music by John B. Dykes

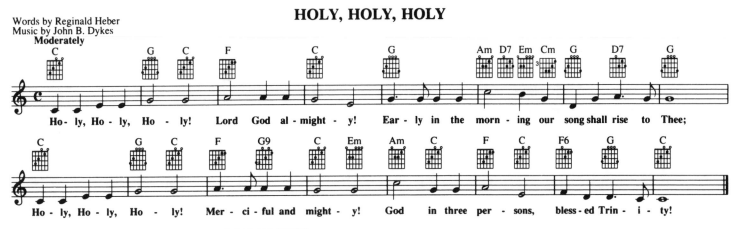

Ho - ly, Ho - ly, Ho - ly! Lord God al - might - y! Ear - ly in the morn - ing our song shall rise to Thee;

Ho - ly, Ho - ly, Ho - ly! Mer - ci - ful and might - y! God in three per - sons, bless - ed Trin - i - ty!

HONEY, WON'T YOU COME BACK TO ME?

Hon - ey, Won't You Come Back To Me?___ I'm as lone - ly as a man can be.___

Since you went a - way I'm cry - ing ev - 'ry day. Can't you hear me call - ing? Can't you hear me say?___ Oh,

Hon - ey Won't You Come Back To Me?___ Hon - ey, won't you hear my plea?___ It's

break - ing my heart,___ hon - ey, since we're a - part.___ Hon - ey, Won't You Come Back To Me?___

HOW DRY I AM!

How Dry I Am!_____ How Dry I Am!_____ No - bod - y knows_____ How Dry I Am._____

HOME SWEET HOME

Lyrics by John Howard Payne
Music by Sir Henry Bishop

1. 'Mid _ pleas - ures and pal - a - ces though _ we may roam, Be it ev - er so hum - ble, there's
2, 3. *(See additional lyrics)*

no_____ place like home; A charm___ from the sky seems to hal - low us there, Which,

seek ___ through the world, is ne'er met___ with else - where. Home! Home! Sweet Home. _____ There's

no_____ place like home. Home! Home! Sweet Home. _____ There's no_____ place like home.

Additional Lyrics

2. An exile from home, splendor dazzles in vain,
Oh, give me my lowly thatched cottage again;
The birds singing gaily, that come at my call;
Give me them, with that peace of mind, dearer than all.
Chorus

3. To thee, I'll return, overburdened with care,
The heart's dearest solace will smile on me there.
No more from that cottage again will I roam,
Be it ever so humble, there's no place like home.
Chorus

HOPAK

Modest Moussorgsky

Brightly

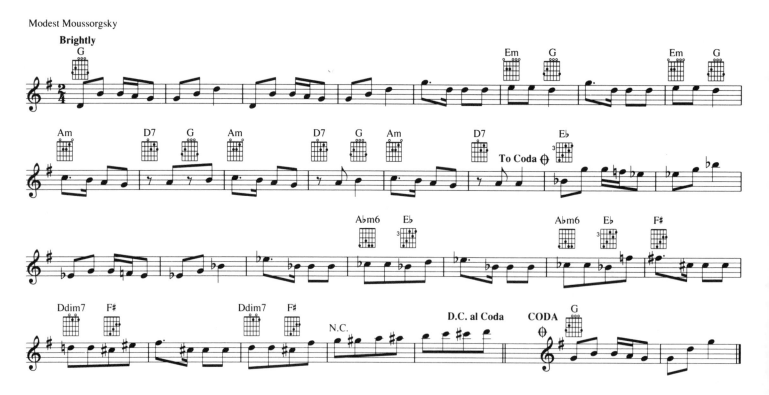

A HOT TIME IN THE OLD TOWN TONIGHT

Words by Joe Hayden; Music by Theodore A. Metz

Brightly

When you hear them-a bells go ding ling ling, All join 'round And __ sweet-ly you must sing, And when the verse is through, In the cho-rus all join in, There'll Be A Hot Time In The Old Town To - night. _____ night. _____

HOUSE OF THE RISING SUN

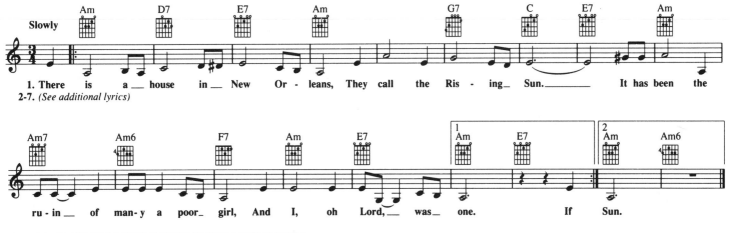

Slowly

1. There is a __ house in __ New Or - leans, They call the Ris - ing __ Sun. _____ It has been the
2-7. *(See additional lyrics)*

ru - in __ of man-y a poor __ girl, And I, oh Lord, __ was __ one. If Sun.

Additional Lyrics

2. If I had listened to what mama said,
   I'd 'a' been at home today.
   Being so young and foolish, poor girl,
   Let a gambler lead me astray.

3. My mother, she's a tailor,
   She sells those new blue jeans.
   My sweetheart, he's a drunkard, Lord,
   Drinks down in New Orleans.

4. The only thing a drunkard needs
   Is a suitcase and a trunk.
   The only time he's satisfied
   Is when he's on a drunk.

5. Go tell my baby, sister,
   Never do like I have done.
   To shun that house in New Orleans,
   They call the Rising Sun.

6. One foot is on the platform,
   And the other one on the train.
   I'm going back to New Orleans
   To wear that ball and chain.

7. I'm going back to New Orleans,
   My race is almost run.
   Going back to end my life
   Beneath the Rising Sun.

HUMORESQUE

Antonin Dvořák

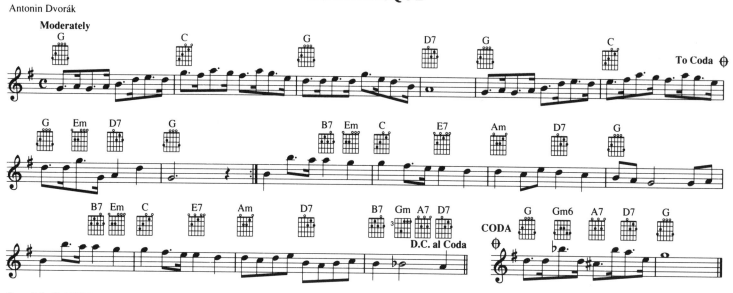

HUMPTY DUMPTY

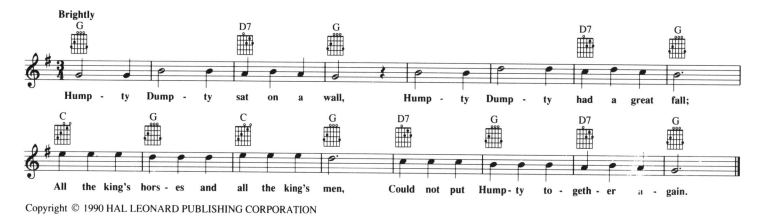

Hump - ty Dump - ty sat on a wall, Hump - ty Dump - ty had a great fall;

All the king's hors - es and all the king's men, Could not put Hump - ty to - geth - er a - gain.

HUNGARIAN DANCE NO. 5

Johannes Brahms

HUSH, LITTLE BABY

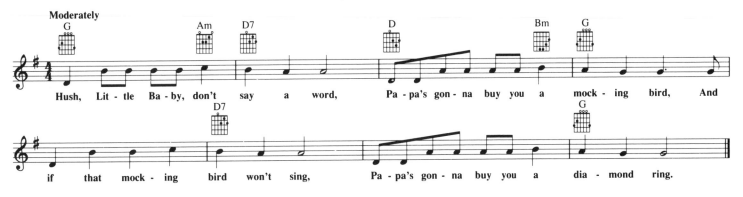

I AM THE CAPTAIN OF THE PINAFORE

By W.S. Gilbert and Arthur Sullivan

HARRIGAN

George M. Cohan

H-A- dou-ble R-I- G-A-N spells Har-ri-gan. Proud of all the I-rish blood that's in me. "Di-vil" a man can say a word a-gin' me. H-A- dou-ble R-I- G-A-N, you see, is a name that a shame nev-er has been con-nect-ed with Har-ri-gan, that's me! Har-ri-gan, Mul-li-gan, Har-ri-gan, Mul-li-gan, Har-ri-gan, that's me!

I WANT A GIRL

Words by William Dalton
Music by Harry Von Tilzer

When I was a boy___ my moth-er oft-en said to me,___ Get mar-ried boy and see,___ how hap-py you will be,___ I have looked all o - ver, but no girl-ie can I find, ___ Who seems to be___ just like the lit - tle girl___ I have in mind,_ I will have to look a-round_ un-til the right one I have found. I Want A Girl, _ just like the girl___ that mar-ried dear old dad, ___ She was a pearl_ and the on-ly girl_ that Dad-dy

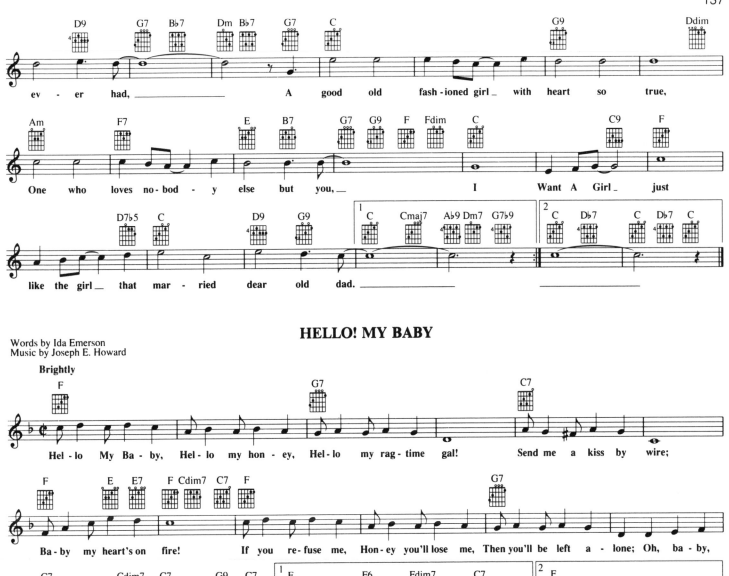

ev - er had, _____ A good old fash-ioned girl _ with heart so true,

One who loves no-bod - y else but you, _ I Want A Girl _ just

like the girl _ that mar - ried dear old dad. _____

HELLO! MY BABY

Words by Ida Emerson
Music by Joseph E. Howard

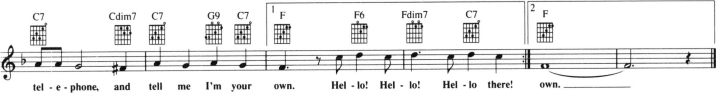

Brightly

Hel - lo My Ba - by, Hel - lo my hon - ey, Hel - lo my rag - time gal! Send me a kiss by wire;

Ba - by my heart's on fire! If you re - fuse me, Hon - ey you'll lose me, Then you'll be left a - lone; Oh, ba - by,

tel - e - phone, and tell me I'm your own. Hel - lo! Hel - lo! Hel - lo there! own. _____

I LOVE YOU TRULY

Carrie Jacobs Bond

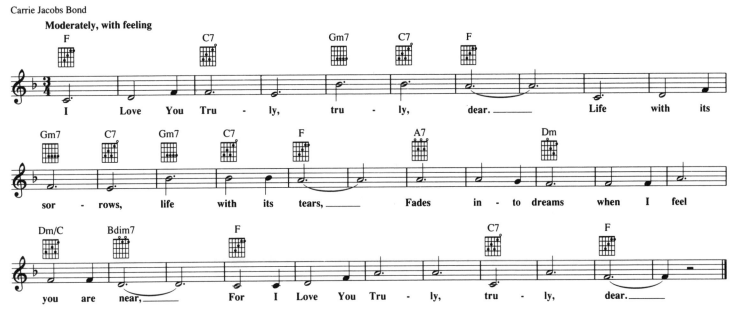

Moderately, with feeling

I Love You Tru - ly, tru - ly, dear. _____ Life with its

sor - rows, life with its tears, _____ Fades in - to dreams when I feel

you are near, _____ For I Love You Tru - ly, tru - ly, dear. _____

I WONDER WHO'S KISSING HER NOW

Words by Will M. Hough and Frank R. Adams
Music by Joseph E. Howard

1. You have loved lots of girls in the sweet long a - go, And each one has meant Heav - en to you, ___ You have
2. If you want to feel wretch - ed and lone - ly and blue, Just im - ag - ine the girl you love best ___ In the

vow'd your af - fec - tion to each one in turn And have sworn to them all you'd be true; ___ You have kissed 'neath the
arms of some fel - low who's steal - ing a kiss From the lips that you once fond - ly pressed; ___ But the world moves a -

moon while the world seemed in tune, Then you've left her to hunt a new game, ___ Does it ev - er oc -
pace and the loves of to - day Flit a - way with a smile and a tear, ___ So you nev - er can

cur to you la - ter, my boy, ___ That she's prob - ably do - ing the same? ___ I Won - der Who's Kiss - ing Her
tell who is kiss - ing her now, Or just whom you'll be kiss - ing next year. ___ } I Won - der Who's Kiss - ing Her

Now, ___ Won - der who's teach - ing her how, ___ Won - der who's look - ing in - to her eyes,

Breath - ing sighs, tell - ing lies; I won - der who's buy - ing the wine ___ For lips that I used to call

mine, ___ Won - der if she ev - er tells him of me, I Won - der Who's Kiss - ing Her Now. ___

I'VE GOT RINGS ON MY FINGERS

Words by Weston and Barnes
Music by Maurice Scott

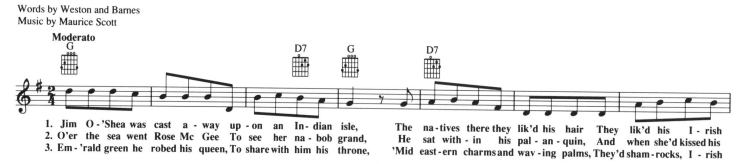

Moderato

1. Jim O - 'Shea was cast a - way up - on an In - dian isle,   The na - tives there they lik'd his hair They lik'd his I - rish
2. O'er the sea went Rose Mc Gee To see her na - bob grand,   He sat with - in his pal - an - quin, And when she'd kissed his
3. Em - 'rald green he robed his queen, To share with him his throne,   'Mid east - ern charms and wav - ing palms, They'd sham - rocks, I - rish

IDA, SWEET AS APPLE CIDER

Words by Eddie Leonard; Music by Eddie Munson

I - da,___ Sweet As Ap - ple Ci - der,___ Sweet - er ___ than all I know. ___

Come out ___ in the sil - v'ry moon - light, ___ Of love we'll whis - per, ___ so soft and low. ___

Seems I ___ can't live with - out ___ you, ___ Lis - ten, ___ oh hon - ey, do. ___

I - da,___ I i - do - lize you, ___ I love you, I - da, 'deed I do. ___

IF I HAD MY WAY

Words by Lou Klein; Music by James Kendis

I'd like to make your gold-en dreams come true, dear, If I on-ly had my way, _____ A
You'd nev-er know a care, a pain, or sor-row, If I on-ly had my way, _____ I'd

par-a-dise this world would seem to you, _____ If I on-ly had my way.
fill your cup of hap-pi-ness to-mor-row, If I on-ly had my way. _____ } If

I Had My Way, dear, for-ev-er there'd be a gar-den of ros-es for

you and for me, A thou-sand and one things, dear, I would do, Just for you, just for

you, just for you. _____ If I Had My Way, we would nev-er grow old, And

sun-shine I'd bring ev-'ry day. _____ You would reign all a-lone Like a

queen on a throne, If I Had My Way. If Way. _____

IN MY MERRY OLDSMOBILE

Vincent P. Bryan and Gus Edwards

Tempo di Valse

Young John-ny Steele has an Olds-mo-bile, He loves a dear lit-tle girl, _____ She is the queen of his
They love to spark in the dark old park, As they go fly-ing a-long, _____ She says she knows why the

gas ma-chine; She has his heart in a whirl._____ Now, when they go for a spin, you know, She
mo-tor goes; The spark-er's aw-ful-ly strong._____ Each day they spoon to the en-gine's tune, Their

tries to learn the au-to, so He lets her steer while he gets her ear, And whis-pers soft and
hon-ey-moon will hap-pen soon, He'll win Lu-cile with his Olds-mo-bile And then he'll fond-ly

low: } Come a-way with me, Lu-cile,_____ In My Mer-ry Olds-mo-bile,_____ Down the road of
croon:}

life we'll fly Au-to-mo-bub-bling, you and I. To the church we'll swift-ly steal,_____ Then our

wed-ding bells will peal,_____ You can go as far as you like with me In My Mer-ry Olds-mo-bile._____

IN THE GLOAMING

By A.F. Harrison and Meta Orred

In The Gloam-ing, Oh, my dar-ling, When the lights are dim and low, soft-ly go.
And the qui-et shad-ows fall-ing, Soft-ly come and long a-go.
Will you think of me and love me, As you did long,

When the winds are sob-bing_____ faint-ly, With a gen-tle un-known woe;

CODA
It was best to leave you thus,_____ Best for you and best for me._____

Additional Lyrics

In The Gloaming, oh my darling!
Think not bitterly of me!
Though I passed away in silence,
Left you lonely, set you free,
For my heart is crushed with longing,
What had been could never be.
It was best to leave you thus, dear,
Best for you and best for me.

IN THE SHADE OF THE OLD APPLE TREE

Words by Harry H. Williams
Music by Egbert Van Alstyne

In The Shade Of The Old Ap-ple Tree, _____ Where the love in your eyes I could see, _____ When the
hear the dull buzz of the bee. _____ In the blos-soms as you said to me, _____ With a

voice that I heard, Like the song of the bird, Seem'd to whis-per sweet mu - sic to me; _____
heart that is

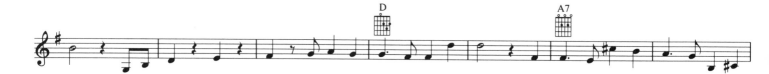

___ I could true, I'll be wait-ing for you, In The Shade Of The Old Ap - ple Tree. _____

JOLLY COPPERSMITH

Carl Peter

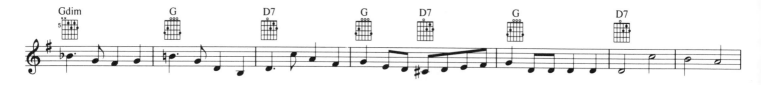

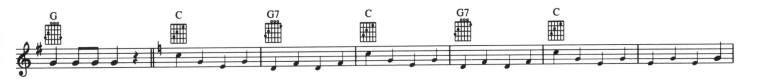

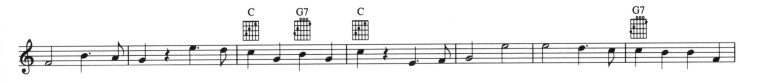

I GAVE MY LOVE A CHERRY
(The Riddle Song)

1. I Gave My Love A Cher - ry that had no stone. I gave my love, a
2,3. *(See additional lyrics)*
chick - en that had no bone. I told my love a sto - ry that had no
end. I gave my love a ba - by with no cry - in'

Copyright © 1990 MILWIN MUSIC

Additional Lyrics

2. How can there be a cherry that has no stone?
How can there be a chicken that has no bone?
How can there be a story that has no end?
How can there be a baby with no cryin'?

3. A cherry, when it's blooming, it has no stone.
A chicken, when it's pipping, it has no bone.
The story that I love you, it has no end.
A baby, when it's sleeping, has no cryin'.

I HEARD THE BELLS ON CHRISTMAS DAY

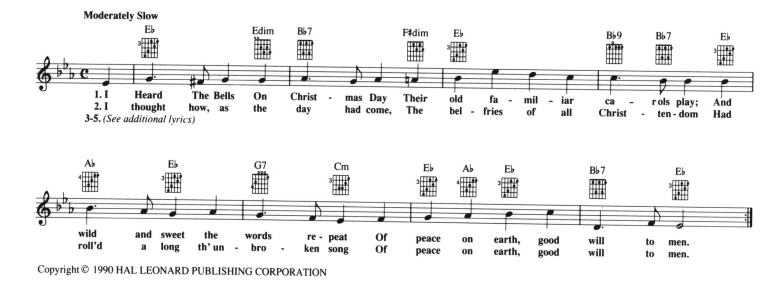

1. I Heard The Bells On Christ - mas Day Their old fa - mil - iar ca - rols play; And
2. I thought how, as the day had come, The bel - fries of all Christ - ten - dom Had
3-5. *(See additional lyrics)*
wild and sweet the words re - peat Of peace on earth, good will to men.
roll'd a long th' un - bro - ken song Of peace on earth, good will to men.

Copyright © 1990 HAL LEONARD PUBLISHING CORPORATION

Additional Lyrics

3. And in despair I bow'd my head:
"There is no peace on earth," I said,
"For hate is strong, and mocks the song
Of peace on earth, good will to men."

4. Then pealed the bells more loud and deep:
"God is not dead, nor doth He sleep;
The wrong shall fail, the right prevail,
With peace on earth, good will to men."

5. Till, ringing, singing on its way,
The world revolved from night to day,
A voice, a chime, a chant sublime,
Of peace on earth, good will to men!

I LOVE YOU WITH ALL MY HEART

I Love You With All My Heart, I do. Yes, I do. _____ I've loved you right from the start. Oh, you're my sweet dream come true. _____ I'll love you till death do us part. My love, I cher - ish you. _____ Yes, I Love You With All My Heart. I do, I do. _____

I SAW THREE SHIPS

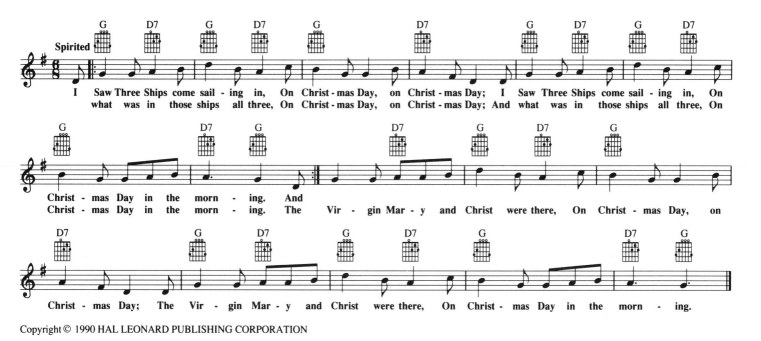

I Saw Three Ships come sail - ing in, On Christ - mas Day, on Christ - mas Day; I Saw Three Ships come sail - ing in, On
what was in those ships all three, On Christ - mas Day, on Christ - mas Day; And what was in those ships all three, On

Christ - mas Day in the morn - ing. And
Christ - mas Day in the morn - ing. The Vir - gin Mar - y and Christ were there, On Christ - mas Day, on

Christ - mas Day; The Vir - gin Mar - y and Christ were there, On Christ - mas Day in the morn - ing.

IF YOU'RE HAPPY
(And You Know It)

clap your hands,
stamp your foot,   clap your hands,
If You're Hap - py and you know it, nod your head,   stamp your foot,
turn a - round,   If You're Hap - py and you know it, nod your head,   If You're
touch your nose,   turn a - round,
                                                    touch your nose,

clap your hands.
stamp your foot.
Hap - py and you know it, then your face will sure - ly show it, If You're Hap - py and you know it, nod your head.
                                                                                                          turn a - round.
                                                                                                          touch your nose.

I WISH I WERE SINGLE AGAIN

By J.C. Beckel

Moderate Waltz

I Wish I Were Sin - gle A - gain, _____ I Wish I Were Sin - gle A - gain! _____
binged me, she banged me, oh then, _____ She binged me, she banged me, oh then. _____

_____ Oh, when I was sin - gle my pock - ets would jin - gle, I Wish I Were Sin - gle A - gain! _____
She binged me, she banged me, she thought she would hang me, I Wish I Were Sin - gle A - gain! _____

_____ I mar - ried a wife, __ oh then, _____ I mar - ried a wife __ oh then, _____ I
_____ She went for the rope __ oh then, _____ She went for the rope __ oh then, _____ She

mar - ried a wife, __ she's ruin - ed my life, Oh I Wish I Were Sin - gle A - gain! _____ She
went for the rope, __ but then it was broke, Oh I Wish I Were Sin - gle A - gain! _____ gain! _____

I'LL TAKE YOU HOME AGAIN, KATHLEEN

T.P. Westendorf

Slowly

I'll Take You Home A - gain Kath - leen, A - cross the o - cean wild and wide, To where your heart has ev - er
I know you love me, Kath - leen dear, Your heart was ev - er fond and true; I al - ways feel when you are
To that dear home be - yond the sea, My Kath - leen shall a - gain re - turn, And when thy old friends wel - come

been, Since first you were my bon - ny bride. The ros - es all have left your cheek, I've
near That life holds noth - ing dear but you. The smiles that once you gave to me, I
thee. Thy lov - ing heart will cease to yearn. Where laughs the lit - tle sil - ver stream, Be -

watched them fade a - way and die; Your voice is sad when - e'er you speak, And tears be - dim your lov - ing
scarce - ly ev - er see them now, Tho man - y, man - y times I see A dark - 'ning shad - ow on your
side your moth - er's hum - ble cot, And bright - est rays of sun - shine gleam, There all your grief will be for -

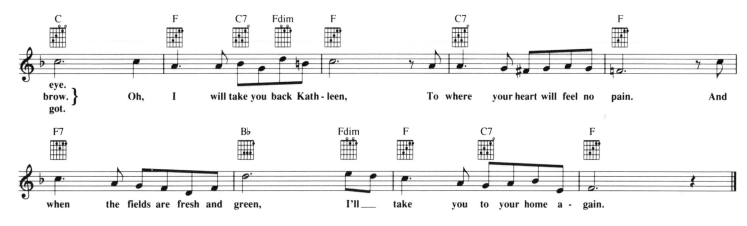

I'VE BEEN WORKING ON THE RAILROAD

ICH LIEBE DICH
(I Love Thee)

Edvard Grieg

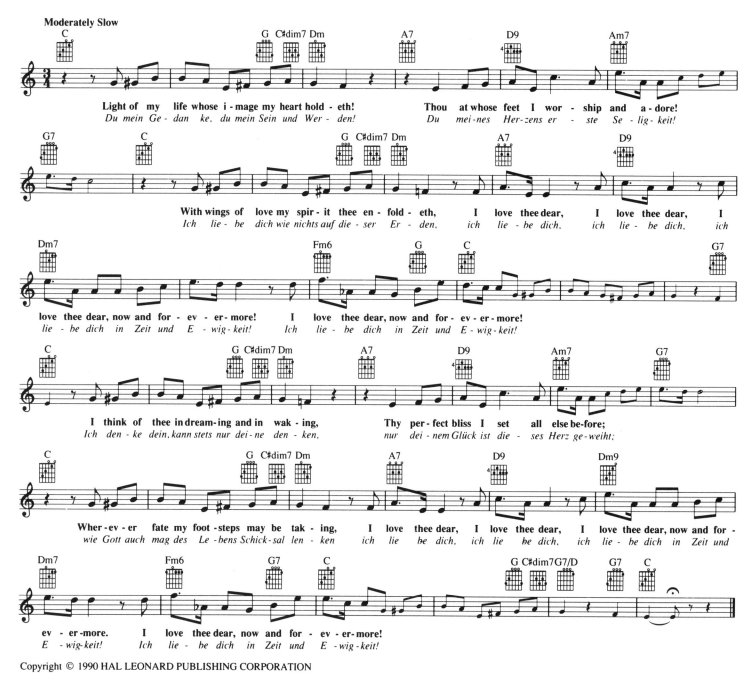

Light of my life whose i - mage my heart hold - eth! Thou at whose feet I wor - ship and a - dore!
Du mein Ge - dan ke, du mein Sein und Wer - den! Du mei - nes Her - zens er - ste Se - lig - keit!

With wings of love my spir - it thee en - fold - eth, I love thee dear, I love thee dear, I
Ich lie - be dich wie nichts auf die - ser Er - den, ich lie - be dich, ich lie - be dich, ich

love thee dear, now and for - ev - er - more! I love thee dear, now and for - ev - er - more!
lie - be dich in Zeit und E - wig - keit! Ich lie - be dich in Zeit und E - wig - keit!

I think of thee in dream - ing and in wak - ing, Thy per - fect bliss I set all else be - fore;
Ich den - ke dein, kann stets nur dei - ne den - ken, nur dei - nem Glück ist die - ses Herz ge - weiht;

Wher - ev - er fate my foot - steps may be tak - ing, I love thee dear, I love thee dear, I love thee dear, now and for -
wie Gott auch mag des Le - bens Schick - sal len - ken ich lie - be dich, ich lie - be dich, ich lie - be dich in Zeit und

ev - er - more. I love thee dear, now and for - ev - er - more!
E - wig - keit! Ich lie - be dich in Zeit und E - wig - keit!

IN OLD NEW YORK

Words by Henry Blossom; Music by Victor Herbert

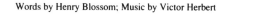
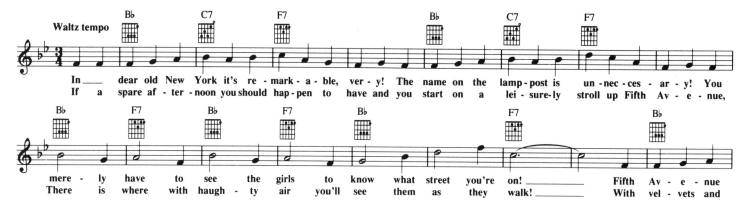

In____ dear old New York it's re - mark - a - ble, ver - y! The name on the lamp - post is un - nec - ces - ar - y! You
If a spare af - ter - noon you should hap - pen to have and you start on a lei - sure - ly stroll up Fifth Av - e - nue,

mere - ly have to see the girls to know what street you're on!____ Fifth Av - e - nue
There is where with haugh - ty air you'll see them as they walk!____ With vel - vets and

beau - ties and dear old Broad-way girls! The tail - or-made shop-pers, the Av - e-nue "A" girls, they're strict - ly all
la - ces and sa - bles en-fold-ing them, real - ly you'll near-ly fall dead on be - hold-ing them, luck-y's the

right but they're dif-fer - ent quite in the dif - f'rent parts of town. _____ In } Old New York, In
earl that can mar-ry a girl from Fifth Av - e-nue, New York. _____ In }

Chorus

Old New York the peach crop's al - ways fine! _____ They're sweet and fair and on the square! The

maids of Man - hat-tan for mine! _____ You can - not see in gay Pa - ree, in Lon - don

or in Cork! _____ The queens you'll meet on an - y street In Old New York. _____

IL BACIO
(The Kiss)

Luigi Arditi

Brightly

IN THE EVENING BY THE MOONLIGHT

By James A. Bland

In The Eve - ning By The Moon - light you could hear those young folks sing - in', In The

Eve - nin' By The Moon - light, you can hear those ban - joes ring - in', How the old folks would en -

joy it, they would sit all night and lis - ten, As we sang In The Eve - ning By The Moon - light.

IN THE HALL OF THE MOUNTAIN KING

Edvard Grieg

IN THE GOOD OLD SUMMERTIME

Words by Ren Shields; Music by George Evans

Copyright © 1990 MILWIN MUSIC

IRISH WASHERWOMAN

Copyright © 1990 HAL LEONARD PUBLISHING CORPORATION

IN THE SWEET BYE AND BYE

Words by S.F. Bennett; Music by J.P. Webster

There's a land that is fair - er than day, and by faith we can see it a - far. For the Fa - ther waits o - ver the
sing on that beau - ti - ful shore the mel - o - di - ous songs of the blest. And our spir - its shall sor - row no
boun - ti - ful Fa - ther a - bove we will of - fer the trib - ute of praise. For the glo - ri - ous gift of His

way to pre - pare us a dwell - ing place there.
more, not a sigh for the bless - ing of rest.   In The Sweet Bye And Bye, we shall meet on that beau - ti - ful
love and the bless - ings that hal - low our days.

shore. In The Sweet Bye And Bye we shall meet on that beau - ti - ful shore. We shall shore.
To our

IT CAME UPON THE MIDNIGHT CLEAR

E.H. Sears/R.S. Willis

It Came Up - on The Mid - night Clear that glo - ri - ous song of old, From
an - gels bend - ing near the earth to
world in sol - emn still - ness lay to

touch their harps of gold. Peace on the earth good will to men from

heav - en's all gra - cious King. The
hear the an - gels sing.

IT'S RAINING, IT'S POURING

It's Rain - ing, It's Pour - ing, The old man is snor - ing. He went to bed and he bumped his head and he could not get up in the morn - ing.

ITALIAN STREET SONG

Lyric by Rida Johnson Young; Music by Victor Herbert

Ah! my heart is back in Na - po - li, ____ Dear Na - po - li, ____ dear Na - po - li, ____ and I seem to hear a - gain in dreams ____ her re - vel - ry, ____ her sweet re - vel - ry ____ The man - do - li - nas play - ing sweet, the pleas - ant fall of dan - cing ____ feet, Oh! could I re - turn oh! joy ____ com - plete! Na - po - li, Na - po - li, Na - po - li! ____ Zing, zing, ziz - zy, ziz - zy, zing, zing, Boom, boom, aye. Zing, zing, ziz - zy, ziz - zy, zing, zing, Man - do - lin - as gay. Zing, zing, ziz - zy, ziz - zy, zing, zing, Boom, __ boom, __ aye, La, la, la, Ha, ha, ha, Zing, boom aye. La, la, la, la, ha, ha, ha, zing, zing, aye. ____

INVITATION TO THE DANCE

By C.M. von Weber

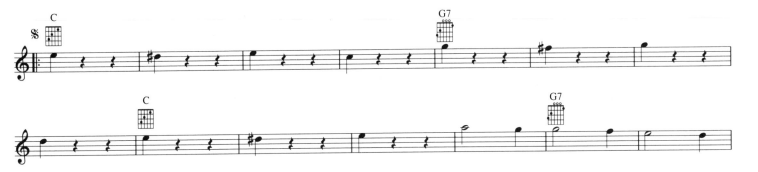

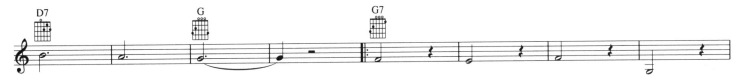

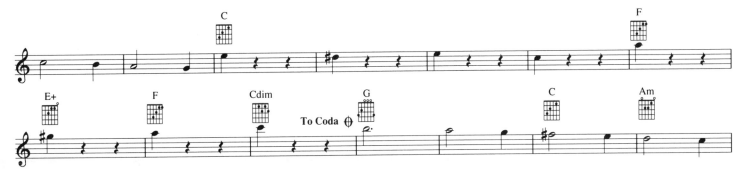

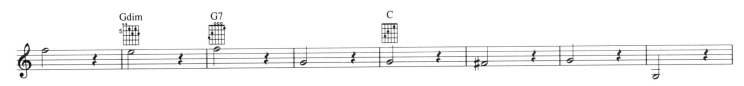

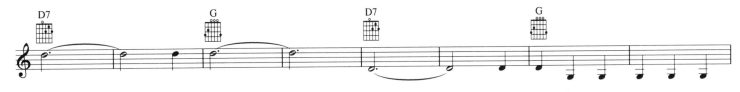

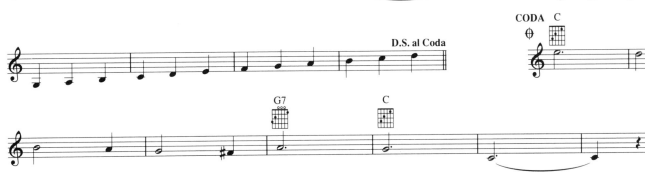

IT'S A LONG, LONG WAY TO TIPPERARY

Words & Music by Jack Judge and Harry Williams

"It's a long way ___ to Tip-per-ar-y, ___ It's a long way ___ to go; ___ It's a long way ___ to Tip-per-ar-y, ___ To the sweet-est girl I know! ___ Good-bye ___ Pic-ca-dil-ly, ___ Fare-well, Leices-ter Square. ___ It's A Long, Long Way To Tip-per-ar-y, But my heart's ___ right there!" ___ "It's a there!" ___

JESU, JOY OF MAN'S DESIRING

J.S. Bach

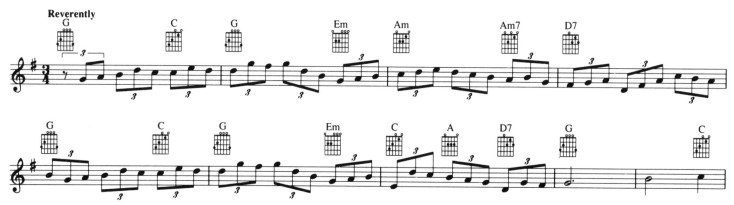

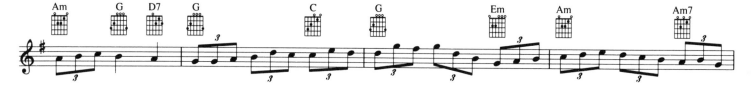

JACK AND JILL

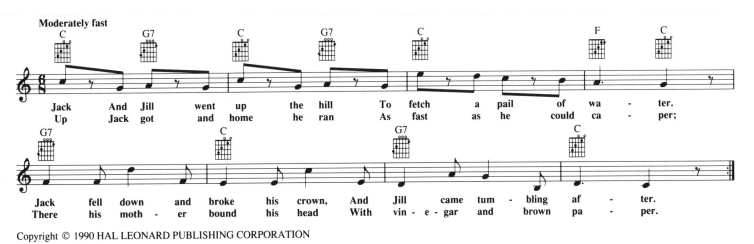

Moderately fast

Jack   And   Jill   went   up   the   hill   To   fetch   a   pail   of   wa - ter.
Up   And   Jack   got   and   home   he   ran   As   fast   as   he   could   ca - per;

Jack   fell   down   and   broke   his   crown,   And   Jill   came   tum - bling   af - ter.
There   his   moth - er   bound   his   head   With   vin - e - gar   and   brown   pa - per.

JEANIE WITH THE LIGHT BROWN HAIR

By Stephen C. Foster

Moderately

1. I   dream   of   Jean - ie   With   The   Light   Brown _ Hair,   Borne,   like   a   va - por
2. I   sigh   for   Jean - ie,   but   her   light   form _ strayed   far   from   the   fond   hearts
3. (See additional lyrics)

on   the   sum - mer   air;   I   see   her   trip - ping   where   the   bright   streams _ play,
round   her   na - tive   glade,   Her   smiles   have   van - ished   and   her   bright   sweet   songs _ flown,

Hap - py   as   the   dai - sies   that   dance   on   her   way.   Man - y   were   the   wild   notes   her
Flit - ting   like   the   dreams _ that   have   cheered   us   and   gone.   Now   the   nod - ding   wild   flow'rs   may

mer - ry   voice   would   pour,   Man - y   were   the   blithe   birds   that   war - bled   them   o'er: I
with - er   on   the   shore,   While   her   gen - tle   fin - gers   will   cull   them   no   more;   I

dream   of   Jean - ie   With   The   Light   Brown _ Hair,   Float - ing   like   a   va - por   on   the   soft,   sum - mer   air.
sigh   for   Jean - ie   With   The   Light   Brown _ Hair,   Float - ing   like   a   va - por   on   the   soft,   sum - mer   air.

Additional Lyrics

2. I long for Jeanie with the day-dawn smile,
Radiant in gladness, warm with winning guile;
I hear her melodies, like joys gone by,
Sighing round my heart o'er the fond hopes that die;
Sighing like the night wind and sobbing like the rain,
Waiting for the lost one that comes not again;
Ah! I long for Jeanie and my heart bows low,
Never more to find her where the bright waters flow.

JENNY LIND POLKA

JESUS LOVES ME!

Je - sus Loves Me! This I know, For the Bi - ble tells me so; Lit - tle ones to Him be - long, they are weak, but He is strong.
Je - sus from His throne on high, come in - to this world to die; That I might from sin be free, Bled and died up - on the tree.

Yes, Je - sus Loves Me! Yes, Je - sus Loves Me! Yes, Je - sus Loves Me! The Bi - ble tells me so.

JINGLE BELLS

J. Pierpont

Bright 2

Dash - ing through the snow, in a one horse o - pen sleigh, O're the fields we go
day or two a - go I thought I'd take a ride; And soon Miss Fan - nie Bright was
Now the ground is white go it while you're young. Take the girls to - night And

Laugh - ing all the way. The Bells on bob - tail ring, Mak - ing spir - its bright, What
seat - ed by my side. The horse was lean and lank, Mis - for - tune seemed his lot, He
sing this sleigh - ing song. Just get a bob - tail bay, Two - for - ty for his speed, Then

fun it is to ride and sing a sleigh - ing song to - night! Oh! Jin - gle Bells, Jin - gle Bells, jin - gle all the
got in - to a drift - ed bank and we, we got up - sot! Oh!
hitch him to an o - pen sleigh and crack! you'll take the lead! Oh!

way. Oh what fun it is to ride in a one horse o - pen sleigh! ___ Jin - gle Bells, Jin - gle Bells,

Jin - gle all the way. Oh what fun it is to ride in a one horse o - pen sleigh! A

JOHN JACOB JINGLEHEIMER SCHMIDT

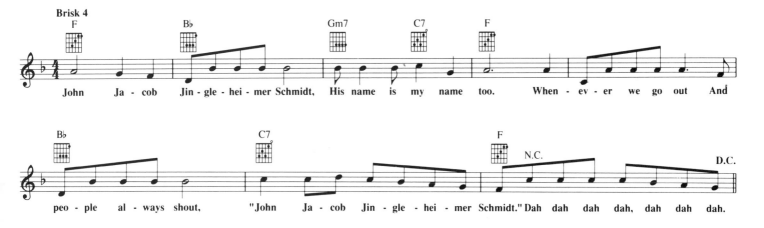

Brisk 4

John Ja - cob Jin - gle - hei - mer Schmidt, His name is my name too. When - ev - er we go out And

peo - ple al - ways shout, "John Ja - cob Jin - gle - hei - mer Schmidt." Dah dah dah dah, dah dah dah.

JOHN PEEL

Words by J.W. Graves

Do you know John Peel with his coat so gay, Do you know John Peel at the break of day, Do you
Do you know John Peel with his coat so gay? He ___ lived at Trout - beck ___ once on a day; But ___

know John Peel when he's far, far a - way, With his hounds and his horn in the morn - ing?
now he has gone far a - way, far a - way, We shall ne'er hear his voice in the morn - ing. } For the

sound of his horn brought me from my bed, And the cry of the hounds which he oft - times led; For

Peel's view hal - loo would ___ awak - en the dead, or the fox from his lair in the morn - ing.

JOHN BROWN'S BODY

March tempo

1. John Brown's ___ Bod - y lies a - mould - 'ring in the grave, John Brown's ___ Bod - y lies a - mould - 'ring in the grave,
2 - 6. (See additional lyrics)

John Brown's ___ Bod - y lies a - mould - 'ring in the grave, But his soul is march - ing on. CHORUS Glo - ry, Glo - ry, hal - le -

lu - jah! Glo - ry, Glo - ry, hal - le - lu - jah! Glo - ry, Glo - ry, hal - le - lu - jah! His soul is march - ing on.

Additional Lyrics

2. The stars of Heaven are looking kindly down, (etc.)
   On the grave of old John Brown.

3. He's gone to be a soldier in the army of the Lord!
   (etc.)
   His soul is marching on.

4. John Brown's knapsack is strapped upon his back,
   (etc.)
   His soul is marching on.

5. His pet lambs will meet him on the way, (etc.)
   And they'll go marching on.

6. They'll hang Jeff Davis to a sour-apple tree (etc.)
   As they march along.

JOHN HENRY

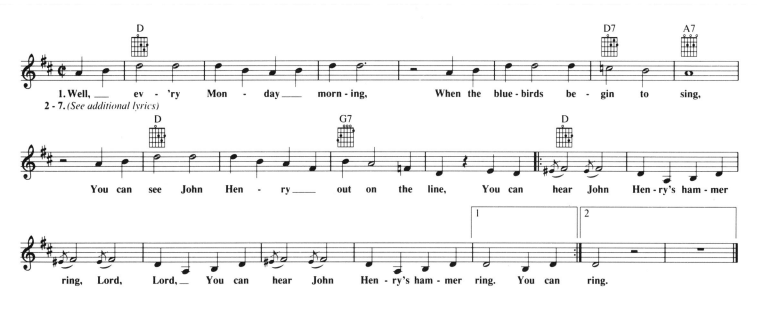

1. Well, ___ ev - 'ry Mon - day ___ morn - ing, When the blue - birds be - gin to sing,
2 - 7. *(See additional lyrics)*

You can see John Hen - ry ___ out on the line, You can hear John Hen - ry's ham - mer

ring, Lord, Lord, ___ You can hear John Hen - ry's ham - mer ring. You can ring.

Additional Lyrics

2. When John Henry was a little baby,
   A-sitting on his papa's knee,
   He picked up a hammer and a little piece of steel,
   Said, "Hammer's gonna be the death of me"...

3. Well, the captain said to John Henry,
   "Gonna bring me a steam drill 'round,
   Gonna bring me a steam drill out on the job,
   Gonna whup that steel on down"...

4. John Henry said to his captain,
   "A man ain't nothin' but a man,
   And before I let that steam drill beat me down,
   I'll die with a hammer in my hand"...

5. John Henry said to his shaker,
   "Shaker, why don't you pray?
   'Cause if I miss this little piece of steel,
   Tomorrow be your buryin' day...

6. John Henry was driving on the mountain
   And his hammer was flashing fire.
   And the last words I heard that poor boy say,
   "Gimme a cool drink of water 'fore I die"...

7. John Henry, he dorve fifteen feet,
   The steam drill only made nine.
   But he hammered so hard that he broke his poor heart,
   And he laid down his hammer and he died...

8. The took John Henry to the graveyard
   And they buried him in the sand.
   And every locomotive comes a-roaring by says,
   "There lies a steel-driving man"...

JOHNNY HAS GONE FOR A SOLDIER

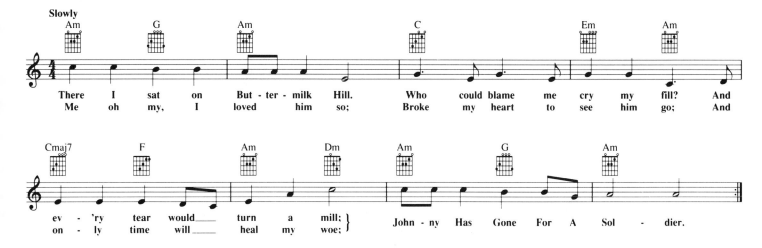

Slowly

There I sat on But - ter - milk Hill. Who could blame me cry my fill? And
Me oh my, I loved him so; Broke my heart to see him go; And

ev - 'ry tear would ___ turn a mill;
on - ly time will ___ heal my woe; } John - ny Has Gone For A Sol - dier.

JOY TO THE WORLD

G.F. Handel

Brightly

1. Joy To The World! The Lord is come; Let earth re-ceive her King;___
2. Joy To The World! The Sav-ior reigns; Let men their songs em-ploy;___

3 - 4. (See additional lyrics)

___ Let ev-'ry heart___ pre-pare _ Him___ room.___ And heav'n and na-ture___ sing. And _
___ while fields _ and___ floods.___ rocks, hills _ and___ plains,___ Re-peat the sound-ing___ joy. Re -

heav'n and na-ture___ sing. And___ heav'n _ and heav'n___ and na-ture sing.
peat the sound-ing___ joy. Re - peat,___ re - peat___ the sound-ing joy.

Additional Lyrics

3. No more let sin and sorrow grow,
   Nor thorns infest the ground,
   He comes to make His blessings flow
   Far as the curse is found,
   Far as the curse is found,
   Far as, far as the curse is found.

4. He rules the world with truth and grace,
   And makes the nations prove
   The glories of His righteousness,
   And wonders of His love,
   And wonders of His love,
   And wonders, and wonders of His love.

JUANITA

Mrs. Norton

Moderately

Soft o'er the foun-tain, ling-'ring falls the south-ern moon, Far o'er the moun-tain
When in thy dream-ing, moons like these shall shine a-gain, And day-light beam-ing

Breaks the day too soon! In thy dark eyes splen-dor, Where the warm light loves to dwell,
Prove thy dreams are vain, Wilt thou not re-lent-ing, For thine ab - sent lov-er sigh,

Wear-y looks yet ten-der, Speak their fond fare-well. Ni-ta! Jua-ni-ta!
In thy heart con-sent-ing To a pray'r gone by? Ni-ta! Jua-ni-ta!

Ask thy soul if we should part! Ni-ta! Jua-ni-ta! Lean thou on my heart.
Let me lin-ger by thy side! Ni-ta! Jua-ni-ta! Be my own fair bride.

JOLLY OLD ST. NICHOLAS

Moderately

Jol - ly Old Saint Nich - o - las, Lean your ear this way! Don't you tell a sin - gle soul What I'm going to say;
When the clock is strik - ing twelve. When I'm fast a - sleep, Down the chim - ney broad and black, With your pack you'll creep;
John - ny wants a pair of skates; Su - sy wants a dolly; Nel - lie wants a sto - ry book; She thinks dolls are folly.

Christ - mas Eve is com - ing soon; Now you dear old man, Whis - per what you'll bring to me; Tell me if you can.
All the stock - ings you will find hang - ing in a row; Mine will be the short - est one, You'll be sure to know.
As for me, my lit - tle brain is - n't ve - ry bright; Choose for me, old San - ta Claus, What you think is right.

JUST A CLOSER WALK WITH THEE

K. Morris

Slowly

I am weak, but thou art strong, Je - sus, keep me from all wrong, __ I'll be sat - is - fied as long _____ As I

walk, let me walk close to Thee. Just A Clo - ser Walk With Thee, Grant it Je - sus is my plea, _____

Dai - ly walk - ing close to Thee _____ Let it be, dear Lord, let it be. Let it be, dear Lord, let it be.

KUM-BAH-YAH

Slowly

1. Kum - bah - yah, my Lord, Kum - bah - yah, Kum - bah - yah, my Lord, Kum - bah -
2. Some - one's pray - in', Lord, Kum - bah - yah, Some - one's pray - in', Lord, Kum - bah -

3 - 6. *(See additional lyrics)*

yah, Kum - bah - yah, my Lord, Kum - bah - yah, Oh, Lord, _____ Kum - bah - yah.
yah, Some - one's pray - in', Lord, Kum - bah - yah, Oh, Lord, _____ Kum - bah - yah.

Additional Lyrics

3. Someone's singin', Lord, Kum-bah-yah. . .
4. Someone's crying', Lord, Kum-bah-yah. . .
5. Someone's dancin', Lord, Kum-bah-yah. . .
6. Someone's shoutin', Lord, Kum-bah-yah. . .

JOSHUA FOUGHT THE BATTLE OF JERICHO

JULIDA POLKA

A. Grill

JUST A SONG AT TWILIGHT

Words by J. Clifton Bingham
Music by James L. Molloy

THE KERRY DANCE

J. L. Molloy

KING COTTON

John Philip Sousa

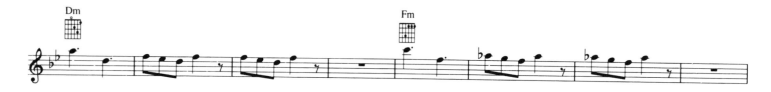

LA CUCARACHA

LA DONNA È MOBILE

Giuseppe Verdi

LA GOLONDRINA

N. Serradell

LA MARSEILLAISE

fright and des - o - late the land
vien - nent jus - que dans nos bras;

While _ peace and lib - er - ty lie bleed - ing?
E - gor - ger nos fils, _ nos com - pagn - es.

To arms, _ you sons of
Aux ar _ mes, ci - toy -

France!
ens!

To arms, _ your ranks ad - vance! _
For - mez _ vos ba - tail - lons!

March on! March on!
Mar - chons! Mar - chons!

all hearts re -
Qu'un Sang im -

solved _ On lib - er - ty or death! _
pur, _ A - breu - ve nos sil -

Al - lons, en -
lons!

LA PALOMA

S. Yradier

Medium Tango

LARGO
(From The "NEW WORLD SYMPHONY")

Anton Dvorak

Very slowly

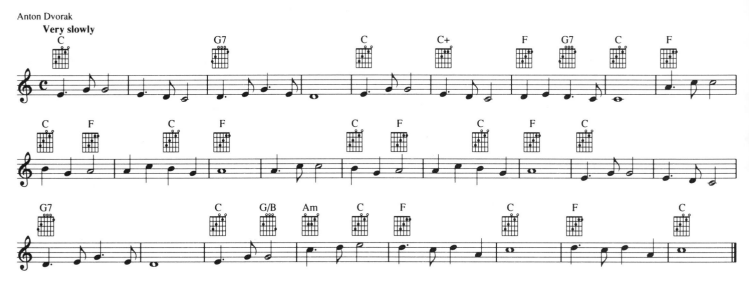

LAVENDER'S BLUE

Moderate waltz

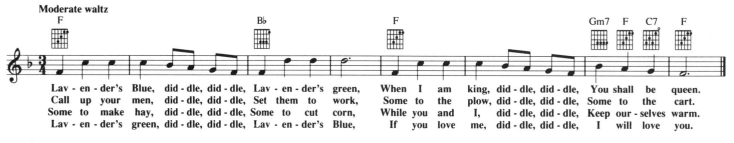

Lav - en - der's Blue, did - dle, did - dle, Lav - en - der's green, When I am king, did - dle, did - dle, You shall be queen.
Call up your men, did - dle, did - dle, Set them to work, Some to the plow, did - dle, did - dle, Some to the cart.
Some to make hay, did - dle, did - dle, Some to cut corn, While you and I, did - dle, did - dle, Keep our - selves warm.
Lav - en - der's green, did - dle, did - dle, Lav - en - der's Blue, If you love me, did - dle, did - dle, I will love you.

LET ME CALL YOU SWEETHEART

Words by Beth Slater Whitson
Music by Leo Freidman
Slowly

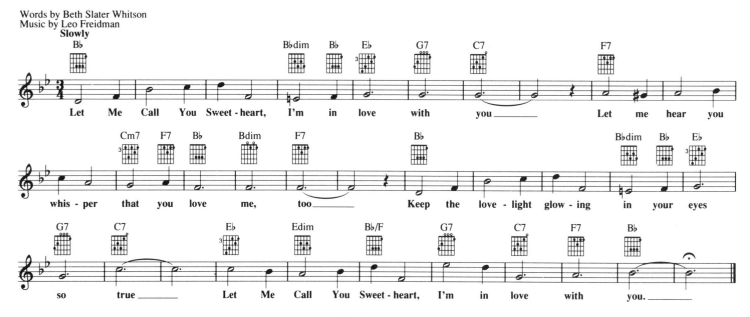

Let Me Call You Sweet - heart, I'm in love with you _____ Let me hear you

whis - per that you love me, too _____ Keep the love - light glow - ing in your eyes

so true _____ Let Me Call You Sweet - heart, I'm in love with you.

LAS MAÑANITAS

Es - tas son Las Ma - ña - ni - tas Que can - ta - ba el rey Da - vid A las mu - cha - chas bo - ni - tas, Te las can -

ta - mos a ti. Es - tas son Las Ma - ña - ni - tas Que can - ta - ba el rey Da - vid, Qué can - ció - nes tan bo -

ni - tas, Las que can - ta - mos a - qui. Des - pier - ta, mi bien, des - pier - ta Por - que ya a - ma - ne -

ció, Ya los pa - ja - ri - llos can - tan, La lu - na ya se me - tió. _____

LAZY MARY, WILL YOU GET UP?

La - zy Ma - ry, Will You Get Up? Will you get up? Will you get up?

La - zy Ma - ry, Will You Get Up? Will you get up to - day? _____

LET US BREAK BREAD TOGETHER

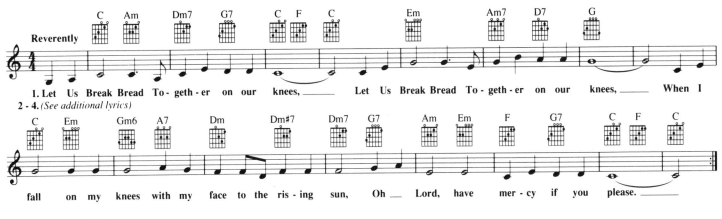

1. Let Us Break Bread To - geth - er on our knees, _____ Let Us Break Bread To - geth - er on our knees, _____ When I
2 - 4. (See additional lyrics)

fall on my knees with my face to the ris - ing sun, Oh __ Lord, have mer - cy if you please. _____

Additional Lyrics

2. Let us drink wine together. . .
3. Let us praise God together. . .
4. Let us all sing together. . .

THE LIBERTY BELL

John Philip Sousa

LISTEN TO THE MOCKING BIRD

Alice Hawthorne

I'm dream-ing now of ___ Hal - ly, ___ sweet ___ Hal - ly, ___ sweet Hal - ly, ___ I'm dream-ing now of ___
sleep-ing in the ___ val - ley, ___ the ___ val - ley, ___ the ___ val - ley, ___ She's sleep-ing in the ___

Hal - ly, ___ For the thought of her is one that nev - er dies. She's
val - ley, ___ And the mock-ing bird is sing-ing where she lies. Lis-ten To The Mock-ing Bird, Lis-ten To The

Mock-ing Bird, The mock-ingbird still sing-ing o'er her grave: Lis-ten To The
Mock-ing Bird, Still sing - ing where the weep-ing wil - lows wave.

LIGHT CAVALRY OVERTURE

Franz von Suppe

LIEBESTRAUM

F. Liszt

A LITTLE BIT OF HEAVEN

Words by Keirn Brennan
Music by Ernest R. Ball

Shure, A Lit-tle Bit Of Heav-en fell from out the sky one day, And nes-tled on the o-cean in a spot so far a-way; And when the An-gels found it, Shure it looked so sweet and fair, They said sup-pose we leave it, for it looks so peace-ful there: So they sprink-led it with star dust just to make the sham-rocks grow: 'Tis the on-ly place you'll find them no mat-ter where you go; Then they dot-ted it with sil-ver, To make it's lakes so grand, And when they had it fin-ished shure they called it Ire-land.

LITTLE ANNIE ROONEY

Michael Nolan

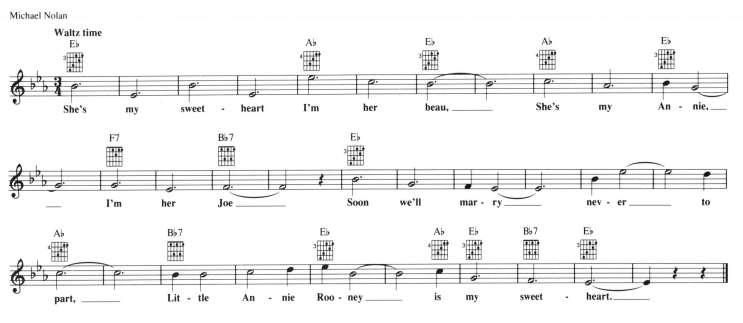

She's my sweet-heart I'm her beau, _____ She's my An - nie, ___ ___ I'm her Joe _____ Soon we'll mar - ry _____ nev - er _____ to part, _____ Lit - tle An - nie Roo - ney _____ is my sweet-heart. _____

LITTLE BO PEEP

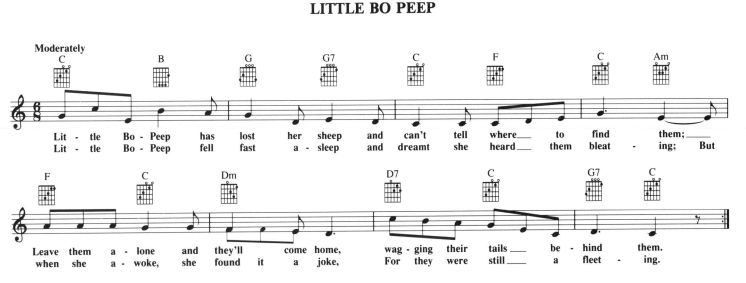

Lit - tle Bo - Peep has lost her sheep and can't tell where___ to find them;
Lit - tle Bo - Peep fell fast a - sleep and dreamt she heard___ them bleat - ing; But
Leave them a - lone and they'll come home, wag - ging their tails ___ be - hind them.
when she a - woke, she found it a joke, For they were still ___ a fleet - ing.

LITTLE BOY BLUE

Lit - tle Boy Blue, come blow on your horn; There's sheep in the mead - ow and cows in the corn.
Where is the boy who looks af - ter the sheep? He lies in the hay - stack, fast a - sleep.

(I'm Called)
LITTLE BUTTERCUP

W. S. Gilbert and Arthur Sullivan

I'm called Lit-tle But-ter-cup, Dear Lit-tle But-ter-cup, Though I could nev-er tell why; But
buy of your But-ter-cup, Dear Lit-tle But-ter-cup, Sail-ors should nev-er be shy; So

still I'm called But-ter-cup, Poor Lit-tle But-ter-cup, Sweet Lit-tle But-ter-cup, I. I've
buy of your But-ter-cup,

snuff and to-bac-cy, and ex-cel-lent jack-y; I've scis-sors and watch-es and knives; I've

rib-bons and lac-es to set off the fac-es Of pret-ty young sweet-hearts and wives. I've

trea-cle and tof-fee, I've tea and I've cof-fee, Soft tom-my and suc-cu-lent chops; I've

chick-ens and co-nies, And pret-ty po-lo-nies, And ex-cel-lent pep-per-mint drops. Then

CODA

Poor Lit-tle But-ter-cup; Come, of your But-ter-cup buy._____

LITTLE JACK HORNER

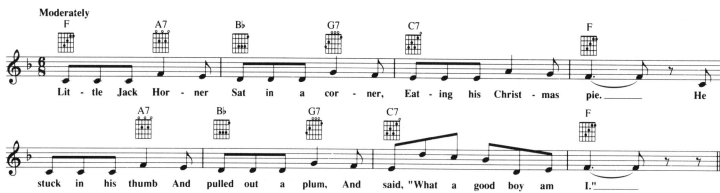

Lit-tle Jack Hor-ner Sat in a cor-ner, Eat-ing his Christ-mas pie._____ He

stuck in his thumb And pulled out a plum, And said, "What a good boy am I."_____

LITTLE BROWN JUG

J.E. Winner

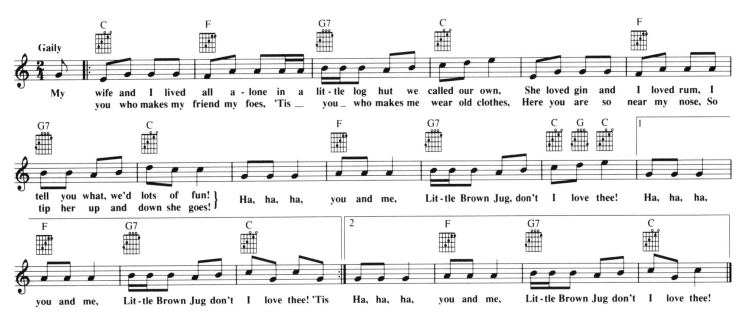

My wife and I lived all a - lone in a lit - tle log hut we called our own, She loved gin and I loved rum, I
you who makes my friend my foes, 'Tis __ you __ who makes me wear old clothes, Here you are so near my nose, So

tell you what, we'd lots of fun! }
tip her up and down she goes! } Ha, ha, ha, you and me, Lit - tle Brown Jug, don't I love thee! Ha, ha, ha,

you and me, Lit - tle Brown Jug don't I love thee! 'Tis Ha, ha, ha, you and me, Lit - tle Brown Jug don't I love thee!

LITTLE MISS MUFFET

Moderately fast

Lit - tle Miss Muf - fet Sat on a tuf - fet, Eat - ing some curds and whey. _____ There

came a big spi - der And sat down be - side her, And fright - ened Miss Muf - fet a - way. _____

LITTLE TOMMY TUCKER

Moderately fast

Lit - tle Tom - my Tuck - er, Sing __ for your sup - per. What shall he sing for? White bread and but - ter.

How can he cut it With - out a - ny knife? How can he mar - ry With - out a - ny wife?

LO, HOW A ROSE E'RE BLOOMING

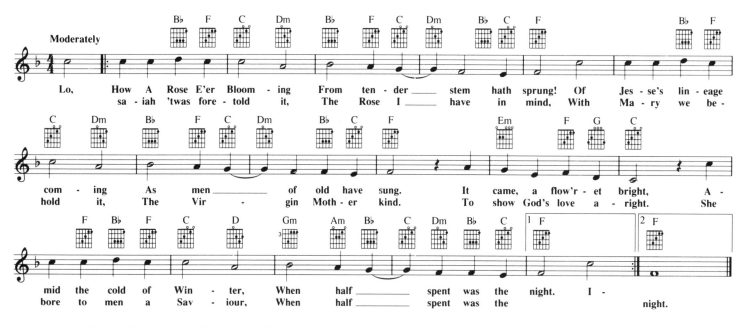

Lo, How A Rose E'er Bloom - ing, From ten - der ____ stem hath sprung! Of Jes - se's lin - eage
sa - iah 'twas fore - told it, The Rose I ____ have in mind, With Ma - ry we be -

com - ing As men ____ of old have sung. It came, a flow'r - et bright, A -
hold it, The Vir - gin Moth - er kind. To show God's love a - right. She

mid the cold of Win - ter, When half ____ spent was the night. I -
bore to men a Sav - iour, When half ____ spent was the night.

LOCH LOMOND

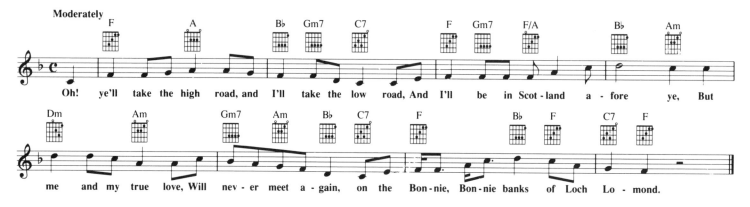

Oh! ye'll take the high road, and I'll take the low road, And I'll be in Scot - land a - fore ye, But

me and my true love, Will nev - er meet a - gain, on the Bon - nie, Bon - nie banks of Loch Lo - mond.

LONDON BRIDGE

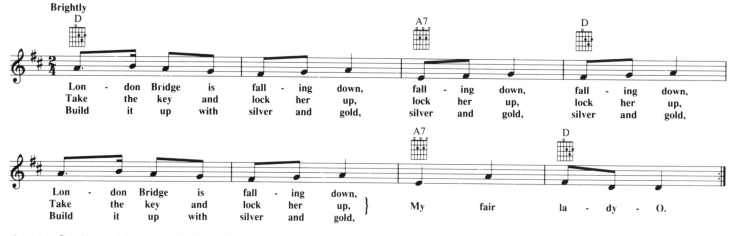

Lon - don Bridge is fall - ing down, fall - ing down, fall - ing down,
Take the key and lock her up, lock her up, lock her up,
Build it up with silver and gold, silver and gold, silver and gold,

Lon - don Bridge is fall - ing down,
Take the key and lock her up,   } My fair la - dy - O.
Build it up with silver and gold,

LONESOME ROAD

Not too fast

| D | D7/C | G/B | Gm/Bb | D | A7 | D |

Look down, look down, that Lone - some Road, _____ Hang down your head and cry. _____
The best of friends must part some day, _____ Then why not you and I? _____
True love, true love, what have I done, _____ That you should treat me so?

LONESOME VALLEY

Traditional Spiritual

Moderately

| F | Bb | F | C | C7 |

1. Je - sus walked _____ this lone-some val - ley. He had to walk _____ it by Him - self. O,
2. walk _____ this lone-some val - ley. We have to walk _____ it by our - selves. O,
3. (See additional lyrics)

| F | Bb | Gm7 | F/C | Gm7/C | 1,2 F | 3 F |

no-bod-y else _____ could walk it for Him. He had to walk it by _ Him - self. We must self.
no-bod-y else _____ can walk it for us. We have to walk it by _ our - selves. You must

Additional Lyrics

3. You must go and stand your trial.
   You have to stand it by yourself.
   O, nobody else can stand it for you.
   You have to stand it by yourself.

LONG, LONG AGO

Thomas Haynes Bayly

Moderately

| F | C7 | F |

Tell me the tales that to me were so dear, Long, Long A - go, Long, Long A - go, Sing me the songs I de -
Do you re - mem - ber the path where we met, Long, Long A - go, Long, Long A - go, Ah yes, you told me you
Tho' by your kind - ness my fond hopes were raised, Long, Long A - go, Long, Long A - go, You, by more el - o - quent

| C7 | F | C7 | F |

light - ed to hear, Long, Long A - go, long a - go. Now you are come, all my grief is re - moved;
ne'er would for - get, Long, Long A - go, long a - go. Then to all oth - ers my smile you pre - ferred;
lips, have been praised Long, Long A - go, long a - go. But by long ab - cense your truth has been tried;

| C7 | F | C | F |

Let me for - get that so long you have rov'd. Let me be - lieve that you love as you loved, Long, Long A - go, long a - go.
Love, when you spoke, gave a charm to each word. Still my heart treas - ures the prais - es I heard, Long, Long A - go, long a - go.
Still, to your ac - cents, I lis - ten with pride. Blest as I was when I sat by your side Long, Long A - go, long a - go.

LOOBY LOO

Brightly
Refrain

Here we go Loo-by Loo, _____ Here we go loo-by light, _____ Here we go Loo-by

Loo, _____ All on a Sat-ur-day night. _____
1. I put my right hand in, _____ I take my
2. I put my left hand in, _____ I take my
3. I put my right foot in, _____ I take my
4-6. *(See additional lyrics)*

right hand out; _____
left hand out; _____ I give my { right hand } { left hand } a shake, shake, shake! And turn my-self a-bout. _____
right foot out; _____ { right foot }

Copyright © 1990 HAL LEONARD PUBLISHING CORPORATION

Additional Lyrics

4. I put my left foot in,
   I take my left foot out;
   I give my left foot. . .

5. I put my big head in,
   I take my big head out;
   I give my big head. . .

6. I put my whole self in,
   I put my whole self out;
   I give my whole self. . .

LOVE'S OLD SWEET SONG

Words by J. Clifton Bingham; Music by James L. Molloy

Slowly

Once in the dear dead days be-yond re-call, When on the world the mists be-gan to fall, Out of the dreams that

rose in hap-py throng, Low to our hearts Love sung an old sweet song; And in the dusk where fell the fire-light gleam,

Soft-ly _____ it-self in-to our dream.

Chorus:

Just a song at twi-light, when the lights are

low, And the flick-'ring shad-ows soft-ly come and go, Tho' the heart be wea-ry,

sad the day and long, Still to us at twi-light comes love's old song, Comes Love's_ Old Sweet _ Song.

Copyright © 1990 HAL LEONARD PUBLISHING CORPORATION

KEEP THE HOMEFIRES BURNING

Words by Lena G. Ford
Music by Ivor Novello

Keep The Home-fires Burn - ing, While your hearts are yearn - ing Though your lads are far a - way They dream of Home; There's a sil - ver lin - ing Through the dark cloud shin - ing, Turn the dark cloud in - side out, Till the boys come Home.

MARY'S A GRAND OLD NAME

Words and Music by George M. Cohan

For it is Ma - ry, Mary, plain as an - y name can be;____ But with pro - pri - e - ty, so - ci - e - ty will say Ma - rie.____
Ma - ry, Mary, long be - fore the fash - ions But it was came;____ And there is some-thing there that sounds so fair, it's a grand old name!

MATILDA

Brightly
Chorus

Ma - til - da____ Ma - til - da____ Ma - til - da she took me mon - ey and run Ven - e - zue - la! ____
1. That wo - man made a wreck of me, (broke me,____ oh) What she done to me you ought to see.____ Ma - til - da she take me mon - ey and gone Ven - e - zue - la!____

2 - 4. (See additional lyrics)

Additional Lyrics

2. I save up, gonna make her my wife.
   But she wanta live another kind of life.
   Chorus

3. We were sleepin' in me bed,
   When she found the money me had hid.
   Chorus

4. What to do and where to go,
   Never trust a woman with your dough.
   Chorus

MEET ME IN ST. LOUIS, LOUIS

Words by Andrew B. Sterling; Music by Kerry Mills

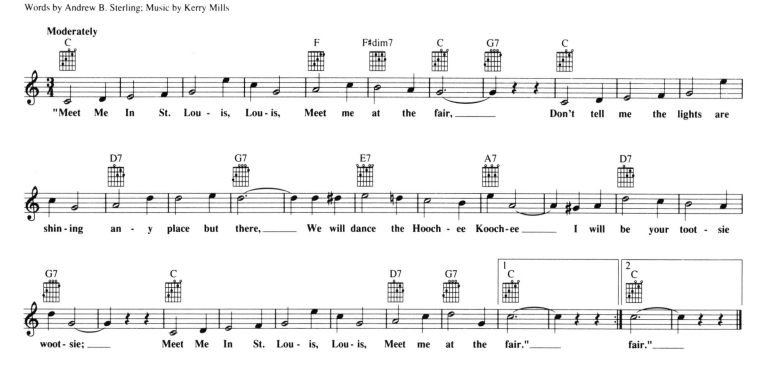

"Meet Me In St. Lou - is, Lou - is, Meet me at the fair, _____ Don't tell me the lights are shin - ing an - y place but there, _____ We will dance the Hooch - ee Kooch-ee _____ I will be your toot - sie woot - sie; _____ Meet Me In St. Lou - is, Lou - is, Meet me at the fair." _____ fair." _____

LA SORELLA

Ch. Borel-Clere

MINUET IN G

Ignace J. Paderewski

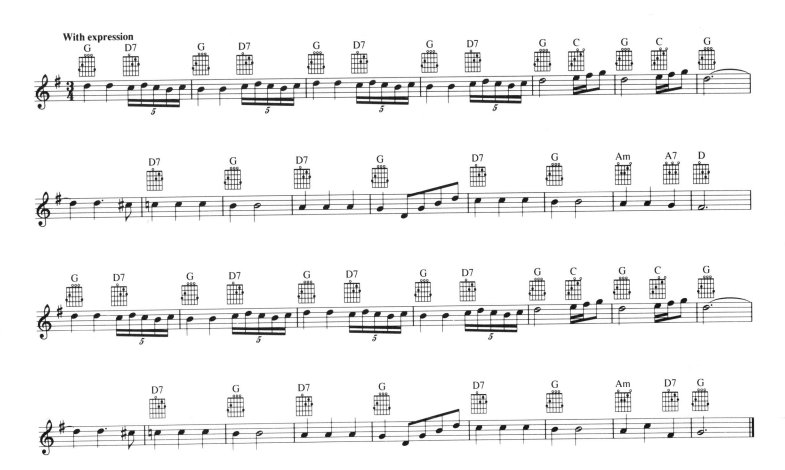

MERRY WIDOW WALTZ

F. Lehar

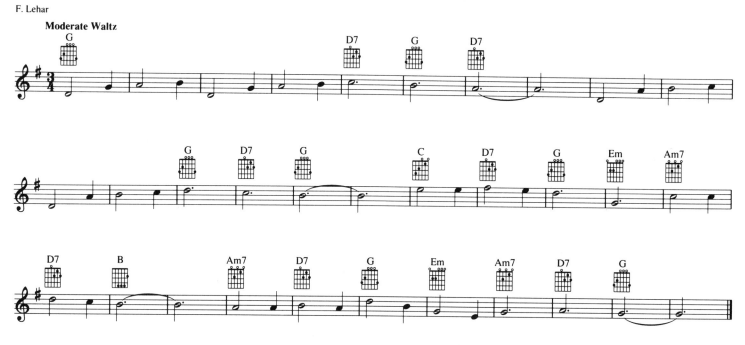

MY HERO

Oscar Straus

Come! come! I love you on - ly my heart is true, _____ Come! come!

my life is lone - ly I long for you; _____ Come! come! naught can ef -

face you, My arms are ach - ing now to em - brace you, Thou art di - vine! _____

Come! come! I love you on - ly come, he - ro mine! _____

MOONLIGHT BAY

Words by Edward Madden; Music by Percy Wenrich

Gracefully

We were sail - ing a - long _____ On Moon - light Bay, _____ We could hear the voic - es ring - ing _____ They seemed to say _____ "You have sto - len my heart, _____ Now don't go 'way!" _____ As we sang love's old sweet song, on Moon - light Bay. _____

MY HEART AT THY SWEET VOICE

Camille Saint-Saens

Slowly

MY MELANCHOLY BABY

Words by George A. Norton; Music by Ernie Burnett

THE MAN ON THE FLYING TRAPEZE

Lyrics by George Leybourne

Moderate Waltz tempo

1. Oh once I was hap-py, but now I'm for-lorn, Just like an old coat that is tat-tered and torn.

2-6. *(See additional lyrics)*

Left in this wide world to fret and to mourn, Be-trayed by a maid in her teens._____ Now, this

girl that I loved she was hand-some,_____ And I tried all I knew her to please._____ But I

nev-er could please her one quar-ter so well As The Man On The Fly-ing Trap-eze. Oh! He'd

float through the air with the great-est of ease, This dar-ing young man on the fly-ing trap-eze. His

move-ments are grace-ful, all girls he does please, And my love he has pur-loined a-way._____

Additional Lyrics

2. Now the young man by name was Señor Boni Slang,
Tall, big and handsome, as well made as Chang.
Where'er he appeared, how the hall loudly rang,
With ovations from all people there.
He'd smile from the bar on the people below
And one night he smiled on my love,
She winked back at him, and she shouted "Bravo!"
As he hung by his nose from above.

3. Her father and mother were both on my side
And tried very hard to make her my bride.
Her father, he sighed, and her mother, she cried
To see her throw herself away.
'Twas all no avail, she went there ev'ry right
And threw her bouquets on the stage,
Which caused him to meet her—how he ran me down,
To tell it would take a whole page.

4. One night I as usual went to her dear home,
And found there her mother and father alone.
I asked for my love, and soon 'twas made known,
To my horror, that she'd run away.
She packed up her boxes and eloped in the night,
With him with the greatest of ease.
From two stories high he had lowered her down
To the ground on his flying trapeze.

5. Some months after that I went into a hall;
To my suprise I found there on the wall
A bill in red letters which did my heart gall,
That she was appearing with him.
He'd taught her gymnastics, and dressed her in tights
To help him live at ease.
He'd made her assume a masculine name,
And now she goes on the trapeze.

Final Chorus:
She floats through the air with the greatest of ease;
You'd think her a man on the flying trapeze.
She does all the work while he takes his ease,
And that's what's become of my love.

188

MADEMOISELLE FROM ARMENTIERS

Ma-de-moi-selle From Ar-men-tières par-ley voo. Ma-de-moi-selle From Ar-men-tières,

par-ley voo. Ma-de-moi-selle From Ar-men-tières, she has-n't been hugged for for-ty years.

Hink-y dink-y par-ley voo. voo.

Copyright © 1990 MILWIN MUSIC

Additional Lyrics

1. She might have been old for all we knew,
Parlez-voo, (*Sing 3 times*)
When Napoleon flopped at Waterloo,
Hinky Dinky Parlez-voo.

2. You might forget the gas and the shell,
Parlez-voo, (*Sing 3 times*)
But you'll never forget the mademoiselle.
Hinky Dinky Parlez-voo.

3. Oh, madam, have you a daughter fair?
Parlez-voo, (*Sing 3 times*)
To wash a soldier's underwear?
Hinky Dinky Parlez-voo.

4. She got the palms and the Croiz-de-Guerre,
Parlez-voo, (*Sing 3 times*)
For washing soldiers' underwear.
Hinky Dinky Parlez-voo.

5. The General got the Croix-de-Guerre,
Parlez-voo, (*Sing 3 times*)
The son-of-a-bitch was never there.
Hinky Dinky Parlez-voo.

6. The officers get all the steak,
Parlez-voo, (*Sing 3 times*)
And all we get is the belly-ache.
Hinky Dinky Parlez-voo.

7. The MPs say they won the war,
Parlez-voo, (*Sing 3 times*)
Standing on guard at the cafe door.
Hinky Dinky Parlez-voo.

8. I didn't care what became of me,
Parlez-voo, (*Sing 3 times*)
So I went and joined the infantry.
Hinky Dinky Parlez-voo.

9. They say they mechanized the war,
Parlez-voo, (*Sing 3 times*)
So what the hell are we marching for?
Hinky Dinky Parlez-voo.

A MAN WITHOUT A WOMAN

Words and Music by Alfred Williams

Oh, A Man With-out A Wom-an is like a ship with-out a sail; Is like a boat with-out a rud-der, Is like a

fish with-out a tail. Oh A Man With-out A Wom-an is like a wreck up-on the sand. There's on-ly

one thing worse in this whole darn u-ni-verse, And that's a wom-an __ I say a wom-an __ I mean a wom-an with-out a man.

Copyright © 1990 HAL LEONARD PUBLISHING CORPORATION

MAPLE LEAF RAG

Scott Joplin

MARCH OF THE TOYS

By Victor Herbert

MARIANNE

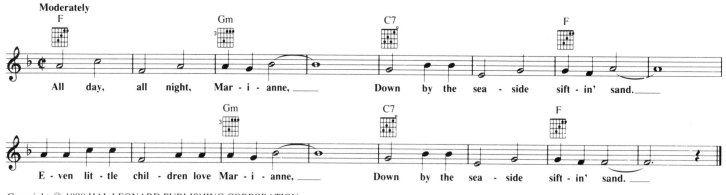

All day, all night, Mar-i-anne, _____ Down by the sea-side sift-in' sand. _____

E-ven lit-tle chil-dren love Mar-i-anne, _____ Down by the sea-side sift-in' sand. _____

MARCH SLAV
(Tchaikovsky)

Peter Tchaikovsky

MARCH MILITAIRE

Franz Schubert

MARINE'S HYMN

From the halls of Mon-te-zu-ma To the shores of Trip-o-li;___ We ___ First to
fight our coun-try's bat-tles, On the land and on the sea.___
proud to claim the ti-tle of U-nit-ed States Ma-rine.

Fine __ fight for right and free-dom, And to keep our hon-or clean;___ We are

MAORI FAREWELL SONG

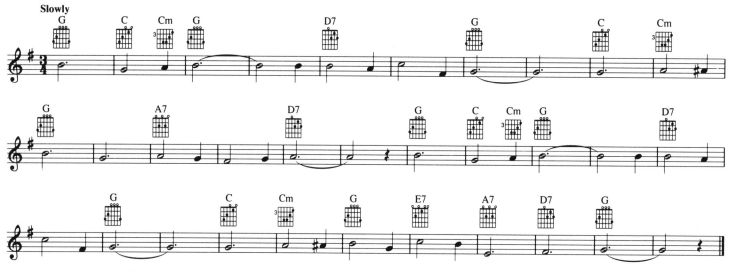

MATTINATA

Ruggiero Leoncavallo

MIDNIGHT SPECIAL

Freely, but not too slow

1. Well you wake up in the morn - ing,_____ hear the ding dong ring, You go march-ing to the
2. If you ev - er go to Hous - ton,_____ you'd bet - ter walk right, And you bet - ter not __
3. *(See additional lyrics)*

ta - ble,_____ see the same __ damn __ thing. Well, it's on - ly one __ ta - ble,_____
stag - ger,_____ and you bet - ter not __ fight. 'Cause the sher - iff will ar - rest you,_____

__ knife and fork __ and a pan, And if you say a thing a - bout it,_____
__ and he'll car - ry you __ down, And you can bet your bot - tom dol - lar,_____

__ you're in trou - ble with the man. } Let the Mid - night Spe - cial _____ shine her light __ on me,
__ you're for Su - gar-land __ bound. }

Chorus:

Let the Mid - night Spe - cial _____ shine her ev - er lov - in' light on __ me._____

Additional Lyrics

3. Lord, Thelma said she loved me, but I believe she told a lie,
   'Cause she hasn't been to see me since last July.
   She brought me little coffee, she brought me little tea,
   She brought me nearly everything but the jail house key.

A MIGHTY FORTRESS IS OUR GOD

Words by Frederick H. Hedge; Music by Martin Luther

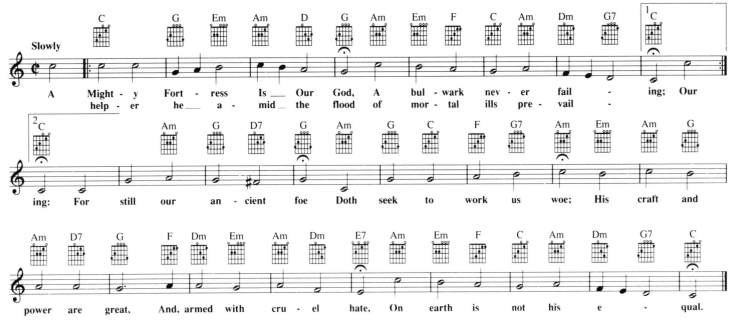

Slowly

A Might - y Fort - ress Is __ Our God, A bul - wark nev - er fail - ing; Our
help - er he __ a - mid __ the flood of mor - tal ills pre - vail -

ing: For still our an - cient foe Doth seek to work us woe; His craft and

power are great, And, armed with cru - el hate, On earth is not his e - qual.

MARTHA POLKA

MEDITATION
(From "THAIS")

Jules Massenet

MARY HAD A LITTLE LAMB

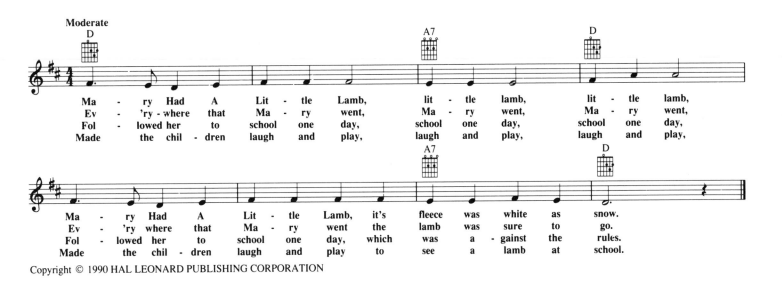

Ma - ry Had A Lit - tle Lamb, lit - tle lamb, lit - tle lamb,
Ev - 'ry-where that Ma - ry went, Ma - ry went, Ma - ry went,
Fol - lowed her to school one day, school one day, school one day,
Made the chil - dren laugh and play, laugh and play, laugh and play,

Ma - ry Had A Lit - tle Lamb, it's fleece was white as snow.
Ev - 'ry where that Ma - ry went the lamb was sure to go.
Fol - lowed her to school one day, which was a - gainst the rules.
Made the chil - dren laugh and play to see a lamb at school.

MAZEL TOV

MEET ME TONIGHT IN DREAMLAND

Words by Beth Slater Whitson; Music by Leo Friedman

MICHAEL FINNEGAN

MERRILY WE ROLL ALONG

MELODY IN A

Brig. Gen Charles G. Dawes

MELODY IN F

Anton G. Rubinstein

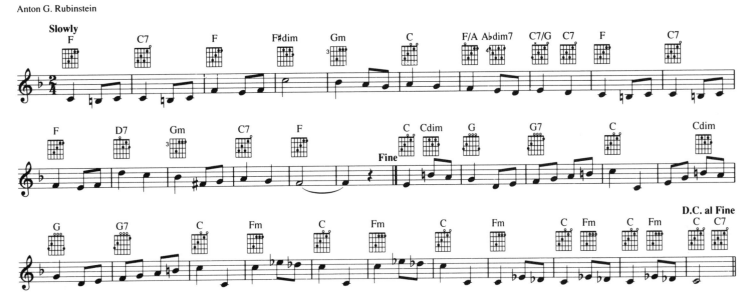

MELODY OF LOVE

H. Engelmann

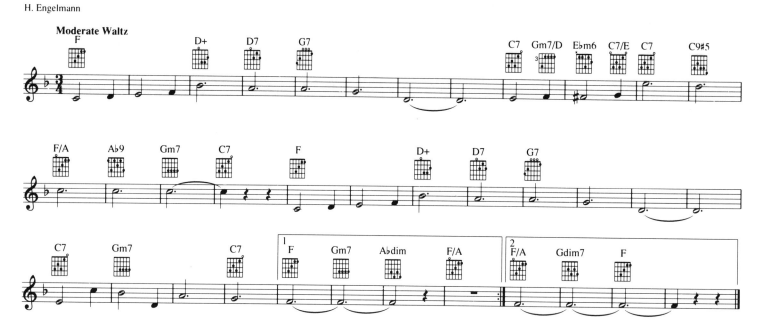

MEXICAN HAT DANCE

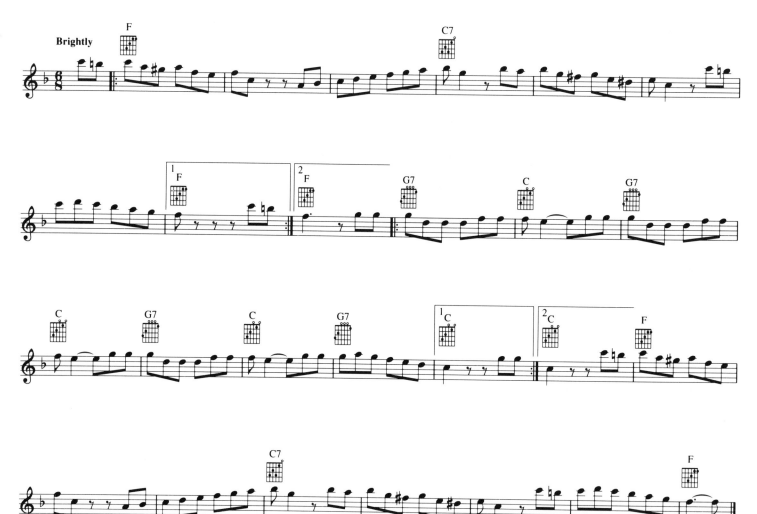

MICHAEL, ROW THE BOAT ASHORE

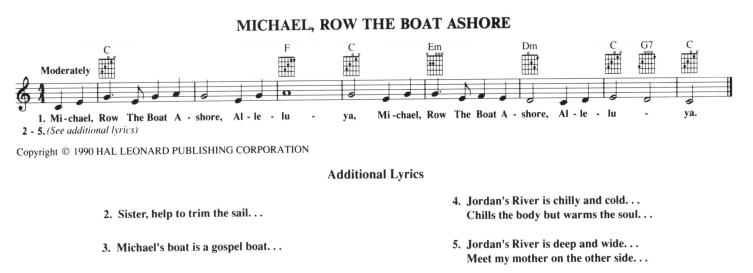

1. Mi-chael, Row The Boat A-shore, Al-le-lu - ya, Mi-chael, Row The Boat A-shore, Al-le-lu - ya.
2 - 5. (See additional lyrics)

Additional Lyrics

2. Sister, help to trim the sail. . .

3. Michael's boat is a gospel boat. . .

4. Jordan's River is chilly and cold. . .
   Chills the body but warms the soul. . .

5. Jordan's River is deep and wide. . .
   Meet my mother on the other side. . .

MIGHTY LAK' A ROSE

Words by Frank L. Stanton; Music by Ethelbert Nevin

Sweet - est lit - tle fel - low, Ev - 'ry - bod - y knows, Don't know what to call him but he's
Look - ing at his mom - my With eyes so shin - y blue, Makes you think __ heav'n _____ is

Might - y Lak A Rose! com - in' close to you! When he's there a - sleep - in' in his ti - ny place,

Think I see the an - gels look - in' thro' the lace. When the dark is fall - in',

When the shad - ows creep, Then they come on tip - toe to kiss him in his sleep. _____

M-I-N-E

If you'll be M - I - N - E mine, I'll be T - H - I - N - E thine, And I'll L - O - V - E love you all the

T - I - M - E time. You are the B - E - S - T best of all the R - E - S - T rest, And I'll

L - O - V - E love you all the T - I - M - E time. __ Wrap 'em up, Stack 'em up an - y old time. __

THE MISSOURI WALTZ

Lyric by J.R. Shannon

MOONLIGHT SONATA
(1st Movement)

thoven

Slow and Sustained

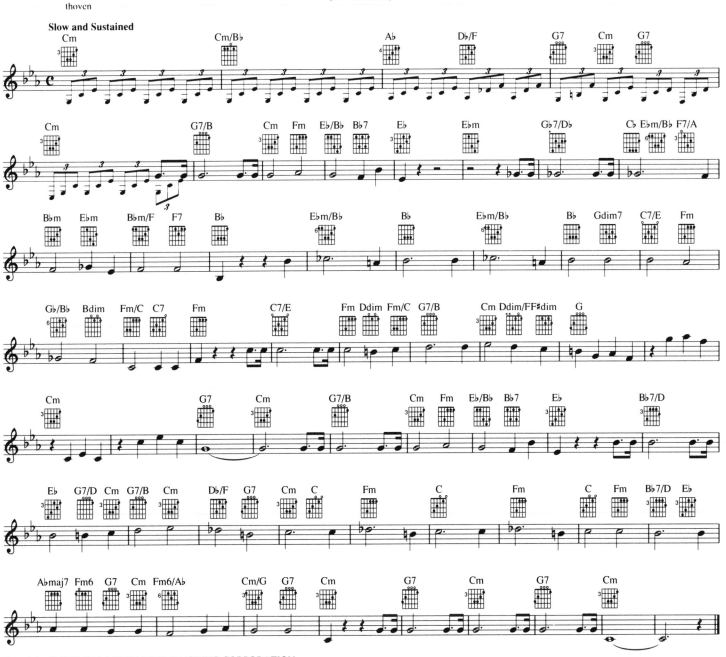

MOMENT MUSICALE
(Schubert)

Franz Schubert

Allegro Moderato

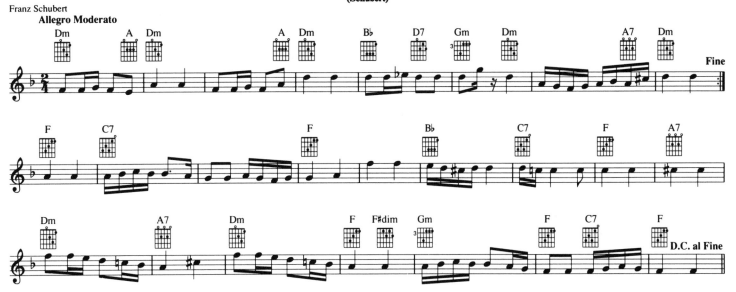

THE MULBERRY BUSH

1. Here we go round The Mul-ber-ry Bush, The Mul-ber-ry Bush, The Mul-ber-ry Bush.
2. This is the way we wash ___ our clothes, We wash ___ our clothes, we wash ___ our clothes.
3. This is the way we i-ron our clothes, We i-ron our clothes, we i-ron our clothes.
4-8. *(See additional lyrics)*

Here we go round The Mul-ber-ry Bush So ear-ly in ___ the morn-ing.
This is the way we wash ___ our clothes So ear-ly Mon-day morn-ing.
This is the way we i-ron our clothes So ear-ly Tues-day morn-ing. morn-ing.

Additional Lyrics

4. This is the way we scrub the floor, etc.
   So early Wednesday morning.

5. This is the way we mend our clothes, etc.
   So early Thursday morning.

6. This is the way we sweep the house, etc.
   So early Friday morning.

7. This is the way we bake our bread, etc.
   So early Saturday morning.

8. This is the way we go to church, etc.
   So early Sunday morning.

MORNING

Edvard Grieg

MUSETTA'S WALTZ

Giacomo Puccini

MY OLD KENTUCKY HOME

By Stephen Foster

1. The sun shines bright on My Old Ken-tuck-y Home 'Tis sum-mer the work-ers are gay. The
young folks roll on the lit-tle cab-in floor, All mer-ry all hap-py and bright. The By'n'
2-3. *(See additional lyrics)*

corn top's ripe and the mead-ow's in bloom, While the birds make mu-sic all the day. The
bye hard times comes a knock-ing at the door, Then My
sing one song for My Old Ken-tuck-y Home, For My

Old Ken-tuck-y Home _ good-night. Weep no more, my la-dy, Oh! Weep no more to-day. We will
Old Ken-tuck-y Home far a-way.

Additional Lyrics

2. They hunt no more for the possum and the coon,
On meadow, the hill and the shore,
They sing no more by the glimmer of the moon,
On the bench by that old cabin door.
The day goes by like a shadow o'er the heart,
With sorrow where all was delight.
The time has come when the darkies have to part,
Then My Old Kentucky Home, good night.

3. The head must bow and the back will have to bend,
Wherever the poor folks may go.
A few more days and the trouble will end,
In the field where sugar-canes may grow.
A few more days for to tote the weary load,
No matter, 'twill never by light.
A few more days till we totter on the road,
The My Old Kentucky Home, good night.

MY WILD IRISH ROSE

Chauncey Olcott

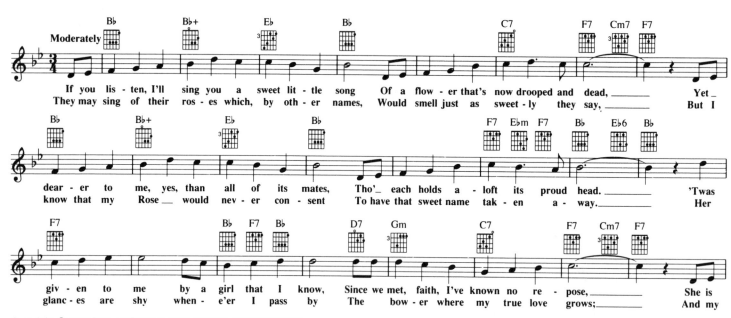

If you lis-ten, I'll sing you a sweet lit-tle song Of a flow-er that's now drooped and dead, _____ Yet _
They may sing of their ros-es which, by oth-er names, Would smell just as sweet-ly they say, _____ But I

dear-er to me, yes, than all of its mates, Tho'_ each holds a-loft its proud head. _____ 'Twas
know that my Rose _ would nev-er con-sent To have that sweet name tak-en a-way. _____ Her

giv-en to me by a girl that I know, Since we met, faith, I've known no re-pose, _____ She is
glanc-es are shy when-e'er I pass by The bow-er where my true love grows; _____ And my

dear-er by far than the world's bright-est star, And I call her My Wild I-rish Rose. _____ } My
one wish has been that some-day I may win The_ heart of My Wild I-rish Rose. _____

With much expression

Wild I - rish Rose, _____ The sweet-est flow'r that grows, _____ You may

search ev - 'ry - where but none can com-pare with My Wild I - rish Rose. _____ My

Wild I - rish Rose, _____ The dear-est flow'r that grows _____ And some

day for my sake, she may let me take The bloom from My Wild I - rish Rose. _____

NORWEGIAN DANCE

Edvard Grieg

Moderately

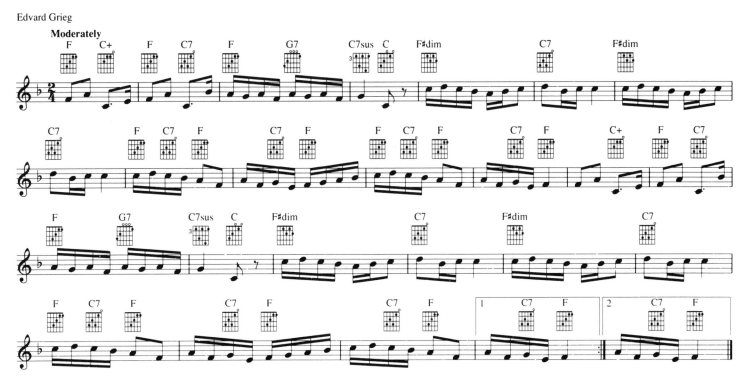

MY BONNIE

My Bon - nie lies o - ver the o - cean, _____ My Bon - nie lies o - ver the sea. _____

_____ My Bon - nie lies o - ver the o - cean, _____ Oh bring back My Bon - nie to

me. _____ Bring back, bring back, Bring back My Bon - nie to me, to

me, Bring back, bring back, Oh bring back My Bon - nie to me. _____

MY GAL SAL

Paul Dresser

They called her friv - o - lous Sal, _____ A pe - cu - liar sort of a gal, _____

_____ With a heart that was mel - low, An all 'round good fel - low, Was my old pal. _____

_____ Your trou - bles, sor - rows and care, _____ She was al - ways will - ing to share. _____ A

wild sort of dev - il, But dead on the lev - el, Was My Gal Sal. _____

NATIONAL EMBLEM

E.E. Bagley

NOEL! NOEL!

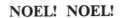

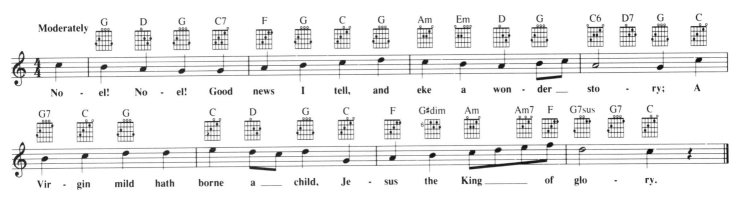

No - el! No - el! Good news I tell, and eke a won - der __ sto - ry; A
Vir - gin mild hath borne a __ child, Je - sus the King __ of glo - ry.

'NEATH THE OLD CHESTNUT TREE

My way-far-ing ways took me a-way from the girl I loved so true. I kissed her on the cheek 'Neath The Old Chest-nut Tree when I bid her a-dieu. The road I did ride was full of tears. I was so lone-some I could cry. Now I think of that girl 'Neath The Old Chest-nut Tree as I lay down to die. So bu-ry me 'Neath The Old Chest-nut Tree that we carved our names up-on. And this lone-some old cow-boy will fi-n'lly rest in peace. And that tree will still stand when I'm gone. I'll lie 'Neath The Old Chest-nut Tree.

NINE HUNDRED MILES

I am walk-ing down this track, I've got tears in my eyes, I'm try'n to read a let-ter from my home; ___ And if this train runs me right I'll be home Sat-ur-day night, 'Cause I'm Nine Hun-dred Miles from ___ my home. ___ And I hate to hear that lone-some whis-tle blow. ___ That long lone-some train whis-tl-ing down.

NOBODY KNOWS THE TROUBLE I'VE SEEN

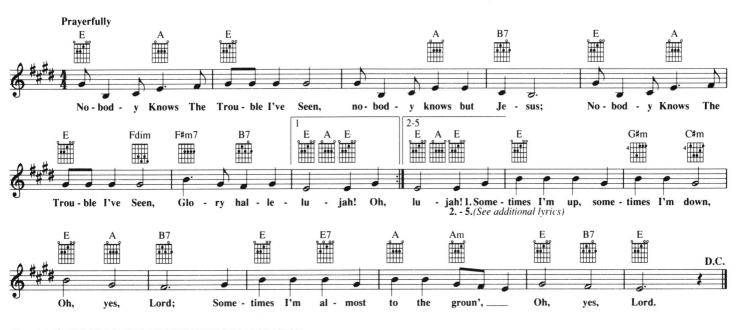

No-bod-y Knows The Trou-ble I've Seen, no-bod-y knows but Je-sus; No-bod-y Knows The

Trou-ble I've Seen, Glo-ry hal-le-lu-jah! Oh, lu-jah! 1. Some-times I'm up, some-times I'm down,
2.-5. *(See additional lyrics)*

Oh, yes, Lord; Some-times I'm al-most to the groun', ____ Oh, yes, Lord.

Additional Lyrics

2. Now, you may think that I don't know, etc.
   But I've had my troubles here below, etc.

3. One day when I was walkin' along,
   The sky opened up and love came down.

4. What make old Satan hate me so?
   He had me once and had to let me go.

5. I never shall forget that day,
   When Jesus washed my sins away.

THE OLD GRAY MARE

Traditional

Oh The Old Gray Mare, She ain't what she used to be, Ain't what she used to be,

Ain't what she used to be. The Old Gray Mare, She ain't what she used to be, man-y long years a-

go. Man-y long years a-go, Man-y long years a-go, Oh The

NOCTURNE
(Chopin)

Frederic Chopin

With expression

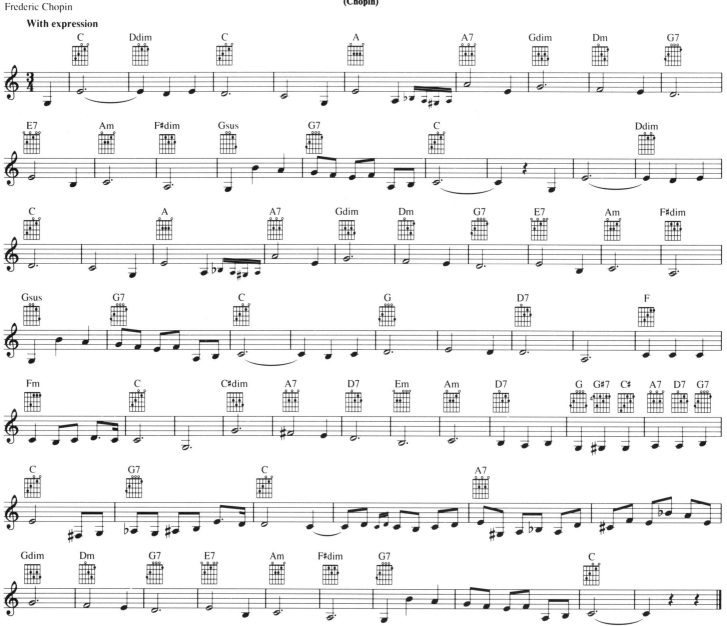

NOW THE DAY IS OVER

Sabine Baring-Gould
Joseph Barnby

Quietly

1. Now The Day Is O - ver, night is draw - ing nigh,
2. Fa - ther, give the wea - ry, calm and sweet re - pose.
3. When the morn - ing wak - ens, then may I a - rise.

shad - ows of the eve - ning steal a - cross the sky.
With Thy ten - d'rest bless - ing may our eye - lids close.
Pure and fresh and sin - less in Thy ho - ly eyes.

NOW THANK WE ALL OUR GOD

Johann Cruger

1. Now Thank We All Our God, with heart and hands and voic - es, who won - drous things hath
2. O may this boun - teous God, thro' all our life be near us! With ev - er joy - ful

done, in whom His world re - joic - es; who from our moth - er's arms, hath
hearts and bless - ed peace to cheer us; and keep us in His grace. hath

blessed ___ us on our way with count - less gifts of love, and still is ours to - day.
guide ___ us when per - plexed. and free us from all ills in this world and the next.

O CANADA!

Calixa Lavallee, l'Hon. Judge Routhier, and
Justice R.S. Weir

1. O Can - a - da! Our home and na - tive land! True pa - triot love in
2. O Can - a - da! Where pines and ma - ples grow, Great prai - ries spread and
French: O Can - a - da! Ter - re de nos aï - eux. Ton front est cient de

all thy sons com - mand, with ___ glow - ing hearts we ___ see thee rise, the ___ true North strong and
lord - ly riv - ers flow, how ___ dear to us thy ___ vast do - main, from ___ east to west - ern
fleu - rons glo - ri - eux! Car ton bras sait por - ter l'é - pé - e. Il ___ sait por - ter la

free, and ___ stand on guard, O ___ Can - a - da, we stand on guard ___ for ___ thee.
sea, thou ___ land of hope for ___ all who toil! Thou true North strong ___ and ___ free. }
croix! Ton his - toire est une é - po - pé - e Des plus bril - lants ___ ex - ploits.

Refrain

O Can - a - da, glo - rious and free, O Can - a - da, we stand on
Et ta va - leur, de foi trem - pée. Pro - té - ge - ra nos foy - ers

guard for thee. O Can - a - da, we stand on guard for thee.
et nos droits. Pro - té - ge - ra nos foy - ers et nos droits.

O COME, ALL YE FAITHFUL

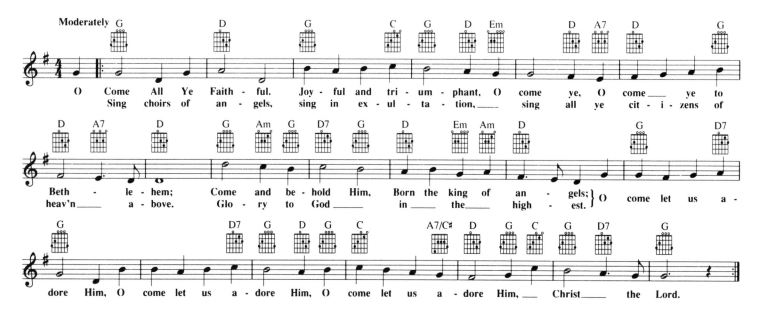

O Come All Ye Faith - ful. Joy - ful and tri - um - phant, O come ye, O come __ ye to
Sing choirs of an - gels, sing in ex - ul - ta - tion, __ sing all ye cit - i - zens of

Beth - le - hem; Come and be - hold Him, Born the king of an - gels; } O come let us a -
heav'n __ a - bove. Glo - ry to God __ in __ the __ high - est.

dore Him, O come let us a - dore Him, O come let us a - dore Him, __ Christ __ the Lord.

O COME, LITTLE CHILDREN

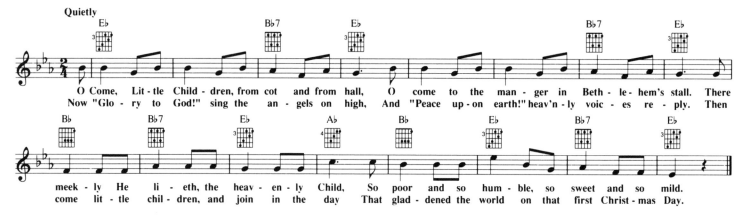

O Come, Lit - tle Child - dren, from cot and from hall, O come to the man - ger in Beth - le - hem's stall. There
Now "Glo - ry to God!" sing the an - gels on high, And "Peace up - on earth!" heav'n - ly voic - es re - ply. Then

meek - ly He li - eth, the heav - en - ly Child, So poor and so hum - ble, so sweet and so mild.
come lit - tle chil - dren, and join in the day That glad - dened the world on that first Christ - mas Day.

O HOLY NIGHT

Words by J.S. Dwight
Music by Adolphe Adam

O Ho - ly Night __ the stars are bright - ly shin - ing, it is the night of the dear Sav - ior's
Tru - ly he taught us to love one an - oth - er, His law is love, and his gos - pel is

birth: __ Long lay the world __ in sin and er - ror pin - ing, till he ap - peared and the
peace: __ Chains shall He break for the slave is our broth - er, and in His name all op -

soul felt its worth. A thrill of hope the wea-ry soul re-joic-es, for yon-der
pres-sion shall cease. Sweet hymns of joy in grate-ful cho-rus raise we, let all with-

breaks a new and glo-rious morn; Fall on your knees, oh, hear the an-gel
in us praise His ho-ly name; Christ is the Lord, oh, praise His name for-

voic-es! O night di-vine o night when Christ was born!
ev-er! His pow'r and glo-ry ev-er more pro-claim

O night O Ho-ly night O night di-vine!
His pow'r

and glo-ry ev-er-more pro-claim!

O CHRISTMAS TREE

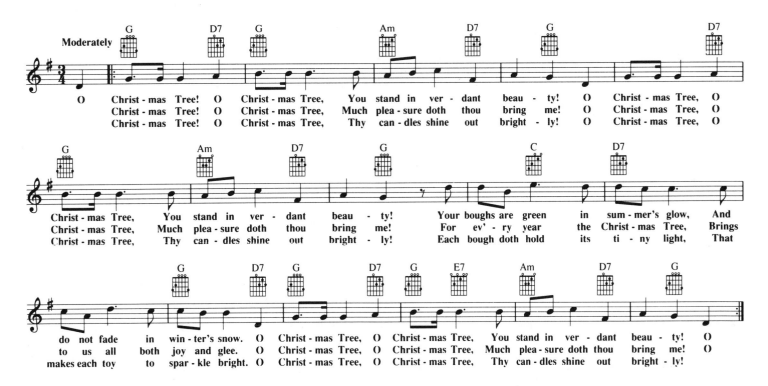

Moderately

O Christ-mas Tree! O Christ-mas Tree, You stand in ver-dant beau-ty! O Christ-mas Tree, O
Christ-mas Tree! O Christ-mas Tree, Much plea-sure doth thou bring me! O Christ-mas Tree, O
Christ-mas Tree! O Christ-mas Tree, Thy can-dles shine out bright-ly! O Christ-mas Tree, O

Christ-mas Tree, You stand in ver-dant beau-ty! Your boughs are green in sum-mer's glow, And
Christ-mas Tree, Much plea-sure doth thou bring me! For ev'-ry year the Christ-mas Tree, Brings
Christ-mas Tree, Thy can-dles shine out bright-ly! Each bough doth hold its ti-ny light, That

do not fade in win-ter's snow. O Christ-mas Tree, O Christ-mas Tree, You stand in ver-dant beau-ty! O
to us all both joy and glee. O Christ-mas Tree, O Christ-mas Tree, Much plea-sure doth thou bring me! O
makes each toy to spar-kle bright. O Christ-mas Tree, O Christ-mas Tree, Thy can-dles shine out bright-ly! O

O COME, O COME EMMANUEL

O LITTLE TOWN OF BETHLEHEM

Brooks/Redner

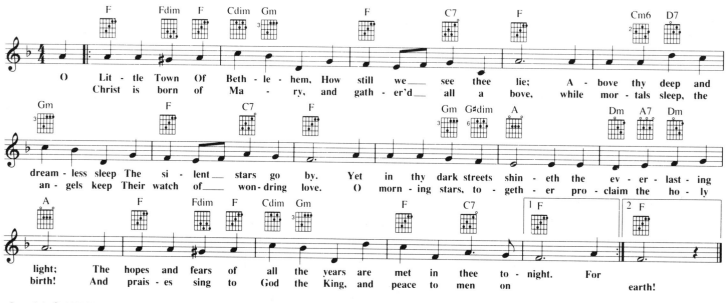

O SANCTISSIMA

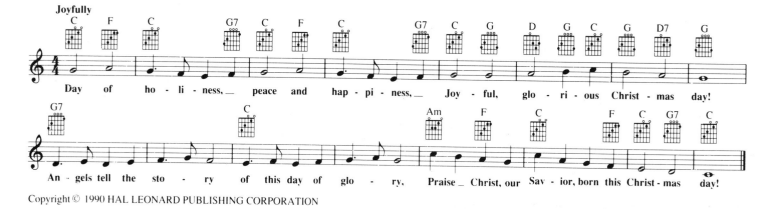

O SOLE MIO

E. Di Capua

OBEREK

ODE TO JOY

Ludwig van Beethoven

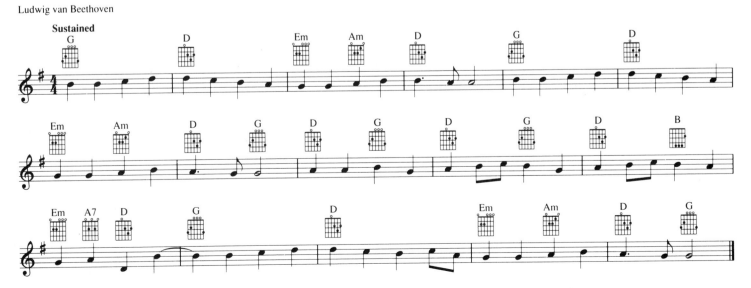

OATS, PEAS, BEANS AND BARLEY GROW

Moderately fast

1. Oats, Peas, Beans, And Bar-ley Grow; Oats, Peas, Beans And Bar-ley Grow; Do
2. First the farm-er sows his seed, Then he stands and takes his ease; He
3. *(See additional lyrics)*

you or I or an-y-one know how Oats, Peas, Beans, And Bar-ley Grow?
stamps his foot and claps his hands, and turns a-round to view the land.

Additional Lyrics

3. Waiting for a partner,
   Waiting for a partner,
   Open the ring and take one in
   While we all gaily dance and sing.

OH MARIE

E. Di Capua

Moderately

Oh Ma-rie, Oh Ma-rie, there is no one but you, dear for me. My heart's re-

peat-ing each word you can hear in it's beat-ing, Oh Ma-rie, Oh Ma-rie, fair-est

flow-er in all It-al-y I beg of thee, hear my plea Oh Ma-rie.

OH WHERE, OH WHERE HAS MY LITTLE DOG GONE?

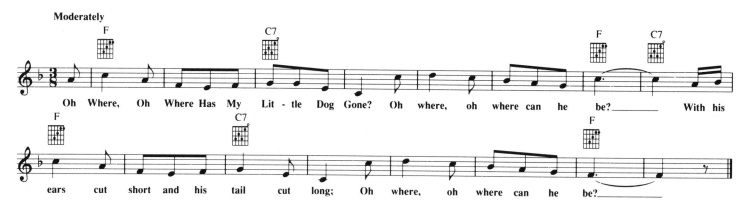

Moderately

Oh Where, Oh Where Has My Lit-tle Dog Gone? Oh where, oh where can he be? With his

ears cut short and his tail cut long; Oh where, oh where can he be?

OH, SUSANNA

Stephen Foster

1. I _____ come from Al - a - bam - a with a ban - jo on my knee. I'm _____ goin' to Lou' - si
rained all night the day I left, the weath - er it was dry. The _____ sun so hot I

2, 3. *(See additional lyrics)*

an - a my Su - san - na for to see. It _____ Oh, Su - san - na, oh
froze to death, Su - san - na don't you cry.

don't you cry for me, for I come from Al - a - bam - a with a ban - jo on my knee.

Copyright © 1990 HAL LEONARD PUBLISHING CORPORATION

Additional Lyrics

2. I had a dream the other night
When everything was still.
I thought I saw Susanna
A-coming down the hill.

3. The buckwheat cake was in her mouth,
The tear was in her eye,
Say I, "I'm coming from the South,
Susanna, don't you cry."

OH, DEAR! WHAT CAN THE MATTER BE?

Oh, Dear! What Can The Mat - ter Be? Dear, dear, what can the mat - ter be? Oh, Dear! What Can The Mat - ter Be?

John - ny's so long at the fair. _____ { He prom - ised to buy me a trin - ket to please me, and then for a smile, oh he
He prom - ised to bring me a bas - ket of po - sies, a gar - land of lil - ies, a

vowed he would tease me, he prom - ised to bring me a bunch of blue rib - bons, to tie up my bon - nie brown hair. _____
gar - land of ros - es, a lit - tle straw hat to set off the blue rib - bons, that tie up my bon - nie brown hair. _____

Copyright © 1990 HAL LEONARD PUBLISHING CORPORATION

OH, THEM GOLDEN SLIPPERS

James A. Bland

1. Oh, my gold-en slip-pers are laid a-way, 'Cause I don't 'spect to wear them till my wed-ding day, and my
2,3. *(See additional lyrics)*

long-tailed coat, that I loved so well, I will wear up in the char-iot in the morn. And my

long white robe that I bought last June, I'm goin' to get changed 'cause it fits too soon, and the

old gray horse that I used to drive, I will hitch him to the char-iot in the morn. Oh, Them

Gold-en Slip-pers Oh, Them Gold-en Slip-pers, gold-en slip-pers I'm goin' to wear, Be-

cause they look so neat. goin' to wear to walk the gold-en street.

Additional Lyrics

2. Oh, my old banjo hangs on the wall,
   'Cause it ain't been tuned since 'way last fall,
   But the folks all say we'll have a good time,
   When we ride up in the chariot in the morn,
   There's old Brother Ben and his sister Luce,
   They will telegraph the news to Uncle 'Bacco Juice,
   What a great camp meeting there will be that day,
   When we ride up in the chariot in the morning.

3. So, it's goodbye children, I will have to go,
   Where the rain don't fall and the wind don't blow,
   And your ulster coats, why, you will not need,
   When you ride up in the chariot in the morn,
   But your golden slippers must be nice and clean,
   And your age must be just sweet sixteen,
   And your white kid gloves you will have to wear,
   When you ride up in the chariot in the morn.

OH, PROMISE ME

Words by Clement Scott
Music by R. de Koven

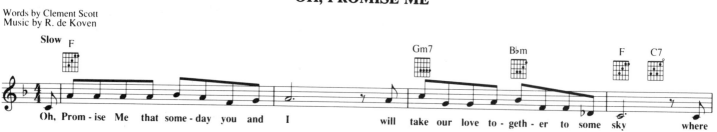

Oh, Prom-ise Me that some-day you and I will take our love to-geth-er to some sky where

we can be a-lone, and faith re-new, and find the hol-lows where those flow-ers grew, _____ those

first sweet vi-o-lets of ear-ly spring, which come in whis-pers, thrill us both, and sing O

love un-speak-a-ble that is to be; Oh, Prom-ise Me! Oh, Prom-ise me! Oh,

Prom-ise Me that you will take my hand, the most un-wor-thy in this lone-ly land, and

let me sit be-side you, in your eyes see-ing the vi-sion of our par-a-dise,

hear-ing God's mes-sage while the or-gan rolls its might-y mu-sic to our ver-y souls; No

love less per-fect than a life with thee; Oh Prom-ise Me! Oh Prom-ise me!

NEARER MY GOD TO THEE

Words by Sarah F. Adams
Music by Lowell Mason

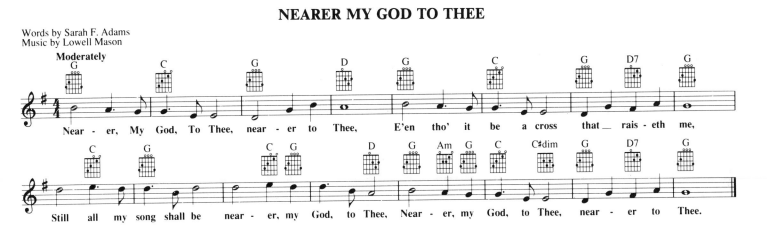

Moderately

Near-er, My God, To Thee, near-er to Thee, E'en tho' it be a cross that __ rais-eth me,

Still all my song shall be near-er, my God, to Thee, Near-er, my God, to Thee, near-er to Thee.

THE OLD CHISHOLM TRAIL

Lively

1. Well, come a - long, boys, and lis - ten to my tale I'll tell you all my trou - bles on The Old Chis - holm Trail. Come a
2-8. *(See additional lyrics)*

ti yi yip - py, yip - py yay, yip - py yay! Come a ti yi yip - py, yip - py yay!

Additional Lyrics

2. On a ten dollar horse and a forty dollar saddle
   I started out a-punchin' those long-horned cattle.
   Refrain

3. I'm up in the morning before daylight
   And before I gets to sleepin' the old moon's
   shining bright.
   Refrain

4. Oh, it's bacon and beans almost every single day
   And I'd sooner be a-eatin' prairie hay.
   Refrain

5. I went to the boss for to draw my roll,
   He had it figured out I was nine dollars in the hole.
   Refrain

6. So I went up to the boss and said I won't take that
   And I slapped him in the face with my old slouch hat.
   Refrain

7. I'll sell my outfit just as soon as I can,
   'Cause I ain't punchin' cattle for no mean boss man.
   Refrain

8. With my knees in the saddle and my seat in the sky,
   I'll quit punchin' cattle in the sweet by and by.
   Refrain

OLD JOE CLARK

Lively

Old Joe Clark, he had a house, six - teen sto - ries high,
I went up to Joe's new house, stepped right in the door,
Old Joe Clark, he had a dog, dumb as he could be,
Old Joe Clark had a mean old cat, nev - er did sing or pray.

Ev - 'ry sto - ry Joe was sleep - in' on a
Barked a lad - y - bug Stuck her head in the

in the house, smelled like ap - ple pie.
feath - er bed, I had to sleep on the floor.
up a stump, a pig up a hol - low tree.
milk - ing pail, washed her sins a - way!

Refrain

'Round and 'round, Old Joe Clark,

'round and 'round, I say; 'Round and 'round, Old Joe Clark, dance your cares a - way.

OLD DAN TUCKER

Quickly

1. Went to town the oth-er night to hear a noise and see a fight, all the peo-ple were run-ning a-round, say-ing,
2. *(See additional lyrics)*

Old Dan Tuck-er's come to town. Get out the way, Old Dan Tuck-er, you're too late to come for sup-per,

sup-per's o-ver and din-ner's cook-ing and Old Dan Tuck-er just stand-ing there look-ing.

Additional Lyrics

2. Old Dan Tucker's a fine old man,
   Washed his face in a frying pan.
   Combed his hair with a wagon wheel,
   And died with a toothache in his heel.

3. Old Dan Tucker come to town,
   Riding a billy goat, leading a hound.
   Hound barked and the billygoat jumped,
   Throwed old Dan right straddle of a stump.

4. Old Dan Tucker clumb a tree,
   His Lord and Master for to see,
   The limb it broke and Dan got a fall,
   Never got to see his Lord at all.

5. Old Dan Tucker he got drunk,
   Fell in the fire and he kicked up a chunk;
   Red hot coal got in his shoe,
   Lord Godamighty, how the ashed flew!

6. Old Dan Tucker he come to town,
   Swinging the ladies 'round and 'round,
   First to the right and then to the left,
   And then to the one that you love the best.

OLD KING COLE

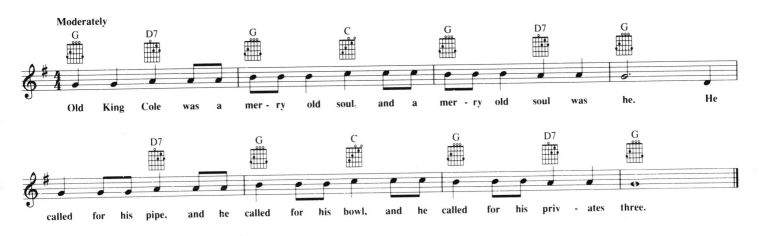

Moderately

Old King Cole was a mer-ry old soul, and a mer-ry old soul was he. He

called for his pipe, and he called for his bowl, and he called for his priv-ates three.

OLD FOLKS AT HOME

Stephen Foster

OLD MacDONALD HAD A FARM

1. Old Mac-Don-ald Had A Farm E - I - E - I - O! And on this farm he had a duck,
2-10. *(See additional lyrics)*
E - I - E - I - O! With a quack-quack here, and a quack-quack there, Here a quack, there a quack,
Ev - 'ry where a quack, quack. Old Mac-Don-ald Had A Farm, E - I - E - I - O!

Additional Lyrics

2. Old MacDonald Had A Farm,
   E - I - E - I - O!
   And on this farm he had a chick,
   E - I - E - I - O!
   With a chick, chick here
   And a chick, chick there,
   Here a chick, there a chick,
   Everywhere a chick, chick
   Old MacDonald Had A Farm,
   E - I - E - I - O!

3. Other verses:

   3. Cow — moo, moo
   4. Dogs — bow, bow
   5. Pigs — oink, oink
   6. Rooster — cock-a-doodle, cock-a-doodle
   7. Turkey — gobble, gobble
   8. Cat — meow, meow
   9. Horse — neigh, neigh
   10. Donkey — hee-haw, hee-haw

OLD OAKEN BUCKET

Words by Samuel Woodworth
Music by Edwin Krallmark

How dear to the heart are the scenes of my child-hood, When fond re-col-
or - chard, the mead-ow, the deep - tan-gled wild-wood, And ev - 'ry loved
Old Oak - en Buck - et, the i - ron-bound buck - et, The moss - cov - ered

lec - tion pre - sents them to view! The wide spread-ing pond, and the mill that stood
spot which my in - fan - cy knew; The
buck - et that hung in the well.

by it, The bridge and the rock where the ca - ta - ract fell. The

D.C. al Fine

ON THE BANKS OF THE WABASH

Paul Dresser

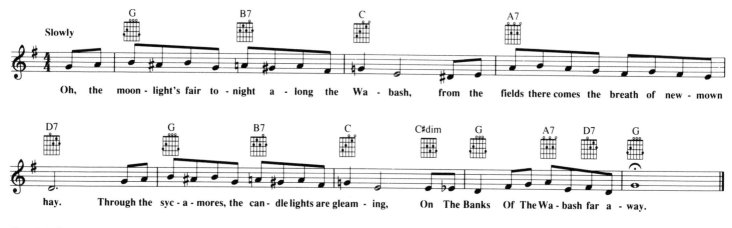

Oh, the moon - light's fair to - night a - long the Wa - bash, from the fields there comes the breath of new - mown hay. Through the syc - a - mores, the can - dle lights are gleam - ing, On The Banks Of The Wa - bash far a - way.

ON TOP OF OLD SMOKY

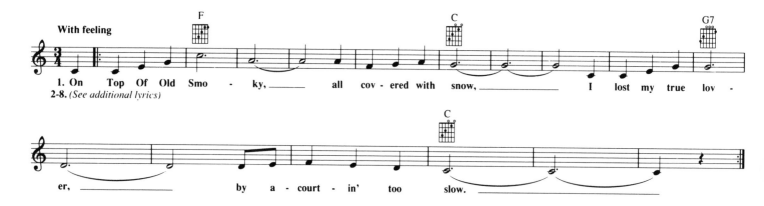

1. On Top Of Old Smo - ky,_____ all cov - ered with snow,_____ I lost my true lov -
2-8. (See additional lyrics)

er,_____ by a - court - in' too slow._____

Additional Lyrics

2. Well, a-courting's a pleasure,
   And parting is grief.
   But a false-hearted lover
   Is worse than a thief.

3. A thief he will rob you
   And take all you have,
   But a false-hearted lover
   Will send you to your grave.

4. And the grave will decay you
   And turn you to dust.
   And where is the young man
   A poor girl can trust.

5. They'll hug you and kiss you
   And tell you more lies
   Than the cross-ties on the railroad,
   Or the stars in the skies.

6. They'll tell you they love you,
   Just to give your heart ease.
   But the minute your back's turned,
   They'll court whom they please.

7. So come all you young maidens
   And listen to me.
   Never place your affection
   On a green willow tree.

8. For the leaves they will wither
   And the roots they will die,
   And your true love will leave you,
   And you'll never know why.

ON WISCONSIN!

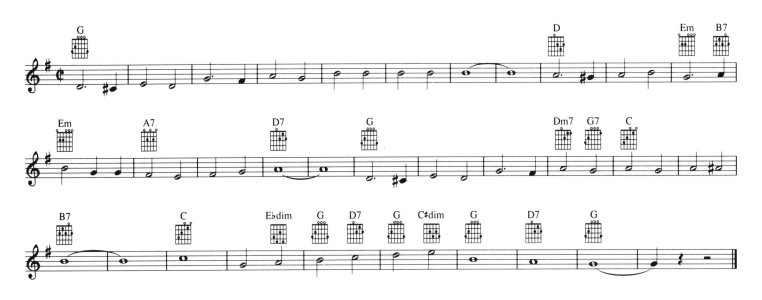

ONCE IN ROYAL DAVID'S CITY

Stately

1. Once In Roy - al Da - vid's __ Cit - y stood a low - ly cat - tle ____ shed, Where a
2. He came down to earth __ from __ heav - en, Who is God and Lord __ of ____ all, And His
3-4. (See additional lyrics)

moth - er laid ____ her ____ Ba - by in a man - ger for ____ His ____ bed; Ma - ry
shel - ter was ____ a ____ sta - ble, And His cra - dle was ____ a ____ stall; With the

was that moth - er mild, Je - sus Christ her lit - tle ____ Child.
poor, and mean, and low - ly, Lived on earth our Sav - iour ____ ho - ly.

Additional Lyrics

3. Jesus is our childhood's pattern,
   Day by day like us He grew;
   He was little, weak and helpless,
   Tears and smiles like us He knew;
   And He feeleth for our sadness,
   And He shareth in our gladness.

4. And our eyes at last shall see Him,
   Through His own redeeming love;
   For that Child so dear and gentle
   Is our Lord in heav'n above:
   And He leads His children on
   To the place where He is gone.

ONWARD CHRISTIAN SOLDIERS

Words by Sabine Baring-Gould
Music by Sir Arthur Sullivan

On - ward, Chris - tian Sol - diers, March - ing as to war. With the cross of Je - sus Go - ing on be - fore: Christ the roy - al mas - ter Leads a - gainst the foe; For - ward in - to bat - tle, __ See His ban - ners go. On - ward Chris - tian Sol - diers, __ March - ing as to __ war. With the cross of Je - sus, Go - ing on be - fore.

Chorus:

OVER THE RIVER AND THROUGH THE WOODS

1. O - ver The Riv - er And Thro' The Woods, To grand - fa - ther's house we go; The horse knows the way to car - ry the sleigh, Thro' the white and drift - ed snow. __ O - ver The Ri - ver And Thro' The Woods, Oh how the wind does blow! __ It stings. the toes. And bites the nose, As o - ver the ground we go.

2. O - ver The Riv - er And Thro' The Woods, To have __ a first - rate play; Oh hear the bells ring, "Ting - a - ling - ling!" Hur - rah for Thanks - giv - ing Day. __ O - ver The Ri - ver And Thro' The Woods, Trot fast my dap - ple gray! __ Spring o - ver the ground, Like a hunt - ing hound! For this is Thanks - giv - ing Day. __

3. O - ver The Riv - er And Thro' The Woods, And straight thro' the barn - yard gate, __ We seem __ to go ex - treme - ly slow It __ is so hard to wait! __ O - ver The Ri - ver And Thro' The Woods, Now grand - moth - er's cap I spy! __ Hur - rah for the fun! Is the pud - ding done? Hur - rah for the pump - kin pie!

OVER THE WAVES

By Juventino Rosas

Moderately

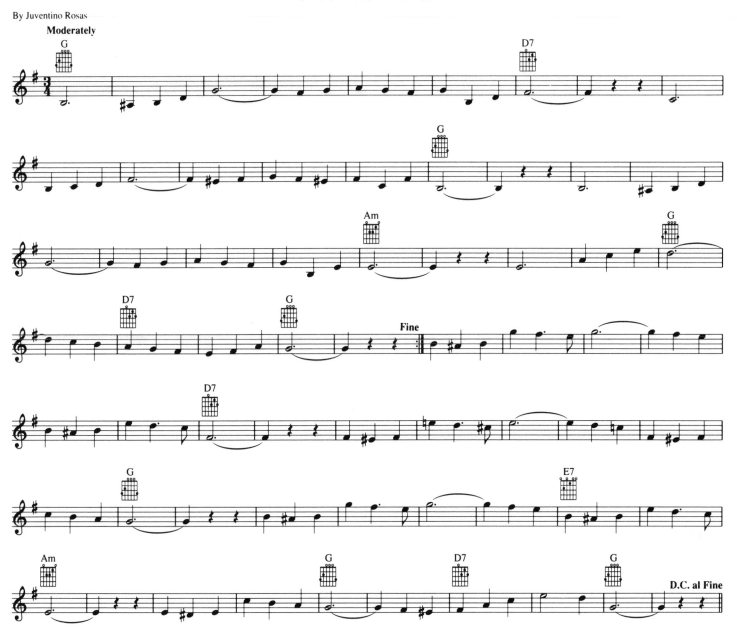

PAT-A-PAN

Bernard de la Monnoye

Quickly

Wil - lie, take your lit - tle drum, Rob - in, bring your flute and come! } Play - ing on the flute and drum, Tu - re - lu - re -
Men of old in an - cient days gave the King of Kings their praise! }
God and man are now as one they com - bine as flute and drum.

lu, pat - a - pat - a - pan, Play - ing on the flute and drum, { We will cel - e - brate this day!
Let us cel - e - brate as they!
Sing and dance for joy this day!

ORANGE MARMALADE RAG

OUR DIRECTOR MARCH

By F.E. Bigelow

Moderate March Tempo

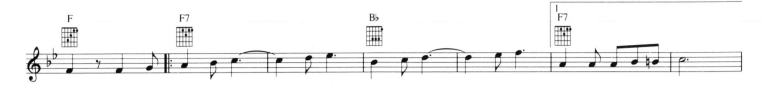

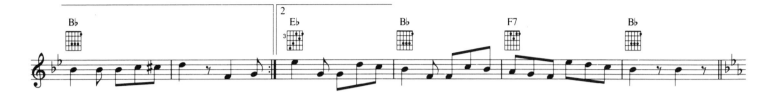

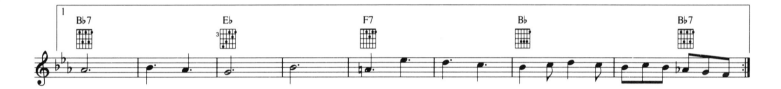

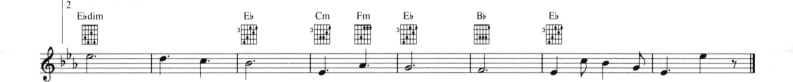

PIZZICATO POLKA

Johann and Josef Strauss

Bright polka tempo

PEG O' MY HEART

Words by Alfred Bryan
Music by Fred Fisher

Peg O' My Heart, _____ I love you, Don't let us part, _____ I love you,
Peg O' My Heart, _____ Your glanc-es make my heart say, _____ "How's chanc-es",

I al-ways knew,__ it would be you, __ Since I heard your lilt-ing laugh-ter,
Come, be my own, __ Come, make your home __ in my heart. _____

it's your I-rish heart I'm af-ter Come, make your home __ in my heart. _____

PLAY A SIMPLE MELODY

Irving Berlin

Won't you Play A Sim-ple Mel - o - dy Like my moth-er sang to me _____

___ One with good old fash-ioned har - mo-ny. Play A Sim-ple Mel-o-

dy. Mus-i-cal de-mon, set your hon-ey a dream-in', Won't you play me a rag __

Just change that clas-si-cal nag __ to some sweet beau-ti-ful drag _ If you will

play from a cop-y of a tune that is chop-py, You'll get all my ap-plause And that is

sim-ply be-cause __ I want to lis-ten to rag.

PUT YOUR ARMS AROUND ME, HONEY

Words by Junie McCree
Music by Albert von Tilzer

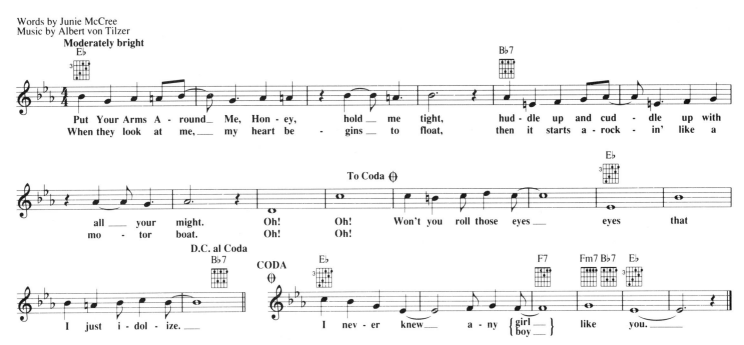

OH! YOU BEAUTIFUL DOLL

Words by A. Seymour Brown
Music by Nat D. Ayers

ON A SUNDAY AFTERNOON

Words by Andrew B. Sterling
Music by Harry von Tilzer

PEGGY O'NEIL

Words and Music by HARRY PEASE,
ED. G. NELSON and GILBERT DODGE

With a lilt

If her eyes are blue as skies, that's Peg - gy O' -
Neil. _____ If she's smil - ing all the while, that's
Peg - gy O' - Neil. _____ If she walks like a sly lit - tle rogue,
if she talks with a cute lit - tle brogue, sweet per - son - al - i - ty full of ras -
cal - i - ty, that's Peg - gy O' - Neil. _____ Neil. _____

PUT ON YOUR OLD GREY BONNET

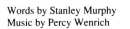

Words by Stanley Murphy
Music by Percy Wenrich

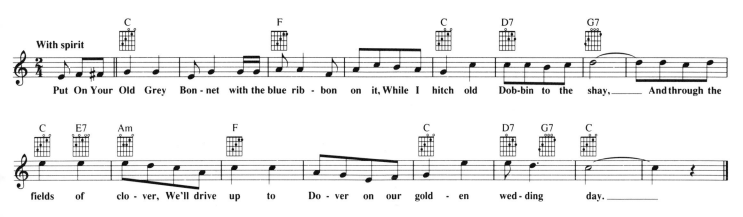

With spirit

Put On Your Old Grey Bon - net with the blue rib - bon on it, While I hitch old Dob - bin to the shay, _____ And through the
fields of clo - ver, We'll drive up to Do - ver on our gold - en wed - ding day. _____

POLOVETZIAN DANCE

Alexander Borodin

RAGTIME COWBOY JOE

Words by Grant Clarke
Music by Lewis F. Muir and Maurice Abrahams

POLLY WOLLY DOODLE

Bright, with humor

1. Oh, I went down South for to see my Sal, Sing-ing Pol-ly-Wol-ly-Doo-dle all the day. My __
2. Sal she is a __ maid-en fair, Sing-ing Pol-ly-Wol-ly-Doo-dle all the day. With __
3. grass-hop-per sit-tin' on a rail-road track, Sing-ing Pol-ly-Wol-ly-Doo-dle all the day. A -

4 - 6. *(See additional lyrics)*

Sal she is a spunk-y gal, Sing-ing Pol-ly-Wol-ly-Doo-dle all the day.
curl-y eyes and laugh-ing hair, Sing-ing Pol-ly-Wol-ly-Doo-dle all the day.
pick-in' his teeth with a car-pet tack, Sing-ing Pol-ly-Wol-ly-Doo-dle all the day.

Chorus

Fare thee

well, Fare thee well, Fare thee well, my fair-y fay, For I'm goin' to Lou'-si-an-a for to

see my Su-zi-an-na, Sing-ing Pol-ly-Wol-ly-Doo-dle all the day. 2. Oh, my day.
3. Oh, a

Additional Lyrics

4. Oh, I went to bed, but it wasn't no use,
Singing Polly-Wolly-Doodle all the day.
My feet stuck out like a chicken roost,
Singing Polly-Wolly-Doodle all the day.
Chorus

5. Behind the barn down on my knees,
Singing Polly-Wolly-Doodle all the day.
I thought I heard a chicken sneeze,
Singing Polly-Wolly-Doodle all the day.
Chorus

6. He sneezed so hard with the whooping cough,
Singing Polly-Wolly-Doodle all the day,
He sneezed his head and tail right off,
Singing Polly-Wolly-Doodle all the day.
Chorus

POMP AND CIRCUMSTANCE

Sir Edward Elgar
Slowly

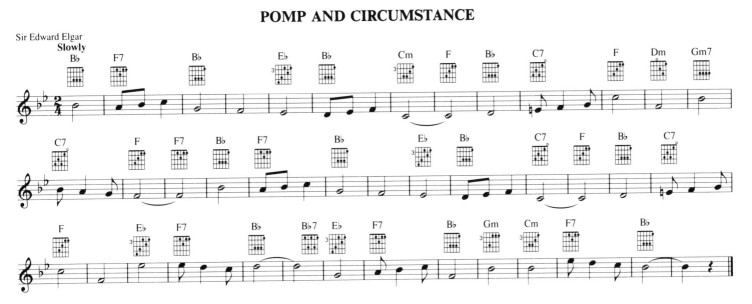

POET AND PEASANT OVERTURE

Franz von Suppe

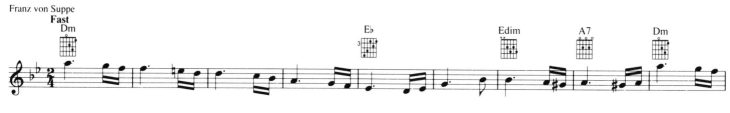

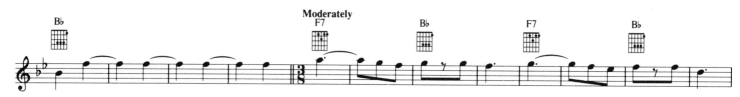

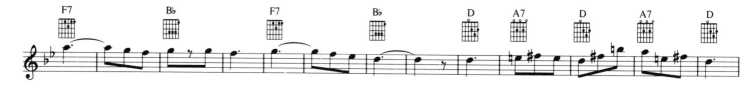

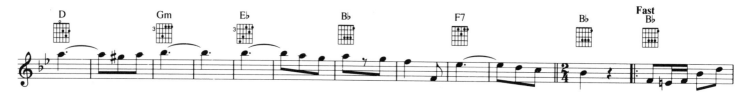

POLONAISE, OPUS 53
(Chopin)

Frederic Chopin

PRAISE GOD FROM WHOM ALL BLESSINGS FLOW

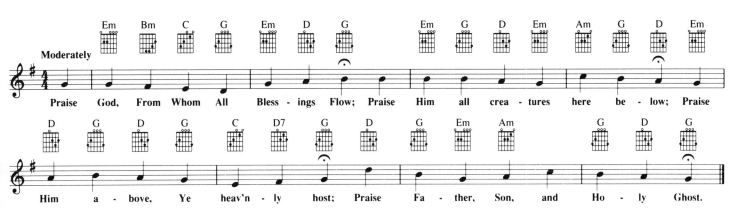

POP! GOES THE WEASEL

All a-round the cob-ler's bench, The mon-key chased the wea-sel. The mon-key thought 'twas
Ru-fus has the whoop-ing cough, And Sal-ly has the meas-les, And that's the way the

all __ in fun, }
doc - tor goes, } Pop! Goes The Wea-sel. A pen-ney for a spool__ of thread, A pen-ney for __ a

nee - dle. That's the way the mon-ey goes, Pop! Goes The Wea-sel.

PRAYER OF THANKSGIVING

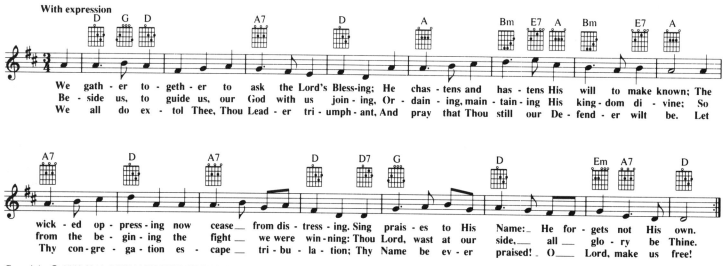

We gath-er to-geth-er to ask the Lord's Bless-ing; He chas-tens and has-tens His will to make known; The
Be - side us, to guide us, our God with us join-ing, Or-dain-ing, main-tain-ing His king-dom di-vine; So
We all do ex-tol Thee, Thou Lead-er tri-umph-ant, And pray that Thou still our De-fend-er wilt be. Let

wick - ed op-press-ing now cease__ from dis-tress-ing. Sing prais-es to His Name:__ He for-gets not His own.
from the be-gin-ing the fight__ we were win-ning: Thou Lord, wast at our side,__ all __ glo-ry be Thine.
Thy con-gre-ga-tion es-cape__ tri-bu-la-tion; Thy Name be ev-er praised! _ O__ Lord, make us free!

PRELUDE
(From "CARMEN")

Georges Bizet

Brightly

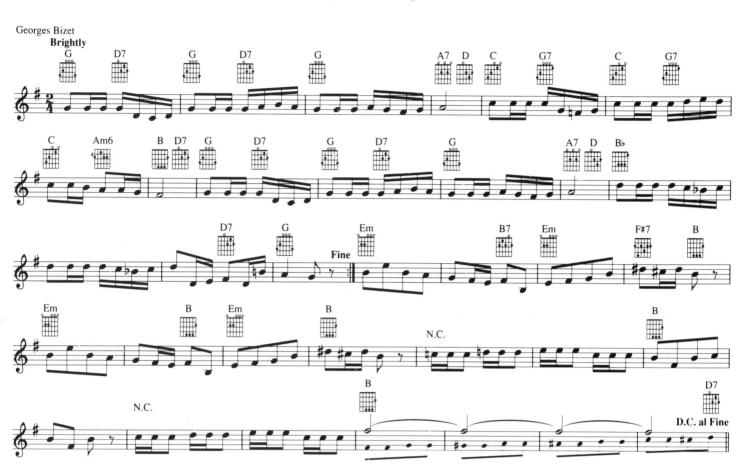

PRETTY BABY

Words by GUS KAHN
Music by EGBERT VAN ALSTYNE
and TONY JACKSON

With a lilt

Ev-'ry-bod-y loves a ba-by that's why I'm in love with you, Pret-ty Ba-by, Pret-ty Ba-by, and I'd

like to be your sis-ter, broth-er, dad and moth-er too, Pret-ty Ba-by, Pret-ty Ba-by. Won't you

come and let me rock you in my cra-dle of love,— and we'll cud-dle all the time.___ Oh! I

want a lov-in' ba-by and it might as well be you, Pret-ty Ba-by of mine.

RED RIVER VALLEY

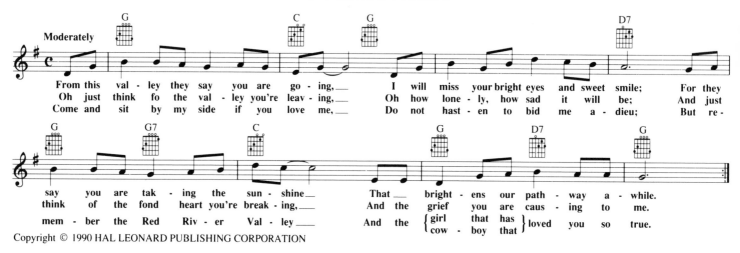

From this val - ley they say you are go - ing, ___ I will miss your bright eyes and sweet smile; For they
Oh just think fo the val - ley you're leav - ing, ___ Oh how lone - ly, how sad it will be; And just
Come and sit by my side if you love me, ___ Do not hast - en to bid me a - dieu; But re -

say you are tak - ing the sun - shine ___ That ___ bright - ens our path - way a - while.
think of the fond heart you're break - ing, ___ And the grief you are caus - ing to me.
mem - ber the Red Riv - er Val - ley ___ And the {girl that has} loved you so true.
{cow - boy that}

RAIN-RAIN POLKA
(Prsi-Prsi)

REUBEN AND RACHEL

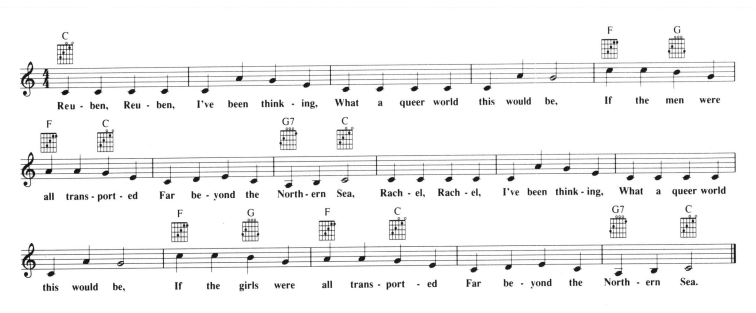

Reu - ben, Reu - ben, I've been think - ing, What a queer world this would be, If the men were

all trans - port - ed Far be - yond the North - ern Sea, Rach - el, Rach - el, I've been think - ing, What a queer world

this would be, If the girls were all trans - port - ed Far be - yond the North - ern Sea.

REVERIE

Claude Debussy

Slowly, with expression

242

RIDE OF THE VALKYRIES

R. Wagner
Moderately

THE ROCK ISLAND LINE

Quickly
Chorus

I say The Rock Is-land Line __ is a migh-ty good road, __ I say The Rock Is-land Line __ is the

road to ride, __ Oh, The Rock Is-land Line __ is a migh-ty good road, __ If you ev-er want to

ride it, got to ride it like you're fly-in'. Buy your tic-ket at the sta-tion on The Rock Is-land Line. __

Now A, B, C, dou-ble X, Y, Z, Cat's in the cup-board, but he can't see me. __
Now Je-sus died to save our sins, Glo-ry be to God, we're gon-na need Him a-gain. __
I may be right and I may be wrong, I know you're gon-na miss me when I __ am gone.

RING THE BANJO

Stephen Foster

1. The time is nev - er drear - y If a fel - low nev - er groans; The la - dies nev - er wea - ry With the
2. Oh! nev - er count the bub - bles While there's wa - ter in the spring: A fel - low has no trou - bles While he's
3 - 4. *(See additional lyrics)*

rat - tle of the bones: Then come a - gain Su - san - na By the gas - light of the moon; We'll _
got this song to sing. The beau - ties of cre - a - tion Will _ nev - er lose their charm While I

play the old Pi - a - no When the ban - jo's out of tune. } Ring! Ring The Ban - jo! I
roam the old plan - ta - tion With my true love on my arm.

like that good old song, Come a - gain my own true love! Oh, where you been so long.

Additional Lyrics

3. Once I was so lucky,
   My master set me free,
   I went to old Kentucky
   To see what I could see:
   I could not go no farther
   I return to master's door,
   I love him all the harder,
   I'll go away no more.

4. Early in the morning
   On a lovely summer day,
   My master send me warning
   He'd like to hear me play.
   On the banjo tapping,
   I come with dulcet strain;
   Master fall a-napping,
   He'll never wake again.

ROCK-A-BYE, BABY

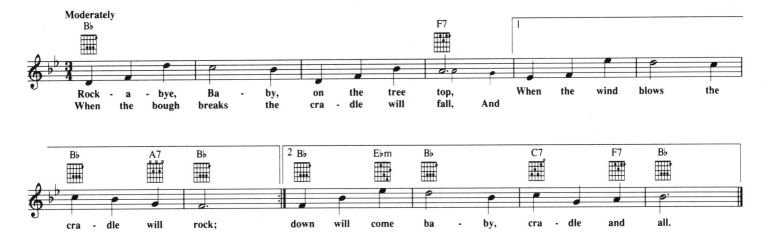

Rock - a - bye, Ba - by, on the tree top, When the wind blows the
When the bough breaks the cra - dle will fall, And

cra - dle will rock; down will come ba - by, cra - dle and all.

ROCK OF AGES

Rock Of A - ges, cleft for me. Let me hide my - self in thee. Let the
tears for - ev - er flow Could my zeal no lan - gour know. These for
draw this fleet - ing breath, When my eye lids close in death. When I

wa - ter and the blood from Thy wound - ed side which flowed, be of sin, the dou - ble
sin could not a - tone, Thou must save, and Thou a - lone. In my hand, no price I
rise to worlds un - known, and be - hold Thee on Thy throne. Rock Of A - ges, cleft for

cure, save from wrath and make me pure. Could my
bring, sim - ply to Thy cross I cling. While I
me, Let me hide my - self in Thee, Let me hide my - self in Thee.

ROMANCE
(Rubenstein)

A. Rubinstein

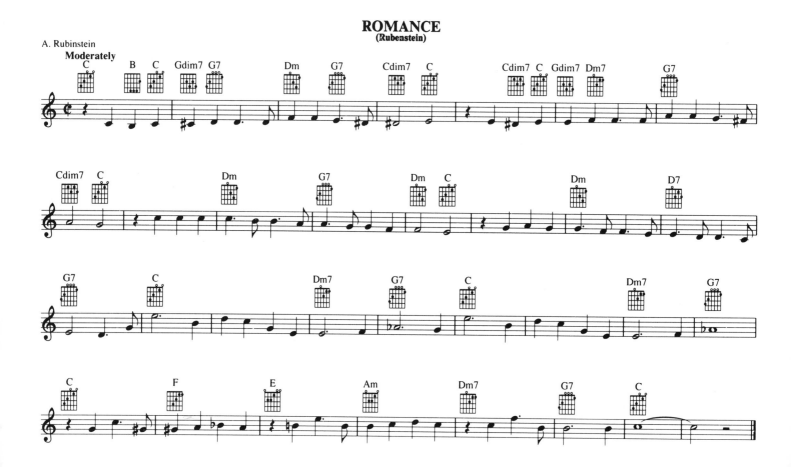

ROMEO AND JULIET

Peter Tschaikovsky
Slowly

THE ROSE OF TRALEE

Words by C. Mordaunt Spencer
Music by Charles W. Glover

The pale moon was ris - ing a - bove the green moun - tain, The sun was de - clin - ing be -
The cool shades of eve - ning their man - tle were spread - ing, And Ma - ry all smil - ing was

neath the blue sea, When I stray'd with my love to the pure crys - tal foun - tain, That
list - 'ning to me, The moon thro' the val - ley, her pale rays was shed - ding, When

stands in the beau - ti - ful vale of Tra - lee; She was love - ly and fair as the
I won the heart of The Rose Of Tra - lee; Though love - ly and fair as the

rose of ___ the ___ sum - mer, Yet 'twas not her beau - ty a - lone that won me. Oh, no! 'Twas the
rose of ___ the sum - mer, Yet 'twas not her beau - ty a - lone that won me. Oh, no! 'Twas the

truth in her eye ev - er dawn - ing, That made me love Ma - ry, The Rose Of Tra - lee.
truth in her eye ev - er dawn - ing, That made me love Ma - ry, The Rose Of Tra - lee.

ROSES FROM THE SOUTH

Johann Strauss

ROW, ROW, ROW YOUR BOAT

Row, Row, Row Your Boat, Gent - ly down the stream;

Mer - ri - ly, mer - ri - ly, mer - ri - ly, mer - ri - ly; Life is but a dream.

RED WING

Words by Thurland Chattaway; Music by Kerry Mills

There once lived an In - dian maid, A shy lit - tle prai - rie maid, Who sang a __ lay, a
She watched for him day and night, She kept all the camp-fires bright, And un - der the sky, each

love song __ gay, As on the plain she'd while a - way the day. She loved a __ war - rior bold,
night she would lie, And dream a - bout his com-ing by and by; But when all the braves re - turned,

shy lit - tle maid of old, But brave and __ gay, he rode one __ day to bat - tle far __ a -
heart of __ Red Wing yearned, For far, far a - way, her war - ri - or gay, fell brave - ly in __ the

way.
fray. } Now, the moon shines to - night on pret - ty Red Wing, _____ the breeze is sigh - ing, _____

__ the night bird's cry - ing, _____ For a - far 'neath his star her brave is sleep - ing, _____

__ While Red Wing's weep - ing _____ her heart a - way.   Now, the   way. _____

ROAMIN' IN THE GLOAMIN'

Words and Music by Harry Lauder

Roam - in' In The Gloam - in' on the bon - nie banks o' Clyde.   Roam - in' In The

Gloam - in' wae my las - sie by my side.   When the sun has gone to rest, That's the time that we love

best   O, it's love - ly Roam - in' In The Gloam - in'!   in'!

ROW, ROW, ROW

Words by William Jerome
Music by Jimmie V. Monaco

And then he'd Row, Row, Row, Way up the riv-er he would Row, Row, Row, A hug he'd give her Then he'd kiss her now and then. She would tell him when He'd fool a-round and fool a-round and then they'd kiss a-gain. And then he'd Row, Row, Row, A lit-tle fur-ther he would row, oh, oh, oh, oh! ___ Then he'd drop both his oars, ___ take a few more en-cores, ___ And then he'd Row, Row, Row. ___

SCARBOROUGH FAIR

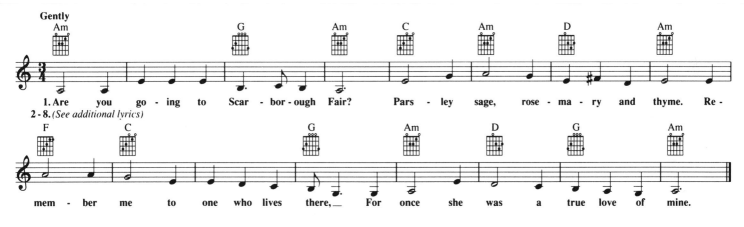

1. Are you go-ing to Scar-bor-ough Fair? Pars-ley sage, rose-ma-ry and thyme. Re-
2 - 8. (See additional lyrics)

mem-ber me to one who lives there, ___ For once she was a true love of mine.

Additional Lyrics

2. Tell her to make me a cambric shirt. . .
   Without any seam or fine needlework. . .

3. Tell her to wash it in younder dry well. . .
   Where water ne'er spring, not drop of rain fell. . .

4. Tell her to dry it on yonder thorn. . .
   Which never bore blossom since Adam was born. . .

5. Will you find me an acre of land. . .
   Between the sea foam and the sea sand. . .

6. Will you plough it with a lamb's horn. . .
   And sow it all over with one peppercorn. . .

7. Will you reap it with sickle of leather. . .
   And tie it all up with a peacock's feather. . .

8. When you've done and finished your work. . .
   Then come to me for your cambric shirt.
   And you shall be a true love of mine.

RONDEAU
(Mouret)

Jean-Joseph Mouret

ROSALIE SCHOTTISCHE

Sep. Winner

SAILING, SAILING

Godfrey Marks

Brightly

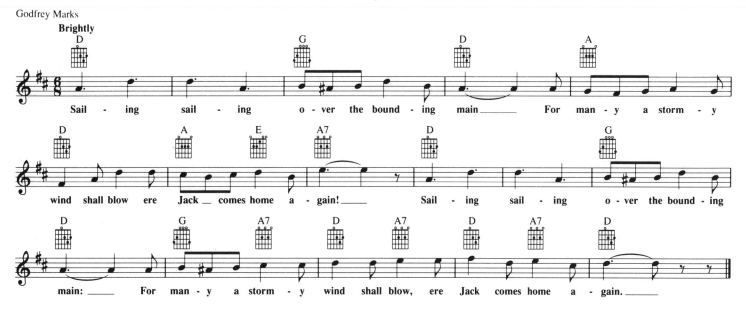

Sail - ing sail - ing o - ver the bound - ing main ___ For man - y a storm - y wind shall blow ere Jack ___ comes home a - gain! ___ Sail - ing sail - ing o - ver the bound - ing main: ___ For man - y a storm - y wind shall blow, ere Jack comes home a - gain. ___

SALTY DOG

In bright two

Salt - y Dog, Salt - y Dog, I don't wa - na be your man at all, Hon - ey, let me be your Salt - y Dog. ___ Down in the wild - wood sit - ting on a log, sing - ing a song a - bout a Salt - y Dog, Hon - ey, let me be your Salt - y Dog. ___

SCOTLAND THE BRAVE
(Tunes of Glory)

Moderately

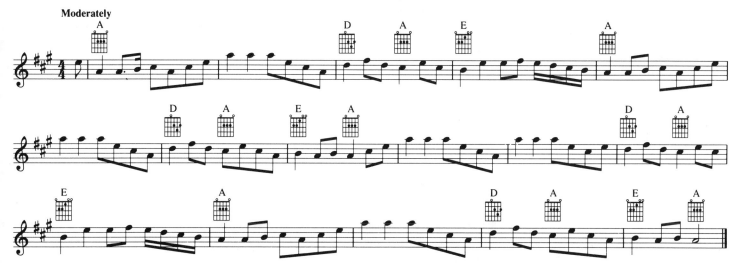

SAILOR'S HORNPIPE

SANTA LUCIA

1. Now 'neath the sil - ver moon o - cean is glow - ing o'er the calm bil - lows
Here balm - y breez - es blow pure joys in - vite___ us and as we gent - ly row,
2. (See additional lyrics)

soft winds are blow - ing.
all things de - light us. } Hark, how the sail - ors cry Joy - ous - ly ech - oes nigh

San - ta ___ Lu - ci - a, San - ta Lu - ci - a. San - ta Lu - ci - a.

Additional Lyrics

2. When o'er the waters light winds are playing,
   They spell can sooth us, all care allaying.
   The thee, sweet Napoli, what charms are given,
   Where smiles creation, toil blessed by Heaven.

SCHNITZELBANK

1. Ei du schoe - ne ei du schoe - ne, ei du schoe - ne Schnit - zel - bank. Ist das nicht eine Schnit-zel-bank?
2 - 6. *(See addtitional lyrics)*

Ja, das ist eine Schnit-zel - bank. Ist das nicht eine kurz und lang? Ja, das ist eine kurz und lang. Kurz und lang un'er Schnit-zel - bank.

Additional Lyrics

2. Ei du schoene, ei du schoene,
Ei du schoene Schnitzelbank.
Is das nicht ein Hin und Her?
Ja, das ist ein Hin und Her.
Ist das nicht eine Lichtputzschere?
Ja, das ist eine Lichtputzschere.
Lichtputzschere, Hin und Her,
Kurz und lang un'er Schnitzelbank.

3. Ei du schoene, ie du schoene,
Ei du schoene Schnitzelbank.
Ist das nicht ein gold'ner Ring?
Ja das ist ein gold'ner Ring.
Ist das nicht ein schoenes Ding?
Ja, das ist ein schoenes Ding.
Schoenes Ding, gold'ner Ring, Lichtputzschere,
Hin und Her, kurz und lang un'er Schnitzelbank.

4. Ei du schoene, ei du schoene,
Ei du schoene Schnitzelbank.
Ist das nicht ein Krum und Grad?
Jas das ist ein Krum und Grad.
Ist das nicht ein Wagenrad?
Ja, das ist ein Wagenrad.
Wagenrad, Krum und Grad,
Schoenes Ding, gold'ner Ring,
Lichtputzschere, Hin und Her,
Kurz und lang un'er Schnitzelbank.

5. Ei du schoene, ei du schoene,
Ei du schoene Schnitzelbank.
Ist das nicht ein Geisenbock?
Ja das ist ein Geisenbock.
Ist das nicht ein Reifenrock?
Jas das ist ein Reifenrock.
Reifenrock, Geisenbock, Wagengrad,
Krum und Grad, Schoenes Ding,
Gold'ner Ring, Lichtputzschere, Hin und Her,
Kurz und lang un'er Schnitzelbank.

6. Ei du schoene, ei du schoene,
Ei du schoene Schnitzelbank.
Ist das nicht eine gute Wurst?
Ja das ist eine gute Wurst.
Ist das nicht ein grosser Durst?
Jas das ist ein grosser Durst.
Grosser Durst, Gute Wurst, Reifenrock,
Geisenbock, Wagengrad, Krum und Grad,
Schoenes Ding, gold'ner Ring,
Lichtputzschere, Hin und Her,
Kurz und lang un'er Schnitzelbank.

SERENADE
(Drigo)

Riccardo Drigo

Moderately

SERENADE
(Schubert)

Franz Schubert

With expression

SERENADE
(Toselli)

Toselli

Moderately

SHALL WE GATHER AT THE RIVER

Words and Music by Robert Lowry

Moderate Country Gospel Tempo

Shall We Gath-er At The Riv-er Where bright an-gel feet have trod,_____
Ere we reach the shin-ing riv-er, Lay we ev-'ry bur-den down;_____
Soon we'll reach the shin-ing riv-er; Soon our pil-grim-age will cease;_____

With its crys-tal tide for-ev-er Flow-ing by the___ throne of ___ God?
Grace our spir-its will de-liv-er And pro-vide us a robe and a crown.
Soon our hap-py hearts will quiv-er With the mel-o-dy of ___ peace.

Chorus

Yes, we'll gath-er at the riv-er, The beau-ti-ful, the beau-ti-ful___ riv-er,

Gath-er with the saints___ at the riv-er That flows by the throne of ___ God.   God.

SEMPER FIDELIS

John Philip Sousa

SHE WORE A YELLOW RIBBON

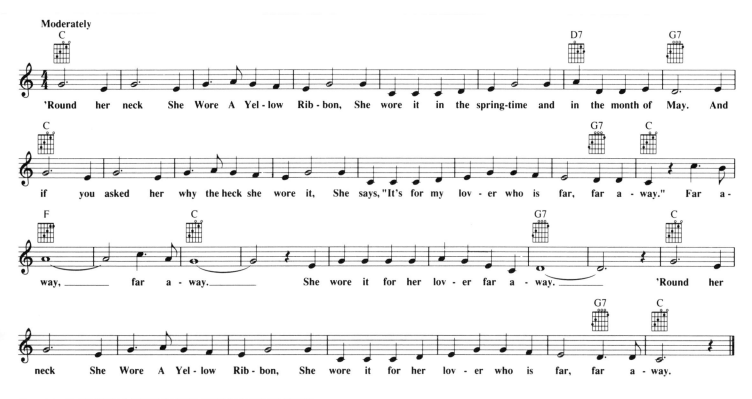

'Round her neck She Wore A Yel-low Rib-bon, She wore it in the spring-time and in the month of May. And if you asked her why the heck she wore it, She says, "It's for my lov-er who is far, far a-way." Far a-way, ___ far a-way. ___ She wore it for her lov-er far a-way. ___ 'Round her neck She Wore A Yel-low Rib-bon, She wore it for her lov-er who is far, far a-way.

SHE IS MORE TO BE PITIED THAN CENSURED

She Is More To Be Pit-ied Than Cen-sured, ___ She is more to be helped than de-spised, ___ She is on-ly a las-sie who ven-tured, ___ On life's storm-y path ill ad-vised, ___ Do not scorn her with words fierce and bit-ter, ___ Do not laugh at her shame and down-fall, ___ For a mo-ment just stop and con-sid-er, ___ That a man was the cause of it all. ___

SHE'LL BE COMIN' 'ROUND THE MOUNTAIN

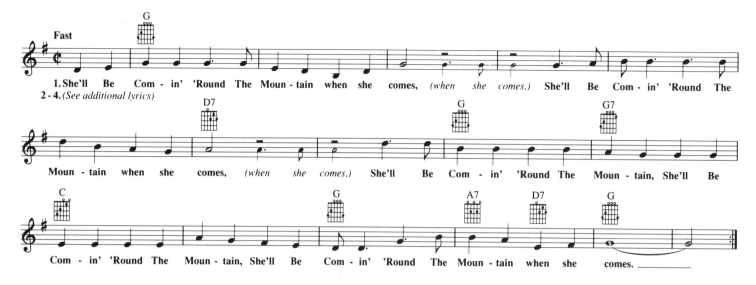

1. She'll Be Com-in' 'Round The Moun-tain when she comes, (when she comes,) She'll Be Com-in' 'Round The Moun-tain when she comes, (when she comes,) She'll Be Com-in' 'Round The Moun-tain, She'll Be Com-in' 'Round The Moun-tain, She'll Be Com-in' 'Round The Moun-tain when she comes. _____

2-4. (See additional lyrics)

Additional Lyrics

2. She'll be drivin' six white horses when she comes,
   She'll be drivin' six white horses when she comes,
   She'll be drivin' six white horses,
   She'll be drivin' six white horses,
   She'll be drivin' six white horses when she comes.

3. Oh, we'll all go out to meet her when she comes,
   Oh, we'll all go out to meet her when she comes,
   Oh, we'll all go out to meet her,
   Yes, we'll all go out to meet her,
   Yes, we'll all go out to meet her when she comes.

4. She'll be wearin' a blue bonnet when she comes,
   She'll be wearin' a blue bonnet when she comes,
   She'll be wearin' a blue bonnet,
   She'll be wearin' a blue bonnet,
   She'll be wearin' a blue bonnet when she comes.

SHENANDOAH

1. O Shen-an-doah, __ I love to see you, A - way _____ you roll-ing riv-er, Oh Shen-an-doah, __ I long to see you, A - way ___ I'm bound a-way, _____ A-cross the wide _____ Mis-sour-i. __

2-4. (See additional lyrics)

Additional Lyrics

2. O Shenandoah, I love your daughter,
   Away, you rolling river,
   For her I've crossed the rolling water,
   Away, I'm bound away,
   Across the wide Missouri.

3. The trader loved this Indian maiden,
   Away, you rolling river,
   With presents his canoe was laden,
   Away, I'm bound away,
   Across the wide Missouri.

4. O Shenandoah, I'm bound to leave you,
   Away, you rolling river,
   O Shenandoah, I'll not deceive you.
   Away, I'm bound away,
   Across the wide Missouri.

5. O Shenandoah, I long to hear you,
   Away, you rolling river,
   O Shenandoah, I long to hear you.
   Away, I'm bound away,
   Across the wide Missouri.

SHORTNIN' BREAD

Put on the skil-let, put on the lid, Mam-my's gon-na make a li-ttle Short-nin' Bread.

That ain't all she's gon-na do, Mam-my's gon-na make a li-ttle cof-fee too.

Mam-my's lit-tle ba-by loves short-nin', short-nin', Mam-my's lit-tle ba-by loves Short-nin' Bread.

Mam-my's lit-tle ba-by loves short-nin', short-nin', Mam-my's lit-tle ba-by loves Short-nin' Bread.

SILVER THREADS AMONG THE GOLD

H.P. Daniels

Dar - ling, I am grow - ing old, _____ Sil - ver Threads A - mong The Gold, Shine up - on my brow to - day, _____
When your hair is sil - ver white, __ And your cheeks no lon - ger bright, With the ro - ses of the May, _____
Love can nev - er more grow old, _____ Locks may lose their brown and gold, Cheeks may fade and hol - low grow, _____
Love is al - ways young and fair, _____ What to us is sil - ver hair, Fad - ed cheeks or steps grown slow, _____

Life is fast fad - ing a - way; But my dar - ling you will be, will be, Al - ways young and fair to me,
I will kiss your lips and say; Oh! my dar - ling mine a - lone, a - lone, You have nev - er old - er grown,
But the hearts that love will know; Nev - er, nev - er win - ter's frost and chill, Sum - mer warmth is in them still,
To the hearts thet beat be - low? Since I kissed you mine a - lone, a - lone, You have nev - er old - er grown,

Refrain

Yea, my dar - ling you will be, _____ Al - ways young and fair to me.
Yes, my dar - ling mine a - lone, _____ You have nev - er old - er grown.
Nev - er win - ter's frost and chill, _____ Sum - mer warmth is in them still.
Since I kissed you, mine a - lone, _____ You have nev - er old - er grow.

Dar - ling, I am grow - ing, grow - ing old,

Sil - ver Threads A - mong The Gold, Shine up - on my brow to - day, _____ Life is fad - ing fast a - way.

SILENT NIGHT

Words by Joseph Mohr
English Tr. by John F. Young
Music by Franz Grüber

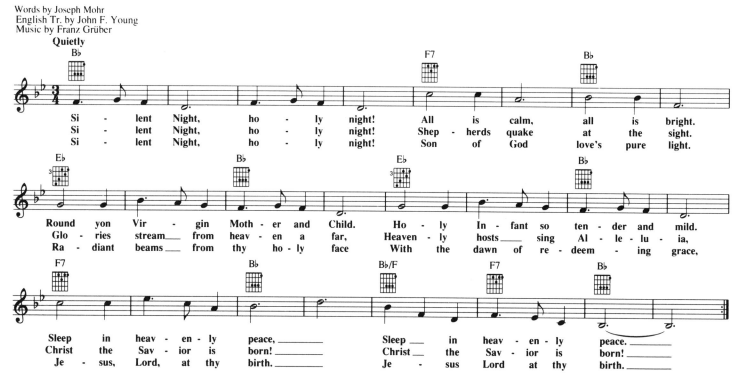

Si - lent Night, ho - ly night! All is calm, all is bright.
Si - lent Night, ho - ly night! Shep - herds quake at the sight.
Si - lent Night, ho - ly night! Son of God love's pure light.

Round yon Vir - gin Moth - er and Child. Ho - ly In - fant so ten - der and mild.
Glo - ries stream__ from heav - en a far, Heaven - ly hosts__ sing Al - le - lu - ia,
Ra - diant beams__ from thy ho - ly face With the dawn of re - deem - ing grace,

Sleep in heav - en - ly peace,_____ Sleep __ in heav - en - ly peace. _____
Christ the Sav - ior is born! _____ Christ __ the Sav - ior is born! _____
Je - sus, Lord, at thy birth. _____ Je - sus Lord at thy birth. _____

Copyright © 1990 HAL LEONARD PUBLISHING CORPORATION

THE SIDEWALKS OF NEW YORK

Words by Charles B. Lawlor
Music by James W. Blake

East Side, West Side, All a - round the town, _____ The tots sang

"Ring __ a - Ros - ie", "Lon - don Bridge is Fall - ing Down!"_____ Boys and

girls to - geth - er, _____ Me and Ma - mie O' - Rorke, _____ Tripped the light __ fan -

tas - tic on The Side - walks Of New York. York. _____

Copyright © 1990 MILWIN MUSIC

SIMPLE SIMON

With a steady beat

Sim - ple Si - mon met a pie - man Go - ing to the fair. Said Sim - ple Si - mon to the pie - man, "Let me taste your ware." Said the man to Sim - ple Si - mon, "Show me first your pen - ny." Said Sim - ple Si - mon to the pie - man, "In - deed, I have not an - y."

THE SKATERS

Emil Wauldteufel

Moderate Waltz

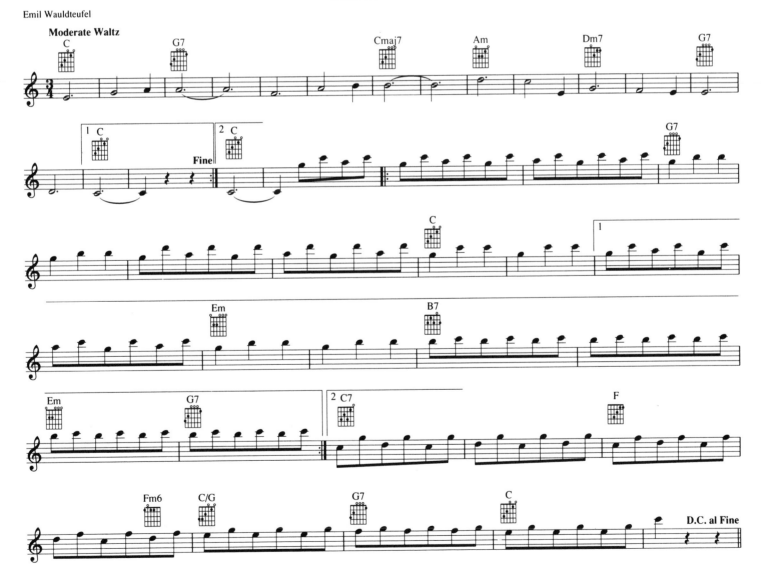

Fine

D.C. al Fine

SING WE NOW OF CHRISTMAS

Sing We Now Of Christ - mas, No - el sing we here. Sing our grate - ful prais - es To the maid so dear.

Sing we No - el! The King is born. No - el! Sing We Now Of Christ - mas, Sing we here No - el.

SKIP TO MY LOU

Skip, skip, Skip To My Lou, Skip, skip, Skip To My Lou, Skip, skip, Skip To My Lou,

Skip To My Lou, my dar - lin'.

Flies in the but - ter - milk, shoo, shoo, shoo! Flies in the but - ter - milk,
Lost my part - ner, what'll I do? Lost my part - ner,
I'll get an - oth - er one, purtier than you, I'll get an - oth - er one,
Can't get a red bird, a blue bird'll do, Can't get a red bird, a

shoo, shoo, shoo! Flies in the but - ter - milk, shoo, shoo, shoo!
what'll I do? Lost my part - ner, what'll I do?
purtier than you, I'll get an - oth - er one, purtier than you,
blue bird'll do, Can't get a red bird, a blue bird'll do,

Skip To My Lou, my dar - lin'.

SLEEP HOLY BABE

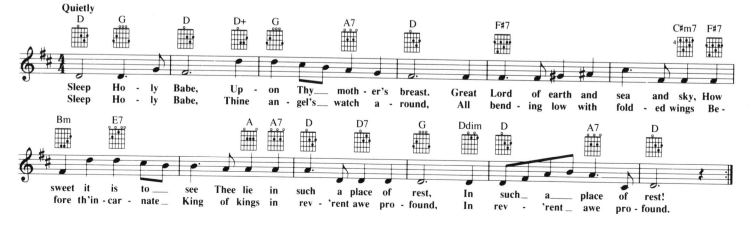

Sleep Ho - ly Babe, Up - on Thy moth - er's breast. Great Lord of earth and sea and sky, How
Sleep Ho - ly Babe, Thine an - gel's watch a - round, All bend - ing low with fold - ed wings Be -

sweet it is to see Thee lie in such a place of rest, In such a place of rest!
fore th'in - car - nate King of kings in rev - 'rent awe pro - found, In rev - 'rent awe pro - found.

SCHOOL DAYS

Words by Will D. Cobb
Music by Gus Edwards

SLEEPING BEAUTY WALTZ
(Tchaikovsky)

Peter Ilyich Tchaikowsky

Moderately

SONG OF INDIA

Nikolai Rimsky-Korsakov

Slowly

SOMETIMES I FEEL LIKE A MOTHERLESS CHILD

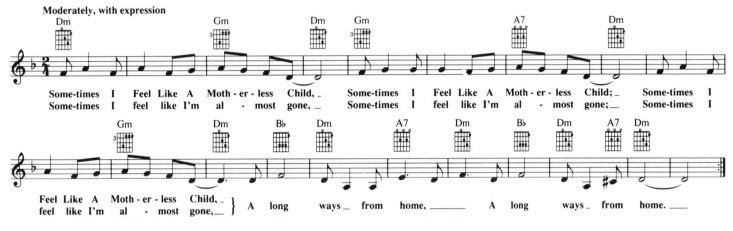

Moderately, with expression

Some-times I Feel Like A Moth-er-less Child, _ Some-times I Feel Like A Moth-er-less Child; _ Some-times I
Some-times I feel like I'm al-most gone, _ Some-times I feel like I'm al-most gone; _ Some-times I

Feel Like A Moth-er-less Child, _ } A long ways _ from home, _____ A long ways _ from home. ___
feel like I'm al-most gone, _ }

SONG OF THE VOLGA BOATMAN

Slowly

SPRING SONG
(Mendelssohn)

Felix Mendelssohn

SOUND OFF

John Philip Sousa

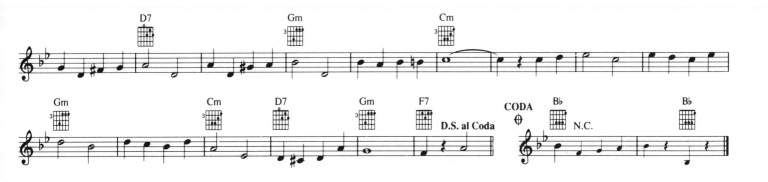

ST. JAMES INFIRMARY

Slowly

1. I went down to the St. James In - firm - 'ry; To see my ba - by there. She was ly - in' on a long white

3 - 8. (See additional lyrics)

ta - ble, So __ sweet, so __ cool, _ so fair. 2. Went up to see the doc - tor, "She's ve - ry low," he

said; Went back to see my ba - by; Great _ God! She was ly - in' there dead.

Additional Lyrics

3. I went down to old Joe's barroom,
   On the corner by the square;
   They were servin' the drinks as usual,
   And the usual crowd was there.

4. On my left stood Joe McKennedy,
   his eyes bloodshot red;
   He turned to the crowd around him,
   These are the words he said:

5. Let her go, let her go, God bless her;
   Wherever she may be;
   She may search this wide world over
   She'll never find a man like me.

6. Oh, when I die, please bury me
   In my high-top Stetson hat;
   Put a gold piece on my watch chain
   So they'll know I died standin' pat.

7. Get six gamblers to carry my coffin,
   Six chorus girls to sing my song,
   Put a jazz band on my tail gate
   To raise Hell as we go along.

8. Now that's the end of my story;
   Let's have another round of booze;
   And if anyone should ask you, just tell them
   I've got The St. James Infirmary blues.

THE STAR SPANGLED BANNER

Words by Francis Scott Key
Music by John Stafford Smith

With spirit

O___ say, can you see, by the dawn's ear - ly light, What so proud - ly we hail'd at the
On the shore dim - ly seen thro' the mists of the deep, Where the foe's haugh - ty host in dread
And ___ where is the band who so vaunt - ing - ly swore, 'Mid the hav - oc of war and the

twi - light's last gleam - ing? Whose broad stripes and bright stars, thro' the per - il - ous fight, O'er the ram - parts we
si - lence re - pos - es, What is that which the breeze, o'er the tow - er - ing steep. As it fit - ting - ly
bat - tle's con - fu - sion, A ___ home and a coun - try they'd leave us no more? Their blood has wash'd

watch'd were so gal - lant - ly stream - ing? And the rock - et's red glare, the bombs burst - ing in air Gave
blows, half con - ceals, half dis - clos - es? Now it catch - es the gleam of the morn - ing's first beam, In full
out their foul foot - step's pol - lu - tion. No ref - uge could save the ___ hire - ling and slave From the

proof thro' the night that our flag was still there. O say, does that ___ star - span - gled
glo - ry re - flect - ed now ___ shines in the stream. 'Tis the star - span - gled ___ ban - ner o
this be our mot - to, "In God is our trust!" And the star - span - gled ___ ban - ner in

ban - ner ___ yet ___ wave ___ O'er the land ___ of the free and the home of the brave.
long may ___ it ___ wave ___ O'er the land ___ of the free and the home of the brave.
tri - umph ___ doth ___ wave ___ O'er the land ___ of the free and the home of the brave.
tri - umph ___ shall ___ wave ___ O'er the land ___ of the free and the home of the brave.

STARS AND STRIPES FOREVER

John Philip Sousa

March tempo
N.C.

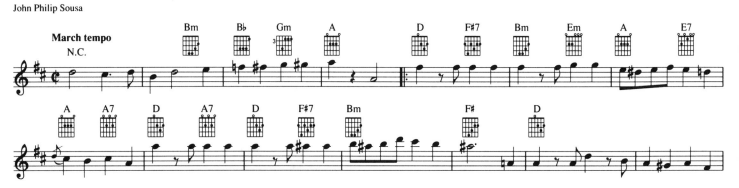

THE STREETS OF LAREDO

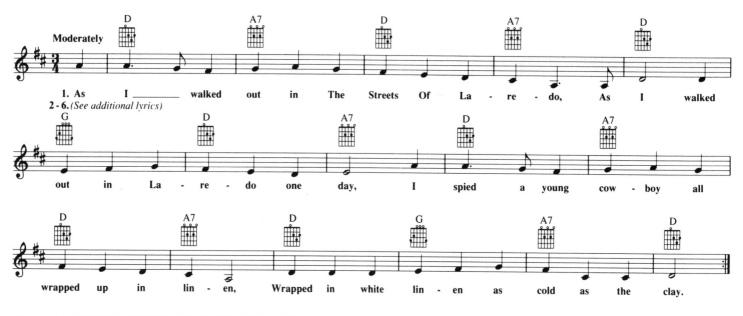

Additional Lyrics

2. I see by your outfit that you are a cowboy,"
   These words he did say as I proudly stepped by,
   "Come sit down beside me and hear my sad story,
   Got shot in the breast and I know I must die.

3. "'Twas once in the saddle I used to go dashing,
   'Twas once in the saddle I used to go gay;
   'Twas first to drinkin', and then to card-playing,
   Got shot in the breast and I'm dying today.

4. "Let six jolly cowboys come carry my coffin,
   Let six pretty gals come carry my pall;
   Throw bunches of roses all over my coffin,
   Throw roses to deaden the clods as they fall.

5. "Oh, beat the drum slowly, and play the fife lowly,
   And play the dead march as you carry me along,
   Take me to the green valley and lay the earth o'er me,
   For I'm a poor cowboy and I know I've done wrong."

6. Oh we beat the drum
   slowly and we played the fife lowly,
   And bitterly wept as we carried him along,
   For we all loved our comrade, so brave, young and handsome,

SURPRISE SYMPHONY
(Theme)

Joseph Haydn

SWAN LAKE
(Theme)

Peter Tschaikovsky

SWEET AND LOW

Poem by Alfred Tennyson
Music by Joseph Barnby

SWEET GENEVIEVE

Lyrics by George Cooper
Music by Henry Tucker

O Gen-e-vieve, I'd give the world, to live a-gain the lone-ly past, The rose of youth was dew im-pearled;But
Fair Gen-e-vieve, My ear-ly love the years but make thee dear-er fair, My heart shall nev-er nev-er rove, Thou

now it with-ers in the blast, I see thy face in ev-'ry dream, My wak-ing thoughts are full of thee; Thy
art my on-ly guid-ing star, For me thy past has no re-gret, What-e'er the years may bring to thee; I

glance is in the star-ry beam, That falls a-long the sum-mer sea! — } Oh! Gen-e-vieve, Sweet Gen-e-vieve, The
bless the hour when we first met, The hour that gave me love and thee! —

days may come, the days_ may go, But still the hand of mem-'ry weave, the bliss-ful dreams of long a-go.

SWEETHEARTS

Victor Herbert

Sweet-hearts make love their ver-y own, Sweet-hearts can live on love a-lone,

For them the eyes where love-light lies O-pen the gates to Par-a-dise!

All oth-er love is doomed to fade, It is like sun-shine veiled in shade,

Such joys of life as love im-parts Are all of them yours, Sweet-hearts! _____

SING A SONG OF SIXPENCE

Moderately

Sing A Song Of Six - pence, a pock - et full of rye; Four and twen - ty black - birds Baked in a pie.

When the pie was o - pened, The birds be - gan to sing. Was - n't that a dain - ty dish to set be - fore a king? The

king was in the count - ing-house, Count-ing out his mon - ey. The queen was in the par - lor, Eat - ing bread and hon - ey. The

maid was in the gar - den, Hang - ing out the clothes; A - long_ came a black - bird And pecked_ off her nose.

SWING LOW, SWEET CHARIOT

Moderately fast, steady tempo

Swing Low Sweet Char - i - ot, _ Com - in' for to car - ry me home; Swing_ Low Sweet Char - i - ot, _

Com - in' for to car - ry me home;

I looked o - ver Jor - dan and what did I see?_ Com - in' for to car - ry me home, A
I'm on the_ up - ward heav - en-ly way,_ Com - in' for to car - ry me home, Since
If you get_ there_ be - fore _ I do, _ Com - in' for to car - ry me home, Tell
Some - times I'm_ up _ and some - times down,_ Com - in' for to car - ry me home, But

1,2,3 — 4

band_ of an - gels com - in' af - ter me,_ Com - in' for to car - ry me home. Swing
Je - sus washed my sins_ a - way,_ Com - in' for to car - ry me home. Swing
all _ my friends I'm a com - in'_ too,_ Com - in' for to car - ry me home. Swing
still _ my soul feels heav'n - ly bound, _ Com - in' for to car - ry me home.

SWEET BETSY FROM PIKE

Moderately

1. Oh don't you re-mem-ber Sweet Bet-sy From Pike, Who crossed the big moun-tains with
2 - 8. *(See additional lyrics)*

her lov-er Ike; With two yoke of cat-tle, a large yel-low dog, A ___ tall Shang-hai roos-ter, and

one spot-ted Hog, Say-ing good-bye, Pike Coun-ty, Fare-well for a while.
We'll ___ come back a-gain when we've panned out our pile.

Additional Lyrics

2. One evening quite early they camped on the Platte,
'Twas near by the road on a green shady flat,
Where Betsy, sore-footed, lay down to repose —
With wonder Ike gazed on that Pike County rose.

3. Their wagon broke down with a terrible crash,
And out on the prairie rolled all kinds of trash,
A few little baby clothes done up with care,
'Twas rather suspicious, but all on the square.

4. The Shanghai ran off, and their cattle all died;
That morning the last piece of bacon was fried;
Poor Ike was discouraged and Betsy got mad,
The dog drooped his tail and looked wondrously sad.

5. They soon reached the desert where Betsy gave out,
And down in the sand she lay rolling about;
While Ike, half distracted, looked on with surprise,
Saying, "Betsy, get up, you'll get sand in your eyes."

6. Sweet Betsy got up in a great deal of pain,
Declared she'd go back to Pike County again;
But Ike gave a sigh, and they fondly embraced,
And they travelled along with his arm round her waist.

7. They suddenly stopped on a very high hill,
With wonder looked down upon old Placerville;
Ike sighed when he said, and he cast his eyes down,
"Sweet Betsy, my darling, we've got to Hangtown."

8. Long Ike and sweet Betsy attended a dance;
Ike wore a pair of his Pike County pants;
Sweet Betsy was dressed up in ribbons and rings;
Says Ike, "You're an angel, but where are your wings?"

TAPS

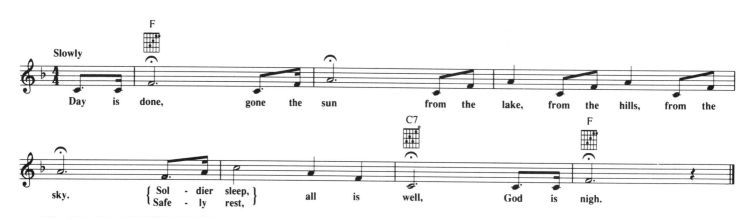

Slowly

Day is done, gone the sun from the lake, from the hills, from the

sky. {Sol-dier sleep, / Safe-ly rest,} all is well, God is nigh.

SHOO, FLY, DON'T BOTHER ME

Shoo, Fly, Don't Both-er Me, Shoo, Fly, Don't Both-er Me, Shoo, Fly, Don't Both-er Me, For

I be-long to some-bod-y. { I feel, I feel, I feel, I feel like a morn-in'
                          { I hear, I hear, I hear, I hear all the an-gels

star; I feel, I feel, I feel, I feel, I feel like a morn-in' star. Oh,
sing; I hear, I hear, I hear, I hear, I hear all the an-gels sing. Oh,

THAT'S WHY I DO LIKE I DO

I took my girl out walk-ing, late one Sat-ur-day night; I took my girl out

walk-ing, the moon was mel-low and bright. I asked her if she'd mar-ry me and

what do you think she said? She said she would-n't mar-ry me if the whole darn world was dead.

Chorus
N.C.

That's Why I Do-Like-I-Do-like-I do-like-I do-like-I-do-like-I-do-do-do. Do-like-I-do-like-I-

do-like-I-do-like-I do-like-I-do-do-do. That's Why I Do-Like-I-Do-like-I do-like-I-do-like-I-

do-like-I-do-do-do. Do-like-I-do-like-I do-like-I do-like-I do-like-I do-like-I do.

SHINE ON HARVEST MOON

Nora Bayes and Jack Norworth

Moderately slow

The night was might-y dark so you could hard-ly see,___ for the moon re-fused to shine.___
I can't see why a boy should sigh, when by his side ___ is the girl he loves so true.___

Coup-le sit-ting un-der-neath a wil-low tree, ___ for love they pine. Lit-tle maid was kind-a 'fraid of
All he has to say is,"Won't you be my bride,___ for I love you." Why should I be tell-ing you this

dark-ness so ___ she said, "I guess I'll go." Boy be-gan to sigh, looked up at the sky,
se-cret when ___ I know _____ that you can guess har-vest moon will smile, shine on all the while,

told the moon his lit-tle tale of woe. Oh, shine on, Shine On Har-vest Moon _____ up in the
if the lit-tle girl should an-swer,"Yes."

sky. I ain't had no lov-in' since Jan-u-ar-y, Feb-ru-ar-y, June or Ju-ly.___

Snow time ain't no time to stay _____ out-doors and spoon. So shine on,

1. Shine On Har-vest Moon, for me and my gal. ___
2. Oh, Moon, for me and my gal. ___

Copyright © 1990 HAL LEONARD PUBLISHING CORPORATION

ST. LOUIS BLUES

W.C. Handy

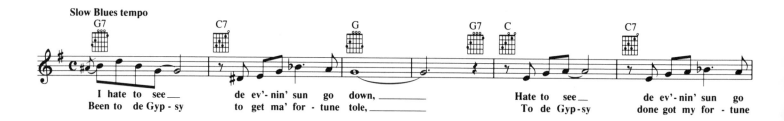

Slow Blues tempo

I hate to see___ de ev'-nin' sun go down, _____ Hate to see___ de ev'-nin' sun go
Been to de Gyp-sy to get ma' for-tune tole, _____ To de Gyp-sy done got my for-tune

Copyright © 1990 HAL LEONARD PUBLISHING CORPORATION

Additional Lyrics

3. You ought to see dat stove pipe brown of mine,
Lak he owns de Dimon' Joseph line.
He'd make a cross-eyed o' man go stone blind,
Blacker than midnight, teeth lak flags of truce,
Blackest man in de whole St. Louis.
Blacker de berry, sweeter is the juice.
About a crap game he knows a pow'ful lot,
But when work-time comes he's on de dot.
Gwine to ask him for a cold ten-spot.
What it takes to git it, he's certainly got.

Chorus

A black-headed gal make a freight train jump the track.
Said a black-headed gal make a freight train jump the track,
But a long tall gal makes a preacher ball the jack.

Extra Choruses

Lawd, a blonde-headed woman makes a good man leave the town,
I said a blonde-headed woman makes a good man leave the town,
But a red-head woman makes a boy slap his papa down.

O ashes to ashes and dust to dust,
I said ashes to ashes and dust to dust,
If my blues don't get you my jazzing must.

THE SWAN

Camille Saint-Saens

Slowly with expression

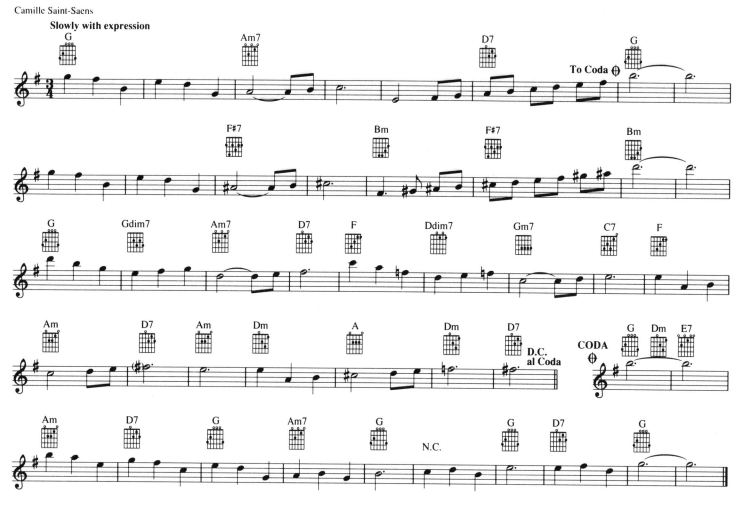

SWEET ROSIE O'GRADY

Maud Nugent

Moderately

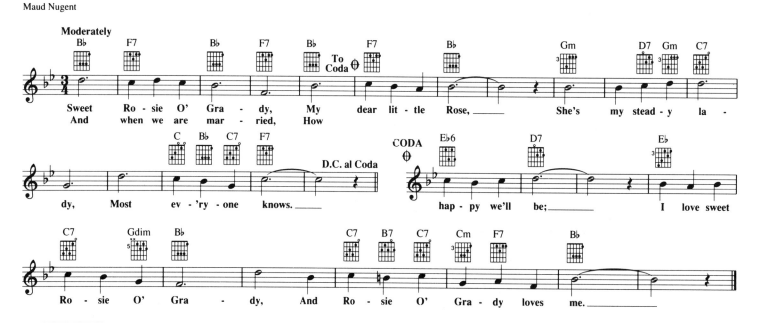

Sweet Ro - sie O' Gra - dy, My dear lit - tle Rose, _____ She's my stead - y la -
And when we are mar - ried, How

dy, Most ev - 'ry - one knows. _____ hap - py we'll be; _____ I love sweet

Ro - sie O' Gra - dy, And Ro - sie O' Gra - dy loves me. _____

SWEET ADELINE

Words by Richard H. Gerard
Music by Harry Armstrong

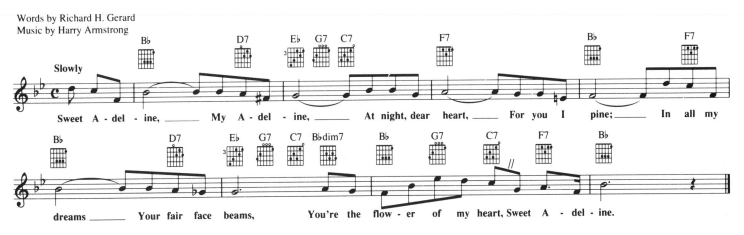

Sweet A-del-ine, _____ My A-del-ine, _____ At night, dear heart, _____ For you I pine; _____ In all my

dreams _____ Your fair face beams, You're the flow-er of my heart, Sweet A-del-ine.

TANGO
(Albeniz)

Isaac Albeniz

Moderately

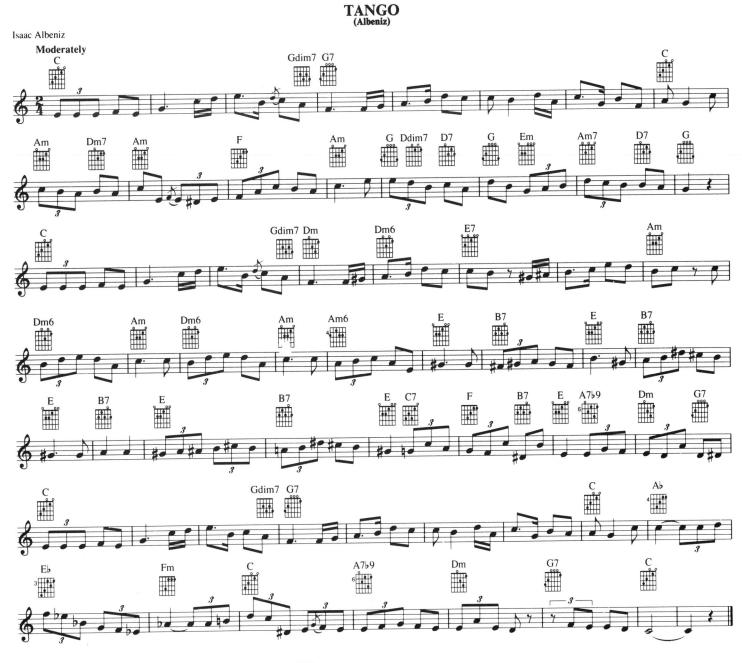

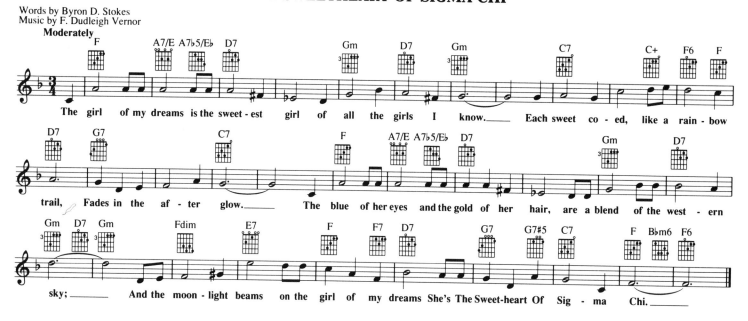

THE SWEETHEART OF SIGMA CHI

Words by Byron D. Stokes
Music by F. Dudleigh Vernor

Moderately

The girl of my dreams is the sweet-est girl of all the girls I know.___ Each sweet co-ed, like a rain-bow trail, Fades in the af-ter glow.___ The blue of her eyes and the gold of her hair, are a blend of the west-ern sky; ___ And the moon-light beams on the girl of my dreams She's The Sweet-heart Of Sig-ma Chi. ___

Copyright © 1990 MILWIN MUSIC

THAT'S A PLENTY

By Lew Pollack

Dixeland

Copyright © 1990 HAL LEONARD PUBLISHING CORPORATION

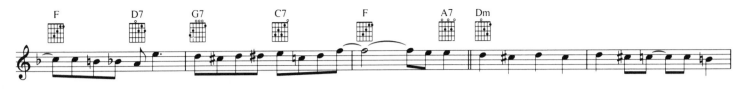

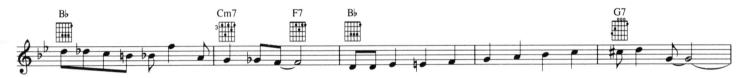

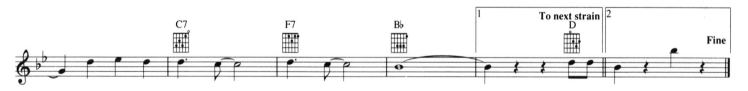

TAKE ME OUT TO THE BALL GAME

Lyrics by Jack Norworth
Music by Albert von Tilzer

THERE'S A LONG, LONG TRAIL

Music by Zo Elliott
Words by Stoddard King

THEY DIDN'T BELIEVE ME

Words by Herbert Reynolds
Music by Jerome Kern

And when I told them how beau-ti-ful you are They Did-n't Be-lieve Me.

They Did-n't Be-lieve Me! Your lips your eyes, your cheeks, your hair Are in a

class be-yond com-pare. You're the love-li-est girl that one could see!

And when I tell them, And I cert-n'ly am goin' to tell them, That I'm the

man whose wife one day you'll be. They'll nev-er be-lieve me. They'll nev-er be-

lieve me That from this great big world you've cho-sen me!

TOO-RA-LOO-RA-LOO-RAL
(That's An Irish Lullaby)

Words and Music by J.R. Shannon

Moderately, with expression

Too - Ra - Loo - Ra- Loo- Ral, Too - ra - loo - ra - li, Too - Ra - Loo - Ra

Loo- Ral, Hush now, don't you cry! Too - Ra - Loo - Ra - Loo- Ral, Too - ra - loo - ra

li, Too - Ra - Loo - Ra - Loo- Ral, That's an I - rish lull - a - by.

284

12TH STREET RAG

By Euday L. Bowman

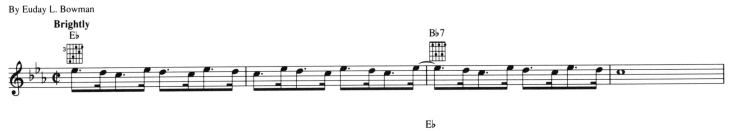

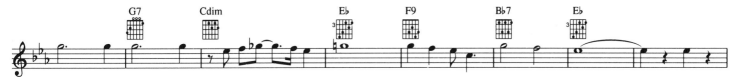

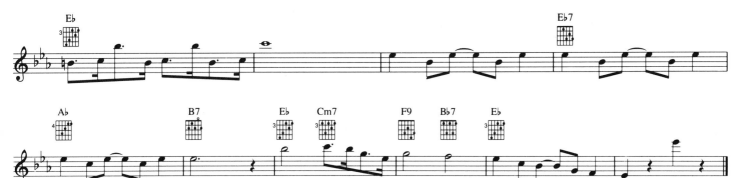

THE TRAIL OF THE LONESOME PINE

Words by Ballard MacDonald
Music by Harry Carroll

TA-RA-RA BOOM-DER-É

Henry J. Sayers

Brightly

A sweet tux - e - do girl you see, Queen of swell so - ci - e - ty, Fond of fun as fond can be, When it's on the
blush - ing bud of in - no - cence, Pa - pa says at big ex - pence, Old maids say I have no sense, Boys de - clare I'm

strict Q. T. I'm not too young, I'm not too old, Not too tim - id, Not too bold, Just the kind you'd
just im - mence, Be - fore my song I do con - clude, I want it strict - ly un - der - stood, Tho' fond of fun, I'm

like to hold, Just the kind for sport I'm told. Ta - ra - ra Boom - der - é Ta - ra - ra Boom - der - é
nev - er rude, Tho' not too bad I'm not too good.

Ta - ra - ra Boom - der - é Ta - ra - ra Boom - der - é Ta - ra - ra Boom - der - é Ta - ra - ra

Boom - der - é Ta - ra - ra Boom - der - é Ta - ra - ra Boom - der - é. I'm a Ta - ra - ra Boom - der - é.

TCHAIKOVSKY PIANO CONCERTO
(1st Movement)

Peter Ilyich Tchaikovsky

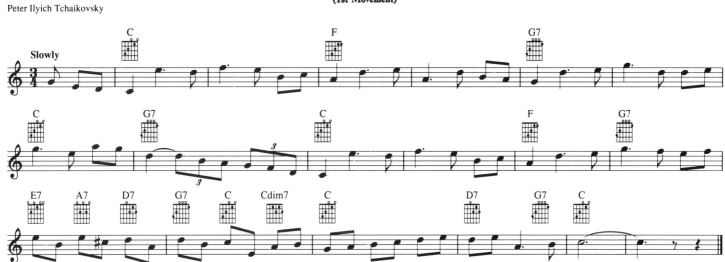

Slowly

TARANTELLA

TEN LITTLE INDIANS

TCHAIKOVKSY SYMPHONY NO. 6
(1st Movement)

Peter Tchaikovsky

TELL ME WHY

Tell __ Me Why__ the stars do shine, Tell __ Me
Be - cause God made __ the stars to shine, Be - cause God

Why__ the i - vy twines. Tell __ Me Why__ the skies are
made __ the i - vy twine. Be - cause God made __ the skies so

blue, And I will tell you why I__ love you.
blue, That is the rea - son why I love you.

TALES FROM THE VIENNA WOODS

Johann Strauss

Waltz tempo

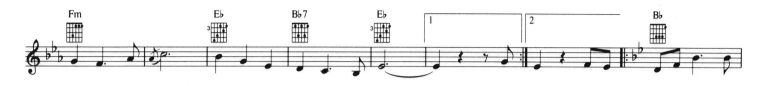

THERE WAS AN OLD WOMAN WHO LIVED IN A SHOE

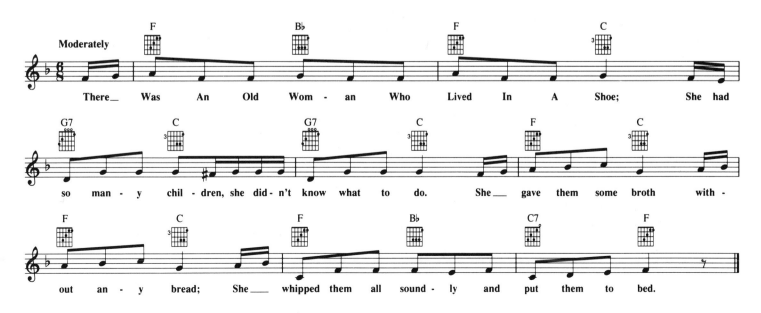

There_ Was An Old Wom - an Who Lived In A Shoe; She had
so man - y chil - dren, she did - n't know what to do. She_ gave them some broth with -
out an - y bread; She_ whipped them all sound - ly and put them to bed.

THIS OLD MAN

Traditional

1. This Old Man, he played one, He played knick - knack on my drum,
2. This Old Man, he played two, He played knick - knack on my shoe,

Chorus

Knick - knack pad - dy - whack, give the dog a bone, This Old Man came roll - ing home.

Additional Lyrics

3. This old man, he played three
   He played knick-knack on my knee. (*Chorus*)

4. This old man, he played four,
   He played knick-knack on my door. (*Chorus*)

5. This old man, he played five,
   He played knick-knack on my hive. (*Chorus*)

6. This old man, he played six,
   He played knick-knack on my sticks. (*Chorus*)

7. This old man, he played seven,
   He played knick-knack up to heaven. (*Chorus*)

8. This old man, he played eight,
   He played knick-knack at the gate. (*Chorus*)

9. This old man, he played nine,
   He played knick-knack on my line. (*Chorus*)

10. This old man, he played ten,
    He played knick-knack over again. (*Chorus*)

TENTING TONIGHT

Words and Music by Walter Kittredge

1. We're Tent - ing To - night on the old camp - ground. Give us a song to
2-4. (*See additional lyrics*)

cheer our wea - ry hearts, A song of home and friends we love so

dear. Man - y are the hearts that are wea - ry to - night

Wish - ing for the war to cease. Man - y are the hearts that are

look - ing for the right to see the dawn of peace. Tent - ing To - night,

Tent - ing To - night, Tent - ing on the old camp - ground.

Additional Lyrics

2. We've been Tenting Tonight on the old camp-ground.
   Thinking of days gone by,
   Of the loved ones at home that gave us the hand,
   And the tear that said, "Goodbye."

3. We are tired of war on the old camp-ground,
   Many are dead and gone,
   Of the brave and true who've left their homes,
   Others been wounded long.

4. We've been fighting
   today on the old camp-ground,
   Many are lying near,
   Some are dead and some are dying,

THIS TRAIN

1. This Train is bound for glo - ry, This Train, _____ This Train is bound for glo - ry,
2-6. *(See additional lyrics)*

This Train, _____ This Train is bound for glo - ry, Don't ride noth- in' but the

right-eous and the ho - ly. This Train is bound for glo - ry, This Train. _____

Additional Lyrics

2. This Train don't carry no gamblers, (*3 times*)
   No hypocrites, no midnight ramblers,
   This Train is bound for glory, This Train.

3. This Train is built for speed now, (*3 times*)
   Fastest train you ever did see,
   This Train is bound for glory, This Train.

4. This Train don't carry no liars, (*3 times*)
   No hypocrites and no high flyers,
   This Train is bound for glory, This Train.

5. This Train you don't pay no transportation, (*3 times*)
   No Jim Crow and no discrimination,
   This Train is bound for glory, This Train.

6. This Train don't carry no rustlers, (*3 times*)
   Sidestreet walkers, two-bit hustlers,
   This Train is bound for glory, This Train.

THERE IS A TAVERN IN THE TOWN

Moderately

There Is A Tav-ern In The Town, in the town, And there my true love sits him down, sits him down, __ and __ drinks his wine as mer-ry as can be, And nev-er, nev-er thinks of me. __ Fare thee well, for I must leave thee, Do not let this part-ing grieve thee, And re-mem-ber that the best of friends must part, must part. A-dieu, a-dieu, kind friends a-dieu, yes a-dieu, I can no long-er stay with you, stay with you __ I'll __ hang my heart on the weep-ing wil-low tree, And may the world go well with thee. __

Chorus

Additional Lyrics

2. He left me for a damsel dark, damsel dark.
   Each Friday night they used to spark, used to spark.
   And now my love who once was true to me,
   Takes this dark damsel on his knee.

3. And now I see him nevermore, nevermore.
   He never knocks upon my door, on my door.
   Oh, woe is me, he pinned a little note,
   And these were all the words he wrote:

4. Oh, dig my grave both wide and deep, wide and deep.
   Put tombstones at my head and feet, head and feet.
   And on my breast you may carve a turtle dove,
   To signify I died for love.

295

THREE BLIND MICE

Copyright © 1990 HAL LEONARD PUBLISHING CORPORATION

Julius Fucik

THUNDER AND BLAZES

Copyright © 1990 HAL LEONARD PUBLISHING CORPORATION

THUNDERER

John Philip Sousa

TOREADOR SONG
(Bizet)

Georges Bizet

TRAMP! TRAMP! TRAMP!

George F. Root

1. In the pris - on cell I sit, Think - ing, Moth - er dear of you, And our bright and hap - py home so far a-
2. In the bat - tle front we stood When their fierc - est charge they made, And they swept us off a hun - dred men or
3. So, with - in the pris - on cell, We are wait - ing for the day, That shall come to o - pen wide the i - ron

way; And the tears they fill my eyes, Spite of all that I can do, Though I
more; But be - fore we reached their lines, They were beat - en back, dis - mayed, And we
door, And the hol - low eye grows bright, And the poor heart al - most gay, As we

try to cheer my com - rades and be gay.
heard the cry of vic - t'ry o'er and o'er.
think of see - ing home and friends once more.

Chorus

Tramp! Tramp! Tramp! the boys are march - ing,

Cheer up, com - rades, they will come, And be - neath the star - ry flag We shall

breathe the air a - gain Of the free land in our own, be - lov - ed home.

TINKER POLKA

TIT-WILLOW

Gilbert and Sullivan

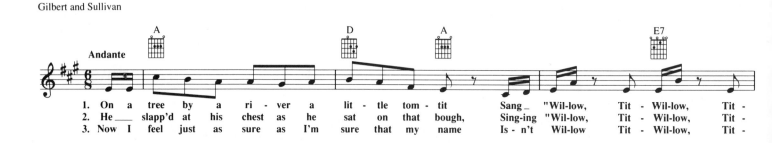

1. On a tree by a ri - ver a lit - tle tom - tit Sang_ "Wil-low, Tit - Wil-low, Tit -
2. He ___ slapp'd at his chest as he sat on that bough, Sing-ing "Wil-low, Tit - Wil-low, Tit -
3. Now I feel just as sure as I'm sure that my name Is - n't Wil-low Tit - Wil-low, Tit -

Wil-low!" And I said to him Dick - y bird, why do you sit Sing - ing
Wil-low!" And a cold pers - pi - ra - tion be - span - gled his brow, Oh___
Wil-low, That 'twas blight - ed af - fec - tion that made him ex - claim, "Oh___

wil - low, Tit - Wil-low, Tit - Wil-low?"___ "Is it weak - ness of in - tel - lect
wil - low, Tit - Wil-low, Tit - Wil-low! ___ He___ sobb'd and he sigh'd, and a
wil - low, Tit - Wil-low, Tit - Wil-low!"___ And if you re - main cal - lous and

bird - ie?" I cried, "Or a rath - er tough worm in your lit - tle in - side?" With a
gar - gle he gave, Then he threw him - self in - to the bil - low - y wave, And a
ob - du - rate, I shall ___ per - ish as he did, And you will know why, Tho' I

shake of his poor lit - tle head he re - plied, "Oh wil - low, Tit - Wil-low, Tit - Wil - low!"___
e - cho a rose from the su - i - cide's grave, "Oh wil - low, Tit - Wil-low, Tit - Wil - low!"___
pro - bab - ly shall not ex - claim as I die, "Oh wil - low, Tit - Wil-low, Tit - Wil - low!"___

TO A WILD ROSE

Edward MacDowell

TOYLAND

Music by Victor Herbert

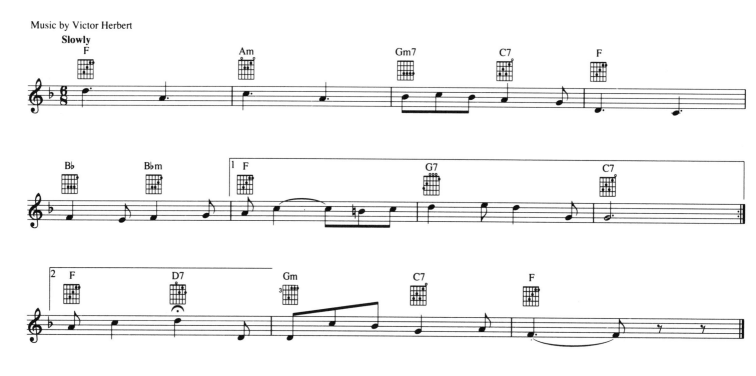

TRAUMEREI

Robert Schumann

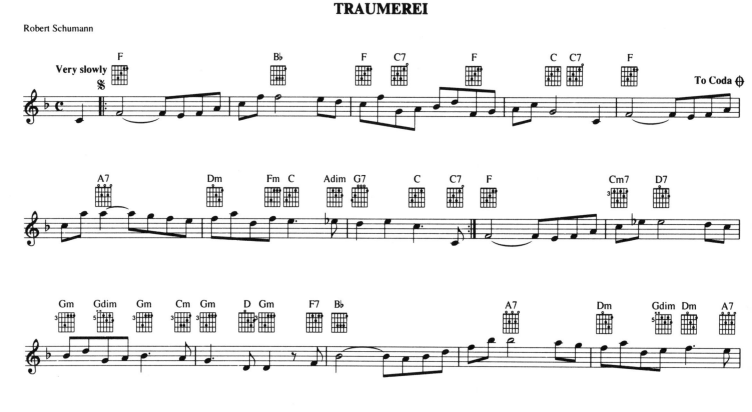

TRUMPET TUNE

Jeremiah Clarke

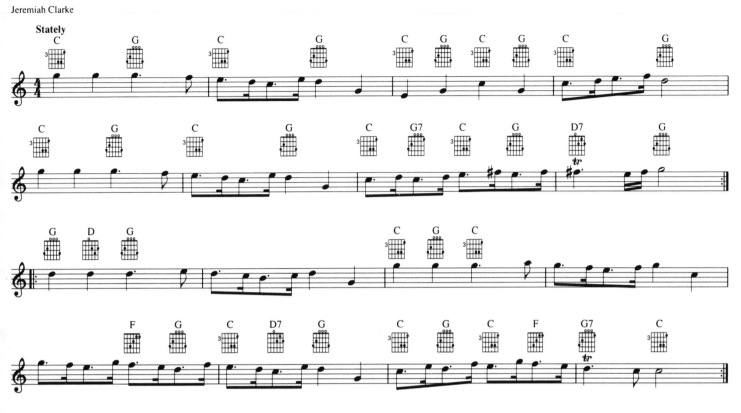

TURKEY IN THE STRAW

Rollicking

As __ I was a-go-ing on __ down the road, With a ti-red team __ and a heav-y load, I __ cracked my __ whip __ and the lead-er sprung, I __ says day-day __ to the wa-gon tongue.

Chorus

Tur-key In The Straw, haw, __ haw, __ haw, Tur-key in the hay, hay, __ hay, __ hay,

Roll 'em up and twist 'em up a high tuck a-haw, And __ hit 'em up a tune __ called __ Tur-key In The Straw.

TOURELAY, TOURELAY

1. Oh, pa - pa is out break - ing rocks on the street, And ba - by is
2. When pa - pa has gum - drops and ba - by has none, If pa - pa is

sleep - ing so co - sy and sweet; O ba - by, don't cry now, but
fool - ish and gives ba - by one, When four o' - clock comes, and the

be ver - y goot, And when pa - pa comes home he'll bring you ci - ga -
child sleeps no more, Then... pa - pa stays up all night pac - ing the

root.
floor! } Tou - re - lay, _____ Tou - re - lay, _____ With my

fil - la - ga dee - sha, Skin - a - ma - roo - sha, bal - der - al - da boom ta - de - ay, Tou - re - lay,

Tou - re - lay, _____ And the pride of the house is pa - pa's ba - bie.

TRIUMPHAL MARCH
(From "AIDA")

Giusseppe Verdi

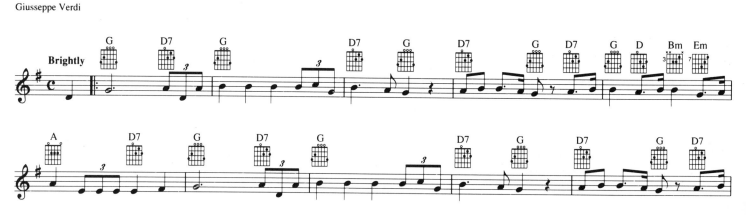

Brightly

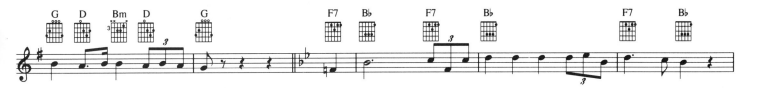

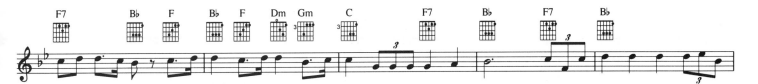

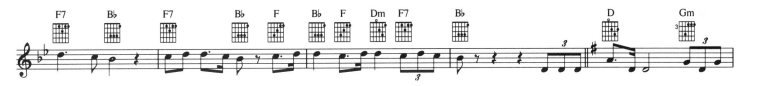

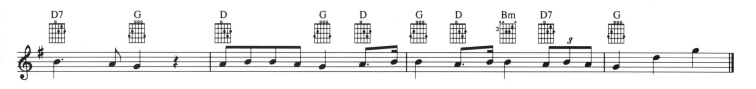

TWINKLE, TWINKLE, LITTLE STAR

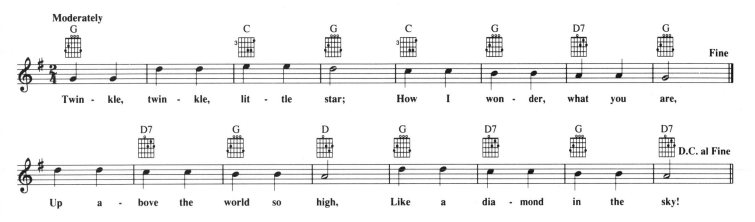

TRUMPET VOLUNTARY

Jeremiah Clarke

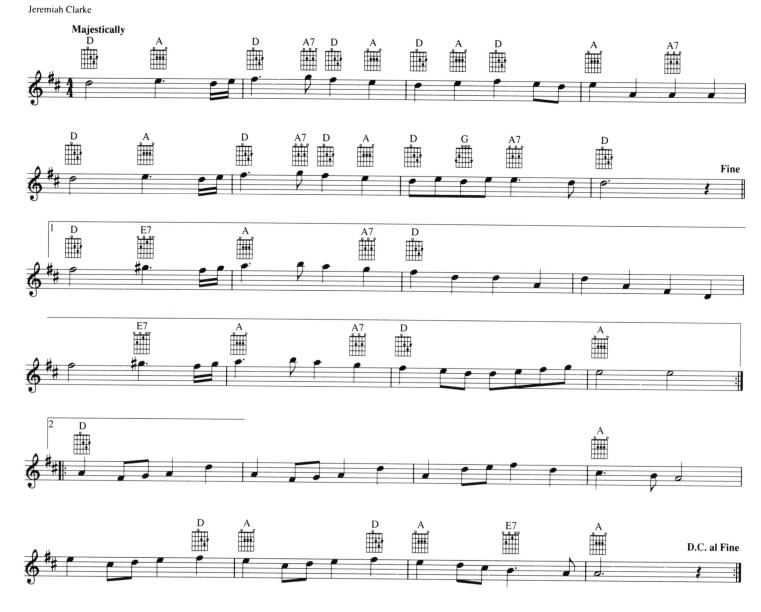

TURKISH MARCH

Ludwig Van Beethoven

THE TWELVE DAYS OF CHRISTMAS

Traditional

On the first day of Christ-mas, my true love gave to me: A par-tridge_ in a pear tree.

Repeat as needed

2. On the sec-ond day of Christ-mas, my true love sent to me: Two tur-tle doves,
3. On the third_ day of Christ-mas, my true love sent to me: Three French hens, And a par-tridge_ in a pear
4. On the fourth_ day of Christ-mas, my true love sent to me: Four call-ing birds,

D.S. for verses 3-4.

tree. On the fifth day of Christ-mas, my true love sent to me: Five gold _____ rings.

Four _ call-ing birds, Three French hens, Two_ tur-tle doves, And a par-tridge_ in a pear tree.

Fine

6. On the sixth _ day of Christ-mas, my true love sent to me: Six ___ geese a-lay-ing,
7. On the sev-enth day of Christ-mas, my true love sent to me: Sev-en swans a-swim-ming,
8. On the eighth_ day of Christ-mas, my true love sent to me: Eight _ maids a-milk-ing,
9. On the ninth _ day of Christ-mas, my true love sent to me: Nine___ la-dies danc-ing, Five gold ___ rings!
10. On the tenth _ day of Christ-mas, my true love sent to me: Ten___ lords a-leap-ing,
11. On the 'lev-enth day of Christ-mas, my true love sent to me: 'Lev-en pi-pers pip-ing,
12. On the twelfth _ day of Christ-mas, my true love sent to me: Twelve_ drum-mers drum-ming,

To ⊕ for verses 7-12.

TWO GUITARS

UNDER THE DOUBLE EAGLE

J. Wagner

UP ON THE HOUSETOP

Brightly
F

Up On The House-top___ rein - deer pause,   Out jumps good old San - ta Claus;
First comes the stock - ing of lit - tle Nell;   Oh, dear San - ta, fill it well;

Down thru the chim - ney with lots of toys,   All for the lit - tle ones, Christ - mas joys.
Give her a dol - lie that laughs and cries,   One that will o - pen and shut her eyes.

Ho, ho, ho! Who would-n't go! Ho, ho, ho! Who would - n't go! ___

Up On The House - top, click, click, click, Down thru the chim - ney with good Saint Nick.

THE UNFINISHED SYMPHONY
(Theme)

Franz Schubert

VENETIAN BOAT SONG

Felix Mendelssohn

UNIVERSITY OF MICHIGAN SONG

Words and Music: Louis Elbert

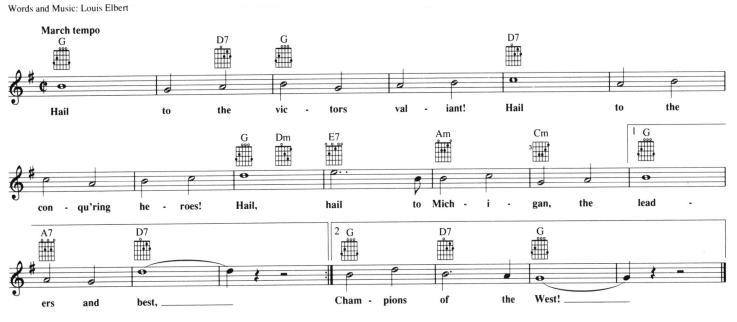

Hail to the vic - tors val - iant! Hail to the

con - qu'ring he - roes! Hail, hail to Mich - i - gan, the lead -

ers and best, _____ Cham - pions of the West! _____

VIENNA LIFE

Johann Strauss

VIVE L'AMOUR

Fast

1. Let ev-'ry good fel-low now fill up his glass, Vi-ve la com-pag-nie, And
2. Let ev-er-y mar-ried man drink to his wife, Vi-ve la com-pag-nie,

drink to the health of our glo-ri-ous class, Vi-ve la com-pag-nie.
joy of his bo-som and plague of his life, Vi-ve la com-pag-nie.

Vi-ve la, vi-ve la, Vi-ve L'a-mour, Vi-ve la, vi-ve la,

Vi-ve L'a-mour, Vi-ve L'a-mour, Vi-ve L'a-mour, vi-ve la com-pag-nie! _____

VALSE BLEUE

Alfred Margis

Waltz tempo

Fine

THE WABASH CANNON BALL

Moderato, not too slowly

I stood on the At - lan - tic O - cean, on the wide Pa - ci - fic shore, Saw the
Lis - ten to the jin - gle, the rum - ble and the roar, From
East - ern states are dan - dies so the West - ern peo - ple say. From
Here's to Dad - dy Clax - ton, may his name for - ev - er stand. May he

queen of flow - ing riv - ers, might - y moun - tains by the score. She's
Rid - ing through the wood - lands, to the hills and by the shore. Hear the
New York to St. Lou - is and Chi - ca - go by the way. Through
ev - er be re - mem - bered through parts of all our land. When his

long and she's tall and hand - some, yes, she's loved by one and all, she's a
might - y rush of the en - gine hear the lone - some ho - bo squall, the
the hills of Min - ne - so - ta where the rip - pling wa - ters fall, no
earth - ly race is o - ver and the cur - tain 'round him fall, we'll

mod - ern com - bi - na - tion called The Wa - bash Can - non - ball.
rid - ing through the jun - gle on The Wa - bash Can - non - ball.
chanc - es can be tak - en on The Wa - bash Can - non - ball.
car - ry him to glo - ry on The Wa - bash Can - non - ball.

VILIA

Franz Lehar

Slowly

Vil - ia, oh Vil - ia, oh where can you be? I'd come to you o - ver
Vil - ia, oh Vil - ia, my heart calls to you, Come back, my love, to my

land, o - ver sea. Vil - ia, oh Vil - ia, oh where have you gone,
love, ev - er true. Vil - ia, oh Vil - ia, I want you to know }

Leav - ing a love that lives on. _____ I love you, I love you

so, I love you so, love you so! _____

WAIT TILL THE SUN SHINES, NELLIE

Words by Andrew B. Sterling
Music by Harry Von Tilzer

Moderately

To Coda

Wait Till The Sun Shines, Nel - lie, And the gray skies turn to
We'll face the years to - geth - er, Sweet - hearts

blue. You know I love you Nel - lie, 'Deed I do. _____

D.C. al Coda   **CODA**

you and I. _____ So won't you Wait

Till The Sun Shines Nel - lie, Bye and bye. _____

WAIT FOR THE WAGON

R. Bishop Buckley

Moderately

1. Will you come with me my Phil - lis, dear, To yon blue moun - tain free, Where the blos-soms smell the sweet - est, Come
   ev - 'ry Sun - day morn - ing, when I am by your side, We'll jump in - to the wag - on, And

rove a - long with me. It's   ride. Wait For The Wag - on, Wait For The
all take a

Wag - on,   Wait For The Wag - on and we'll all take a ride.

WALTZ
(Brahms)

Johannes Brahms

WALTZ
(Chopin)

Chopin

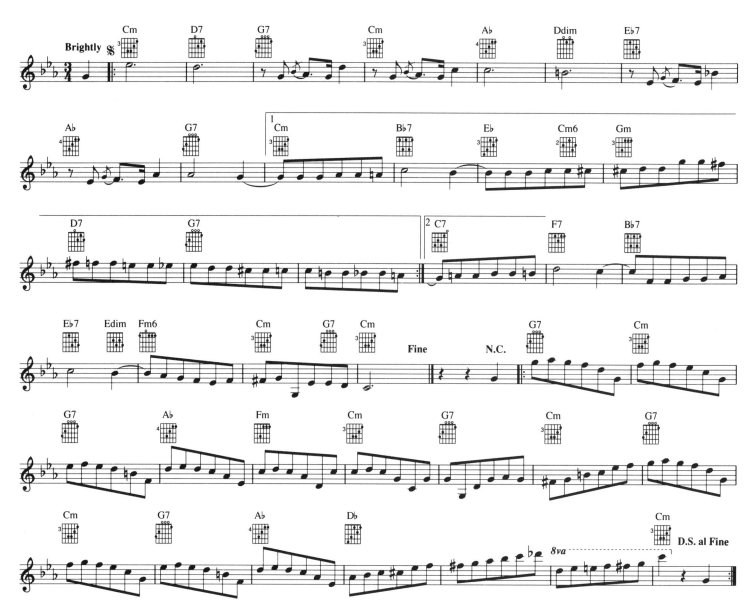

WALTZ OF THE FLOWERS

Peter Tchaikovsky

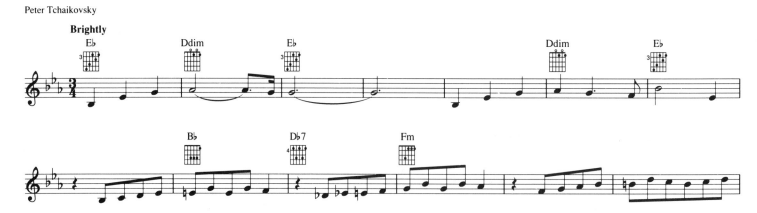

WE THREE KINGS OF ORIENT ARE

Brightly

We Three Kings Of O - ri - ent Are; Bear - ing gifts we trav - erse a - far, Field and foun - tain,

moor and moun - tain, fol - low - ing yon - der star. O___ star of won - der, star of night, Star with

roy - al beau - ty bright, West - ward lead - ing, still pro - ceed - ing, guide us to thy per - fect light.

WAYFARING STRANGER

WASHINGTON POST MARCH

John Phillip Sousa

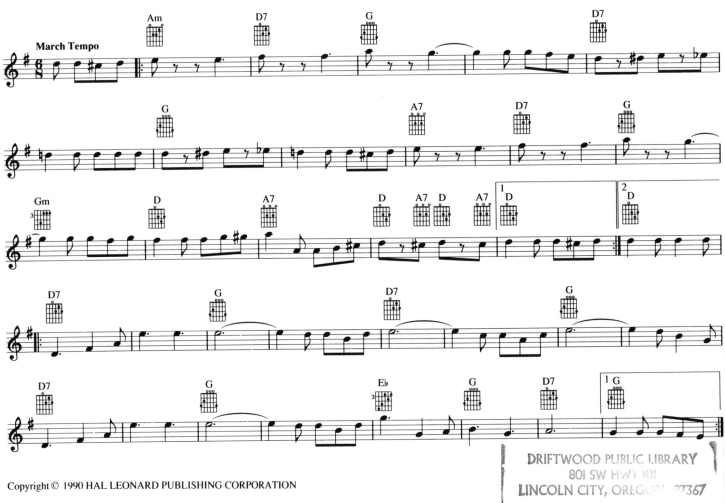

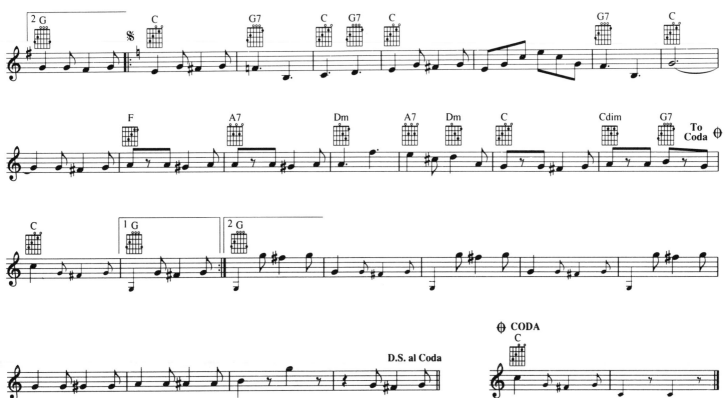

WEDDING MARCH

Felix Mendelssohn

WE WISH YOU A MERRY CHRISTMAS

Gaily

We Wish You A Mer-ry Christ-mas, We Wish You A Mer-ry Christ-mas, We Wish You A Mer-ry Christ-mas, and a Hap-py New Year! Good ti-dings to you, wher-ev-er you are; Good ti-dings for Christ-mas, And a Hap-py New Year!

THE WEARING OF THE GREEN

Moderately

1. O _____ Pad-dy dear, and did you hear the news that's go-ing round, The Sham-rock is for-
2. Then _____ since the col-or we must wear, is Eng-land's cru-el red; Sure Ire-land's sons will
3. But _____ if at last our col-or should be torn from Ire-land's heart, Her sons, with shame and

bid by law, to grow on I-rish ground; And Saint Pat-rick's day no more we'll keep, His
ne'er for-get the blood that they have shed; You may take the sham-rock from your hat, and
sor-row from the dear ould soil will part; I've heard whis-per of a coun-try, that lies

col-or can't be seen, For there's a blood-y law a-gainst the wear-ing of the green; I _____
cast it on the sod, But 'twill take root and flour-ish still, tho' un-der foot 'tis trod, When the
far be-yant the say. Where rich and poor stand e-qual in the light of free-dom's day. O _____

met the Nap-per Tan-dy and he took me by the hand, And he said "How's poor auld
law can stop the blades of grass from grow-ing as they grow, And _____ when the leaves in
E-rin, must we lave you, driv-en by the ty-rant's hand, Must we ask a moth-er's

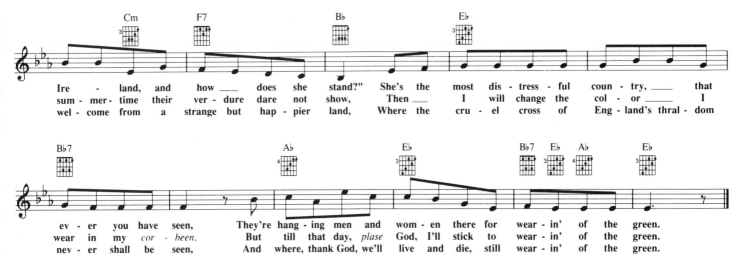

WERE YOU THERE?

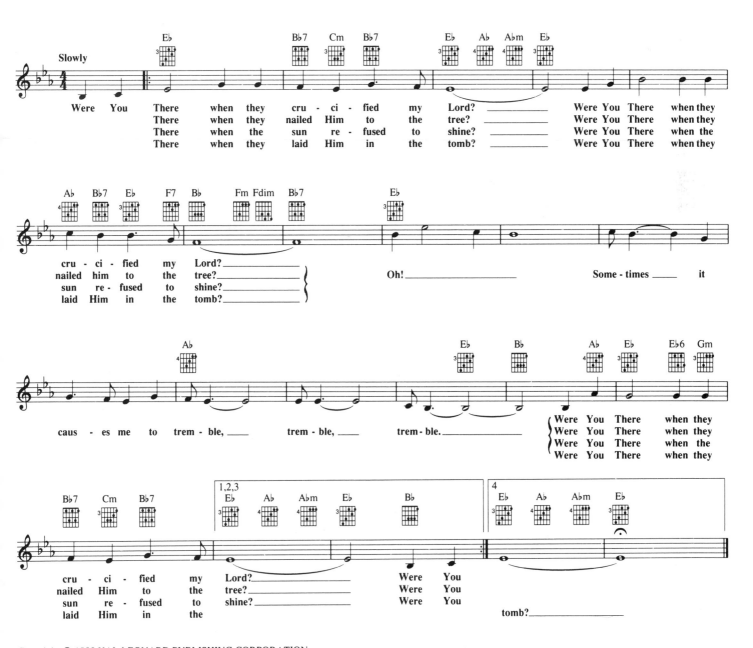

WHAT A FRIEND WE HAVE IN JESUS

Words by Joseph Scriven
Music by Charles C. Converse

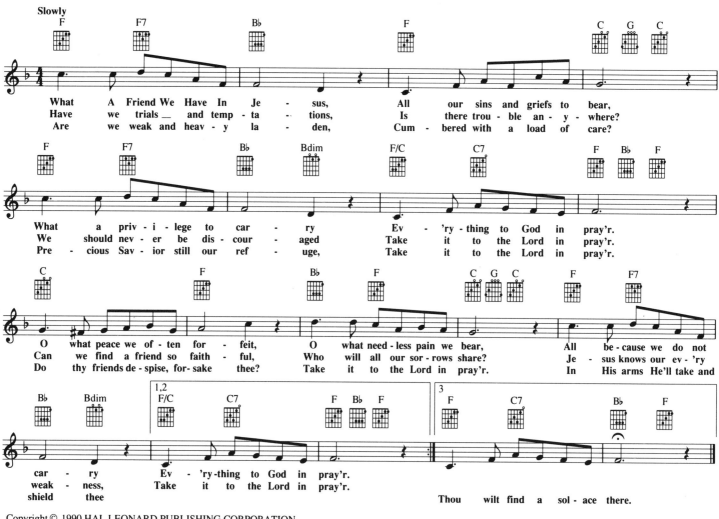

What A Friend We Have In Je - sus, All our sins and griefs to bear,
Have we trials __ and temp - ta - tions, Is there trou - ble an - y - where?
Are we weak and heav - y la - den, Cum - bered with a load of care?

What a priv - i - lege to car - ry Ev - 'ry - thing to God in pray'r.
We should nev - er be dis - cour - aged Take it to the Lord in pray'r.
Pre - cious Sav - ior still our ref - uge, Take it to the Lord in pray'r.

O what peace we of - ten for - feit, O what need - less pain we bear,
Can we find a friend so faith - ful, Who will all our sor - rows share?
Do thy friends de - spise, for - sake thee? Take it to the Lord in pray'r.

All be - cause we do not
Je - sus knows our ev - 'ry
In His arms He'll take and

car - ry Ev - 'ry - thing to God in pray'r.
weak - ness, Take it to the Lord in pray'r.
shield thee

Thou wilt find a sol - ace there.

WHEN JOHNNY COMES MARCHING HOME

Patrick S. Gilmore

Bright March

When John - ny Comes March - ing Home a - gain, Hur - rah! ____ Hur - rah! ____ We'll

give him a heart - y wel - come then, Hur - rah! ____ Hur - rah! ____ Oh the

men will cheer and the boys will shout. The la - dies they __ will all turn out, And we'll

all feel gay, When John - ny Comes March - ing Home. ____

WHAT CHILD IS THIS?

Words by William Dix

1. What Child Is This _ Who, laid to rest _ On Mary's lap, _ is sleep - ing? Whom
2. Why lies He in _ such mean es - tate, _ Where ox and ass _ are feed - ing? Good
3. So bring Him in - cense, gold, and myrrh Come peas - ant, King _ to own Him, The

an - gels greet _ with an - thems sweet, _ While shep - herds watch _ are keep - ing?
Christ - tian, fear: _ for sin - ners here _ The si - lent Word _ is plead - ing.
King of kings, _ sal - va - tion brings, _ let lov - ing hearts _ en - throne Him.

This, this _ is Christ the King; _ Whom shep - herds guard _ and an - gels sing:
Nails, spear, _ shall pierce Him through, _ The Cross be borne, _ for me, for you:
Raise, raise _ the song on high, _ The Vir - gin sings _ her lull - a - by:

Haste, haste _ to bring Him laud, _
Hail, hail, _ the Word made flesh, _ } The Babe, _ the Son _ of Ma - ry!
Joy, joy, _ for Christ is born, _

WHEN IRISH EYES ARE SMILING

Music by Ernest R. Ball
Words by Chauncy Olcott & Geo. Graff Jr.

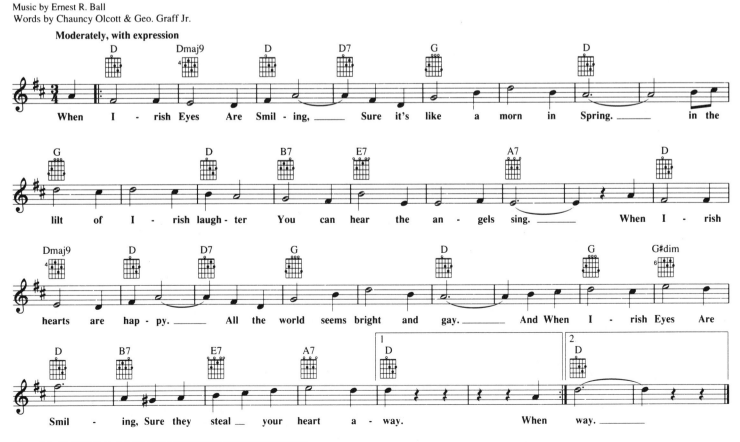

When I - rish Eyes Are Smil - ing, _ Sure it's like a morn in Spring. _ in the

lilt of I - rish laugh - ter You can hear the an - gels sing. _ When I - rish

hearts are hap - py. _ All the world seems bright and gay. _ And When I - rish Eyes Are

Smil - ing, Sure they steal _ your heart a - way. When way. _

WHEN THE SAINTS GO MARCHING IN

Moderately

1 and 5. Oh, When The Saints _____ Go March - ing In, _____ Oh, When The
2. Oh, when the sun _____ re - fuse to shine, _____ Oh, when the
3. Oh, when the stars _____ have dis - ap - peared, _____ Oh, when the
4. Oh, when the day _____ of judg - ment comes, _____ Oh, when the

Saints Go March - ing In, _____
sun re - fuse to shine, _____ Oh Lord, I want to be in that
stars have dis - ap - peared, _____
day of judg - ment comes, _____

num - ber, _____
When The Saints Go March - ing In. _____
When the sun re - fuse to shine. _____
When the stars have dis - ap - peared. _____
When the day of judg - ment comes. _____

WHEN YOU WERE SWEET SIXTEEN

By James Thornton

Slowly

When first I saw the love - light in your eye, And heard the voice like sweet - est mel - o -
night I dreamt I held your hand in mine And once a - gain you were my hap - py

dy Speak words of love to my en - rap - tured soul, The world had nought but joy in store for
bride. I kissed you as I did in Auld Lang Syne, As to the church we wan - dered side by

me. E'en tho we're drift - ing down life's stream a - part, Your face I still can see in dream's do -
side. The love I bear for you can nev - er die; With out you I had rath - er not been

main; I know that it would ease my break - ing heart To hold you in my arms just once a -
born; And e - ven tho we nev - er meet a - gain, I love you as the sun - shine loves the

gain. _____ } I love you as I nev-er loved be-fore, Since
morn. _____

first I met you on the vil-lage green. Come to me, or my dream of love is o'er, I

D.S.
Fine al Fine

love you as I loved you when you were sweet, When You Were Sweet Six-teen. Last

WHISPERING HOPE

Words and Music by Alice Hawthorne

Moderately slow, smoothly

Soft as the voice of an an - gel, Breath - ing a les - son un - heard, _____
If in the dusk of the twi - light, Dim be the re - gion a - far, _____

Hope with a gen - tle per - sua - sion, Whis - pers her com - fort-ing word. _____ Wait till the
Will not the deep-en-ing dark - ness, Bright - en the glim-mer-ing star? _____ Then when the

dark - ness is o - ver, Wait till the tem - pest is done. _____ Hope for the
night is up - on us, why should the heart sink a - way? _____ When the dark

sun - shine to - mor - row, Af - ter the show - er is gone. _____
mid - night is o - ver, Watch for the break - ing of day. _____

Whis - per - ing Hope, _____ Oh, how wel - come thy voice, _____ Mak - ing my

1.
2.

heart, _____ in its sor - row re - joice. joice. _____

WHEN YOU AND I WERE YOUNG, MAGGIE

Words and Music by George W. Johnson and James A. Butterfield

WHEN YOU'RE AWAY

Music by Victor Herbert
Lyrics by Henry Blossum

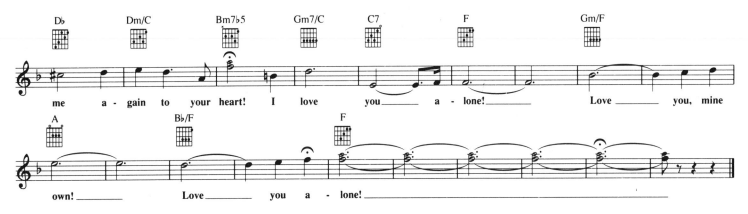

me a - gain to your heart! I love you____ a - lone! Love ____ you, mine

own! ____ Love ____ you a - lone! ____

WHILE STROLLING THROUGH THE PARK ONE DAY

By Ed Haley

While__ Strol - ling Thru The Park One Day, In the mer - ry month of May; I was
me - di - ate - ly rais'd my hat, And fi - nal - ly ____ she re - mark'd: I ___

tak - en by sur - prise, by a pair of ro - guish eyes, In a mo - ment, my poor heart was stole a -
nev - er shall for - get that ____ love - ly af - ter - noon, I ____ met her at the foun - tain in the

way. ____ } A smile was all she gave to me. Of
park. ____

course, we were as hap - py as can be, Ah! I im -

WHITE CORAL BELLS

White cor - al bells up - on a slen - der stalk, Lil - ies of the val - ley deck my gar - den walk.
Oh, don't you wish That you could hear them ring? That will hap - pen on - ly when the fair - ies sing.

WHILE SHEPHERDS WATCHED THEIR FLOCKS

WILL THE CIRCLE BE UNBROKEN

bye and bye, _____ There's a bet - ter _____ home a -
wait - ing _____ in the sky, Lord, _____ in the sky. _____

WHO THREW THE OVERALLS IN MRS. MURPHY'S CHOWDER

Words and Music by George L. Giefer

Moderately

"Who Threw The O - ver - alls In Miss - es Mur - phy's Chow - der?" No - bod - y
spoke so he shout - ed all the loud - er; "It's an I - rish trick that's true, I can
lick the mick that threw The o - ver - alls in Miss - es Mur - phy's chow - der."

WORRIED MAN BLUES

Moderately fast

1. It takes a wor - ried man to sing a wor - ried song. It takes a wor - ried
2. I went a - cross the river and I lay down to sleep. I went a - cross the

man to sing a wor - ried song. It takes a wor - ried man to sing a wor - ried
river and I lay down to sleep. I went a - cross the river and I lay down to

song. I'm wor - ried now but I won't be wor - ried long. _____
sleep, when I woke up, had shack - les on my feet.

WILLIAM TELL OVERTURE

Gioacchino Rossini

Moderately

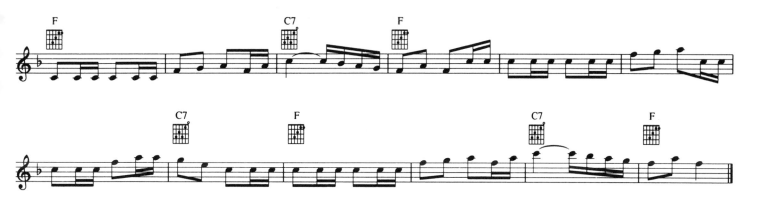

YANKEE DOODLE

Brightly

1. Fath'r and I went down to camp A - long with Cap - tain Good - win, And there we saw the
2. And there was Cap - tain Wash - ing - ton Up - on a slap - ping stal - lion, A - giv - ing or - ders
3. And then the feath - ers in his hat, They looked so ver - y fine, ah, I want - ed pes - ki -

men and boys As thick as hast - y pud - din'.
to his men; I guess there was a mil - lion. } Yan - kee Doo - dle keep it up,
ly to get To give to my Je - mi - ma.

Yan - kee Doo - dle dan - dy; Mind the mu - sic and the step, And with the girls be hand - y

WAITING FOR THE ROBERT E. LEE

Lyric by L. Wolfe Gilbert
Music by Lewis F. Muir

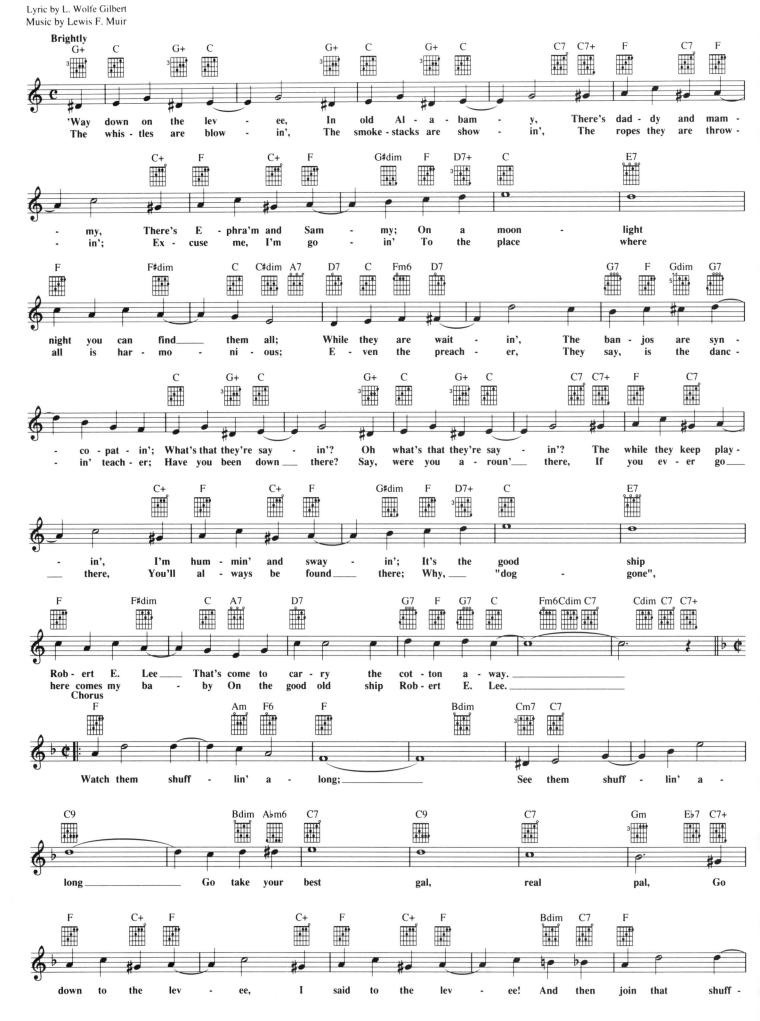

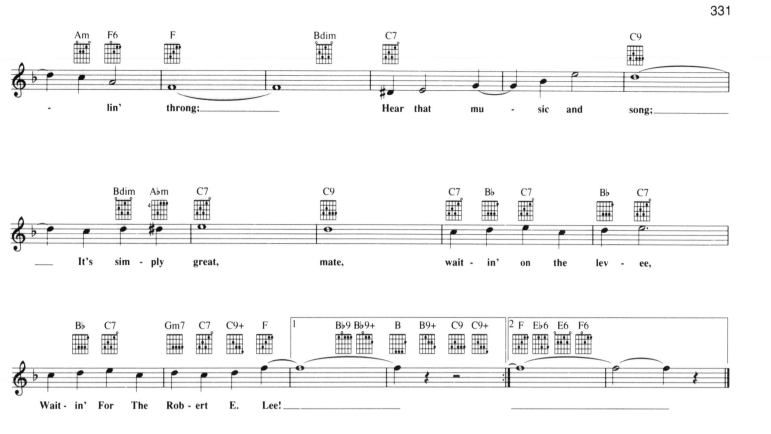

-lin' throng;_____ Hear that mu-sic and song;_____

_____ It's sim-ply great, mate, wait-in' on the lev-ee,

Wait-in' For The Rob-ert E. Lee!_____

WHEN YOU WORE A TULIP

Words by Jack Mahoney
Music by Percy Wenrich

Slowly

When You Wore A Tu-lip, a sweet yel-low tu-lip, and I wore a big red rose,_____

When you ca-ressed me, 'twas then Heav-en blessed me, what a bless-ing, no one knows._____

You made life cheer-y when you called me dear-ie, 'twas down where the blue grass grows,_____ Your lips were

sweet-er than ju-lep when you wore that tu-lip and I wore a big__ red rose._____

THE WHISTLER AND HIS DOG

Arthur Pryor

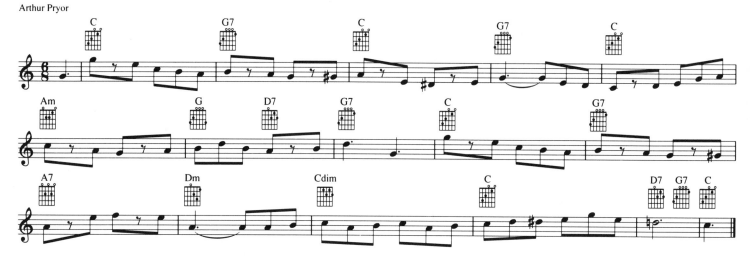

WASHINGTON AND LEE SWING

Words and Music by C.A. Robbins,
T.W. Allen and M.W. Sheafe

YOU MADE ME LOVE YOU

Words by Joseph McCarthy
Music by James V. Monaco

THE YANKEE DOODLE BOY

Words and Music by George M. Cohan

I'm a Yan - kee Doo - dle Dan - dy, a Yan - kee Doo - dle do or die; _____ a
real live neph - ew of my Un - cle Sam's, Born on the Fourth of Ju - ly. _____ I've
got a Yan - kee Doo - dle sweet - heart, She's my Yan - kee Doo - dle joy. _____
Yan - kee Doo - dle came to Lon - don just to ride the po - nies, I am a Yan - kee Doo - dle boy. _____

YOU'RE A GRAND OLD FLAG

George M. Cohan

You're A Grand Old Flag, you're a high fly - ing flag; And for - ev - er in peace may you
wave; _____ You're the em - blem of the land I love, The home of the
free and the brave. _____ Ev - 'ry heart beats true un - der red, white and blue, where there's
nev - er a boast or brag; _____ But, should auld ac - quain - tance be for -
got, Keep your eye on the grand old flag. You're A flag.

YOU TELL ME YOUR DREAM

Lyrics by Ceymour Rice and Albert H. Brown
Music by Charles N. Daniels

You had a dream, Well, I had one, too._____ I know mine's best, 'Cause it was of you._____ Come, sweet-heart, tell me, Now is the time._____ You Tell Me Your Dream, I'll tell you mine._____

Copyright © 1990 MILWIN MUSIC

YOU ARE MY TRUE LOVE

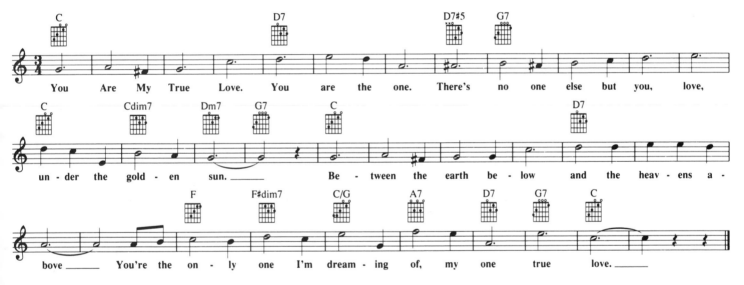

You Are My True Love. You are the one. There's no one else but you, love, un-der the gold-en sun._____ Be-tween the earth be-low and the heav-ens a-bove_____ You're the on-ly one I'm dream-ing of, my one true love._____

Copyright © 1990 MILWIN MUSIC

ZUM GALI GALI

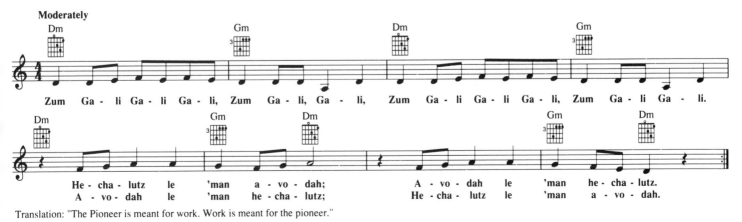

Zum Ga-li Ga-li Ga-li, Zum Ga-li, Ga-li, Zum Ga-li Ga-li Ga-li, Zum Ga-li Ga-li.

He-cha-lutz le 'man a-vo-dah; A-vo-dah le 'man he-cha-lutz.
A-vo-dah le 'man he-cha-lutz; He-cha-lutz le 'man a-vo-dah.

Translation: "The Pioneer is meant for work. Work is meant for the pioneer."

Copyright © 1990 HAL LEONARD PUBLISHING CORPORATION

THE YELLOW ROSE OF TEXAS

Lively, march tempo

1. There's a yel - low rose in Tex - as That I am goin' to see, No
2-3. *(See additional lyrics)*

oth - er fel - low loves her, No - bod - y, on - ly me. She

cried so when I left her, It like to broke my heart And

if I ev - er find ___ her, we nev - er - more will part. She's the

sweet - est rose of col - or This fel - low ev - er knew, Her

eyes are bright as dia - monds ___ They spar - kle like the dew. You may

talk a - bout your dear - est May, And sing of Ro - sa Lee But The

Yel - low Rose Of Tex - as beats the belles of Ten - nes - see.

Additional Lyrics

2. Where the Rio Grande is flowing
And the starry skies are bright,
She walks along the river,
In the quiet summer night.
She thinks, if I remember,
When we parted long ago,
I promised to come back again,
And not to leave her so.

3. Oh, now I'm goin' to find her,
For my heart is full of woe,
And we'll sing the song together,
That we sang so long ago.
We'll play the banjo gaily
And we'll sing the songs of yore
And the Yellow Rose Of Texas
Shall be mine forevermore.

BONUS SECTION

AFTER YOU'VE GONE

Words by HENRY CREAMER
Music by TURNER LAYTON

Easy Swing

Af - ter You've Gone, ___ and left me cry - ing; Af - ter You've Gone, ___
Af - ter I'm gone, ___ af - ter we break up; af - ter I'm gone, ___

there's no de - ny - ing; you'll feel blue, ___ you'll feel sad, ___
you're gon - na wake up; you will find, ___ you were blind, ___

you'll miss the dear - est pal you've ev - er had. ___ There'll come a time, ___
to let some - bod - y come and change your mind. ___ Af - ter the years, ___

now don't for - get it, there'll come a time, ___ when you'll re - gret it; Some day
we've been to - geth - er, through joy and tears, ___ all kinds of weath - er; Some day

when you grow lone - ly, your heart will break like mine and you'll want me on - ly,
blue and down-heart - ed, you'll long to be with me right back where you start - ed;

Af - ter You've Gone, _ Af - ter You've Gone a - way. ___
af - ter I'm gone, _ af - ter I'm gone a - way. ___

AIN'T WE GOT FUN?
from BY THE LIGHT OF THE SILVERY MOON

Words by GUS KAHN and RAYMOND B. EGAN
Music by RICHARD A. WHITING

With a bounce

Ev - 'ry morn - ing, ev - 'ry eve - ning, Ain't We Got Fun? Not much mon - ey,

oh! by hon - ey, Ain't We Got Fun? The rent's un - paid, dear, ___ we have-n't a

car.　But an-y-way,　dear, ___ we'll stay as we are.

E-ven if we owe the gro-cer,　don't we have fun.　Tax col-lec-tor's get-ting clos-er,

still we have fun.　There's noth-ing sur-er,　the rich get rich and the

poor get poor-er.　In the mean-time,　in be-tween time,　Ain't We Got Fun.　Fun.

ALABAMA JUBILEE

Words by JACK YELLEN
Music by GEORGE COBB

Lively

You ought to see Mis-ter Jones ___ when he rat-tles the bones, ___ Old Colo-nel Brown ___

___ fool-in' 'round like a clown, ___ Miss Vir-gin-ia who is past eight-y-three, ___

shout-in' "I'm full ___ o' pep!　*(Spoken:) Watch yo' step, watch ___ yo' step!"* One leg-ged Joe ___ danced a-

roun' on his toe, ___ Threw a-way his crutch and hol-lered, "Let 'er go!" ___ Oh, hon-ey, Hail!

Hail! the gang's all here for an Al-a-ba-ma Ju-bi-lee. ___

ALICE BLUE GOWN

Lyric by JOSEPH McCARTNEY
Music by HARRY TIERNEY

ALL BY MYSELF

Words and Music by
IRVING BERLIN

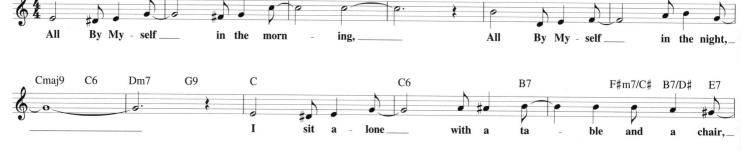

ANY TIME

Words and Music by
HERBERT HAPPY LAWSON

APRIL SHOWERS
from BOMBO

Words by B.G. DeSYLVA
Music by LOUIS SILVERS

With an easy flow

Though A-pril Show-ers may come your way, they bring the flow-ers that bloom in May; so if it's rain-ing, — have no re-grets _____ be-cause it is-n't rain-ing rain you know, it's rain-ing vi-o-lets. And where you see clouds up-on the hills, you soon will see crowds of daf-fo-dils; so keep on look-ing for a blue-bird and lis-t'ning for his song, when-ev-er A-pril Show-ers come a-long. Though A-pril long.

AUF WIEDERSEHN

Words by HERBERT REYNOLDS
Music by SIGMUND ROMBERG

Flowing

Love lives ev-er, know-ing no word like good bye. _____ Hearts may sev-er, true love can nev-er die! _____ Calm all your fears and dry all your tears, love will re-main when all else shall wane. Guid-ing me on thro' the years: Auf Wei-der-sehn, Auf Wei-der-sehn! _____

AVALON

Words by AL JOLSON and B.G. DeSYLVA
Music by VINCENT ROSE

BABY, WON'T YOU PLEASE COME HOME

Words and Music by CHARLES WARFIELD
and CLARENCE WILLIAMS

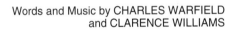

BEALE STREET BLUES

Words and Music by
W. C. HANDY

BEAUTIFUL OHIO

CANADIAN CAPERS

Words by EARL BURTNETT
Music by GUS CHANDLER, BERT WHITE
and HENRY COHEN

COHEN OWES ME NINETY-SEVEN DOLLARS

Words and Music by
IRVING BERLIN

CAROLINA IN THE MORNING

Lyrics by GUS KAHN
Music by WALTER DONALDSON

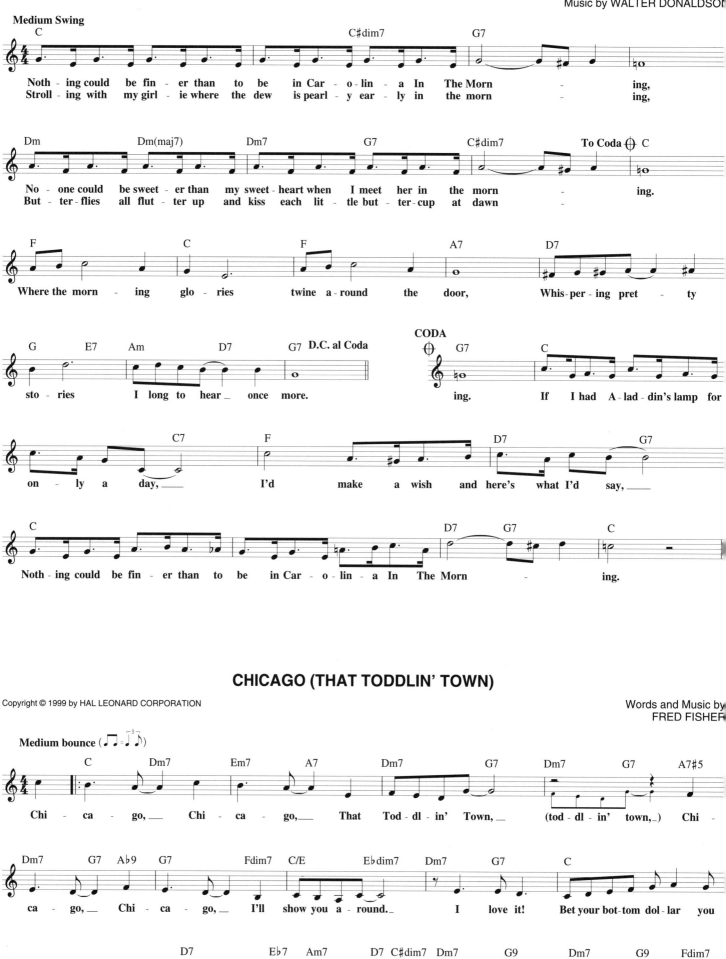

CHICAGO (THAT TODDLIN' TOWN)

Words and Music by
FRED FISHER

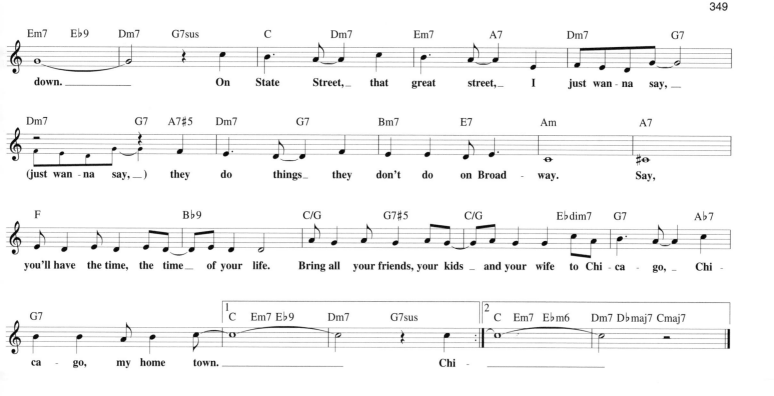

down. _____ On State Street,_ that great street,_ I just wan - na say, _

(just wan - na say, _) they do things_ they don't do on Broad - way. Say,

you'll have the time, the time_ of your life. Bring all your friends, your kids _ and your wife to Chi - ca - go, _ Chi -

ca - go, my home town. _____ Chi - _____

COLONEL BOGEY MARCH

Music by
KENNETH J. ALFORD

Moderately

DARDANELLA

Words by FRED FISHER
Music by FELIX BERNARD and JOHNNY S. BLACK

THE DARKTOWN STRUTTERS' BALL

Words and Music by
SHELTON BROOKS

DO IT AGAIN

Words by B.G. DeSYLVA
Music by GEORGE GERSHWIN

DOLORES WALTZ

By EMIL WALDTEUFEL

DONA NOBIS PACEM

Traditional Canon

Do - na no - bis pa - cem, pa - cem. Do — na — no - bis pa - cem.

Do - na no - bis pa - cem. Do - na no - bis pa - cem.

Do - na no - bis — pa - cem. Do - na no - bis pa - cem.

May be sung as a canon

DOWN YONDER

Words and Music by
L. WOLFE GILBERT

DOWN AMONG THE SHELTERING PALMS

Words by JAMES BROCKMAN
Music by ABE OLMAN

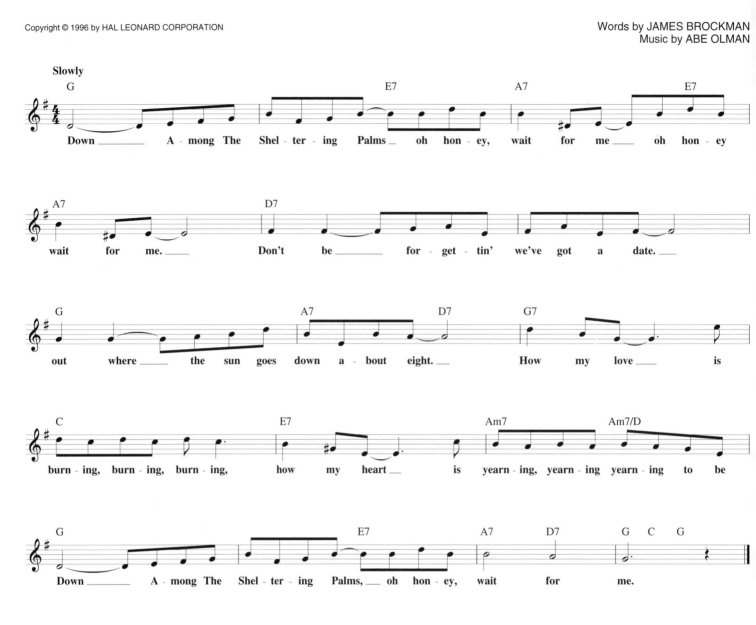

Slowly

Down _____ A - mong The Shel - ter - ing Palms _ oh hon - ey, wait for me _____ oh hon - ey

wait for me. _____ Don't be _____ for - get - tin' we've got a date. _____

out where _____ the sun goes down a - bout eight. _____ How my love _____ is

burn - ing, burn - ing, burn - ing, how my heart ___ is yearn - ing, yearn - ing yearn - ing to be

Down _____ A - mong The Shel - ter - ing Palms, ___ oh hon - ey, wait for me.

ESTUDIANTINA

By EMIL WALDTEUFEL

Waltz Tempo

Fine

ESTRELLITA

Words and Music by
MANUAL M. PONCE

Moderately

Lit - tle star who shines so bright in heav - en, _____ who
Es - tre - lli - ta del le - ja - no cie - lo, _____ Que

knows a - bout my love and sees my bro - ken heart, come and tell me if my
mi - ras mi do - lor que sa - bes mi su - frir, Ba - ja y di - me si me

dear one loves ____ me. ____ Life is sad ____ and ____ des - o - late when
quie - re un po - co _____ Por - que yo no ____ pue - do sin

we ____ are a - part. _____ Oh, love - li - est star, _____ my
su a - more vi - vir. _____ Tu e - res Oh es - tre - lla! mi

bea - con of love, _____ you know that my life will soon ebb and end. ____ Come and
fa - ro de amor, _____ Tú sa - bes que pron - to he de mo - rir. ____ Ba - ja y

tell me if my dear one loves ____ me. _____ Lit - tle star ___ of ____ sil - ver in
di - me si me quie - re un po - co _____ Por - que yo no ____ pue - do sin

heav - en a - bove.
su a - mor vi - vir.

1. Lit - tle
Es - tre

2. bove. _____
vir. _____

FOR ME AND MY GAL

Words by EDGAR LESLIE and E. RAY GOETZ
Music by GEORGE W. MEYER

Moderately, with movement

The bells are ring - ing _____ For Me And My Gal. _____ The birds are

sing - ing _____ For Me And My Gal. _____ Ev - 'ry - bod - y's been know - ing _____ to a wed - ding they're

GO DOWN, MOSES

Traditional American Spiritual

THE GIRL ON THE MAGAZINE COVER

Words and Music by
IRVING BERLIN

A GOOD MAN IS HARD TO FIND

Words and Music by
EDDIE GREEN

GOOD-BYE BROADWAY, HELLO FRANCE

Words by C. FRANCIS REISNER and BENNY DAVIS
Music by BILLY BASKETTE

HE IS AN ENGLISHMAN
from H.M.S. PINAFORE

Words by WILLIAM S. GILBERT
Music by ARTHUR SULLIVAN

HINDUSTAN

Words and Music by OLIVER WALLACE
and HAROLD WEEKS

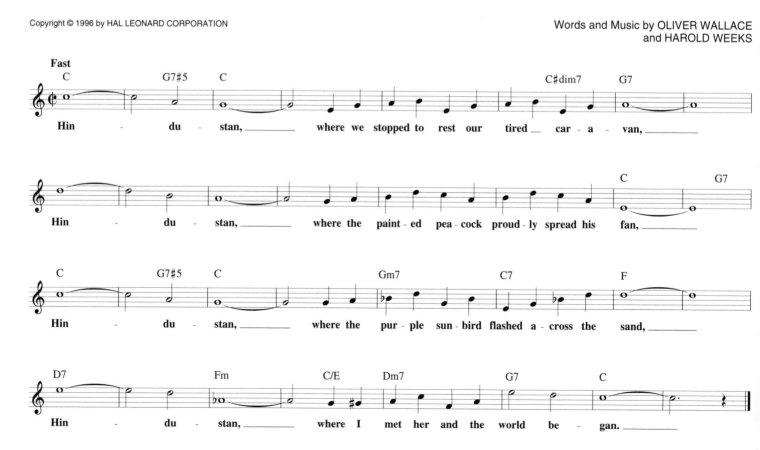

HINKY DINKY PARLEY VOO

Author Unknown

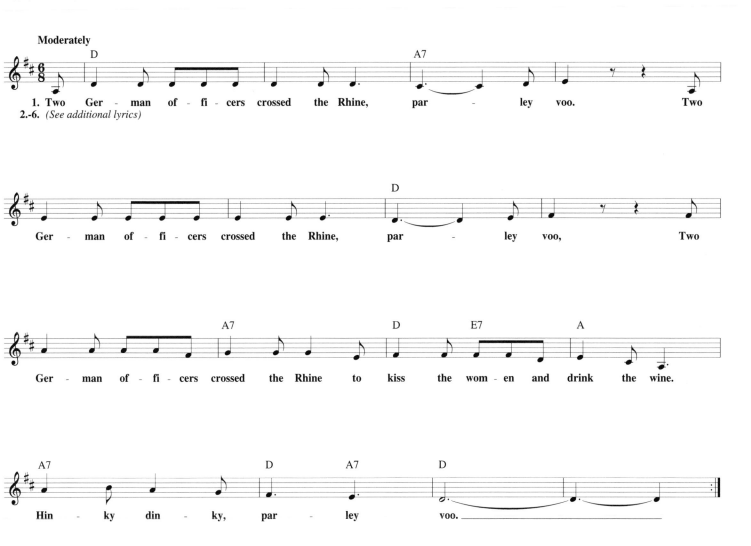

Additional Lyrics

2. The officers get all the steak, parley voo...
   And all we get is the belly-ache...
   Hinky dinky, parley voo.

3. The M.P.s say they won the war, parley voo...
   Standing on guard at a cafe door...
   Hinky dinky, parley voo.

4. The little marine in love with his nurse, parley voo...
   He's taken her now for better or worse...
   Hinky dinky, parley voo.

5. Mademoiselle all dressed in white, parley voo,
   Mademoiselle all dressed in blue, parley voo,
   Mademoiselle all dressed in black
   'Cause her little marine, he didn't come back,
   Hinky dinky, parley voo.

6. You might forget the gas and shell, parley voo...
   You'll never forget the mademoiselle...
   Hinky dinky, parley voo.

HIS EYE IS ON THE SPARROW
from SISTER ACT II

Text by C.D. MARTIN
Music by CHARLES H. GABRIEL

Moderately

Why should I feel dis-cour-aged,
Why should the shad-ows come, _____
Why should my heart be lone-ly _____
And long for heaven and home, _____ When
Je-sus is _____ my por-tion? _____
My con-stant friend _____ is He:
Eye Is On _____ The Spar-row, _____
And I know He watch-es me; _____ His Eye Is On The
Spar-row, _____ And I know He watch-es me. _____
I sing be-cause I'm hap-py, _____ I sing be-cause I'm
free, _____ For His Eye Is On The Spar-row, _____
And I know He watch-es me. _____

"Let not your heart be trou-bled," _____
His ten-der word I hear, _____
And rest-ing on His good-ness, _____
I lose my doubts and fears; _____ Though
by the path _____ He lead-eth, _____
But one step I may see: _____ His

When-ev-er I am tempt-ed, _____
When-ev-er clouds a-rise, _____
When songs give place to sigh-ing, _____
When hope with-in me dies, _____ I
draw the clos-er to Him, _____
From care He sets _____ me free: _____

HOW 'YA GONNA KEEP 'EM DOWN ON THE FARM?
(After They've Seen Paree)

Words by SAM M. LEWIS and JOE YOUNG
Music by WALTER DONALDSON

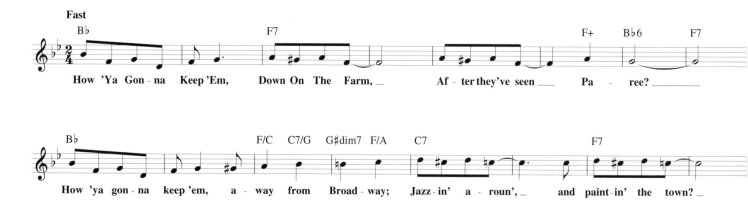

Fast

How 'Ya Gon-na Keep 'Em, Down On The Farm, _____ Af-ter they've seen _____ Pa-ree? _____

How 'ya gon-na keep 'em, a-way from Broad-way; Jazz-in' a-roun', _____ and paint-in' the town? _____

How 'ya gon-na keep 'em, a-way from harm? That's a mys-ter - y; _____

They'll nev-er wnat to see a rake or plow, _ and who the deuce can par-ley - vous a cow? _
Im-ag-ine Reu-ben when he meets his pa, _ He'll kiss his cheek and hol-ler "oo-la - la!" _

How 'Ya Gon-na Keep 'Em, Down On The Farm, _ af - ter they've seen _ Pa - ree? _

I AIN'T GOT NOBODY
(And Nobody Cares for Me)

Words by ROGER GRAHAM
Music by SPENCER WILLIAMS and DAVE PEYTON

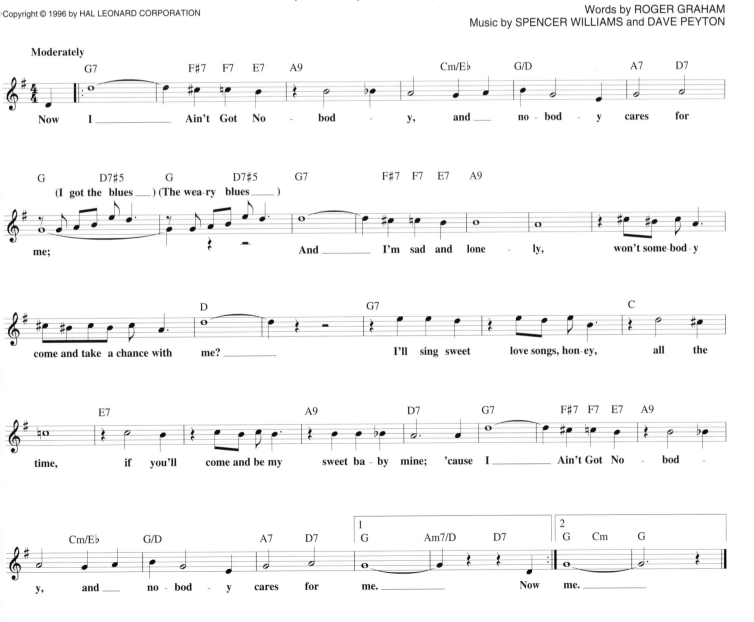

Moderately

Now I _____ Ain't Got No - bod - y, and _ no - bod - y cares for

(I got the blues _) (The wea-ry blues _)

me; _ And _____ I'm sad and lone - ly, won't some-bod-y

come and take a chance with me? _____ I'll sing sweet love songs, hon-ey, all the

time, if you'll come and be my sweet ba - by mine; 'cause I _____ Ain't Got No - bod -

y, and _ no - bod - y cares for me. _____ Now me. _____

I HAVE A SONG TO SING, O!
from THE YEOMAN OF THE GUARD

Words by WILLIAM S. GILBERT
Music by ARTHUR SULLIVAN

Allegro con brio

I Have A Song To Sing, O! _____ (Sing me your song, O!) _____

It is sung to the moon by a

love - lorn ___ loon, Who fled from the mock - ing throng, O! It's the song of a mer - ry man,

mop - ing mum, Whose soul was sad, and whose glance was glum, Who sipped no sup, and who craved no crumb, as he

sighed for the love of a la - dye. Heigh - dy! Heigh - dy! Mi - se - ry me,

lack - a - day dee! He sipped no sup, and he craved no crumb, As he sighed for the love of a la - dye!

I LOVE A PIANO
from the Stage Production STOP! LOOK! LISTEN!

Words and Music by
IRVING BERLIN

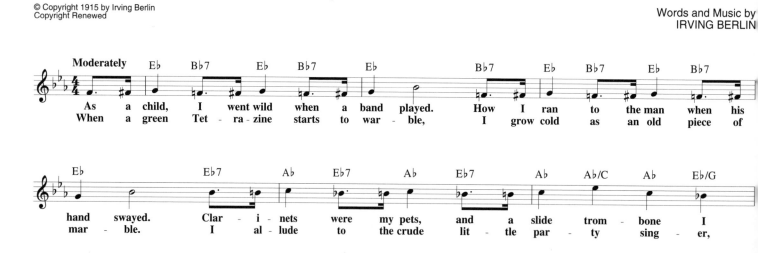

Moderately

As a child, I went wild when a band played. How I ran to the man when his
When a green Tet - ra - zine starts to war - ble, I grow cold as an old piece of

hand swayed. Clar - i - nets were my pets, and a slide trom - bone I
mar - ble. I al - lude to the crude lit - tle par - ty sing - er,

I SURRENDER ALL

Music by W.S. WEEDEN
Words by J.W. VAN DEVENTER

All to Je - sus I sur - ren - der;
all to Him I hum - bly at His
make me, Sav - ior, Lord, I give my
now I feel the

free - ly give; I will ev - er love and trust Him,
feet I bow; world - ly pleas - ures all for - sak - en;
whol - ly thine; let me feel the Ho - ly Spir - it,
self to Thee; fill me with Thy love and pow - er;
sa - cred flame. O the joy of full sal - va - tion!

in His pres - ence dai - ly live.
take me, Je - sus, take me now.
tru - ly know that Thou art mine.
let Thy bless - ing fall on me.
Glo - ry, glo - ry to His name!
I sur - ren - der

all, I sur - ren - der all,

all to Thee, my bless - ed Sav - ior, I sur - ren - der all.

I WISH I COULD SHIMMY LIKE MY SISTER KATE

Words and Music by
ARMAND J. PIRON

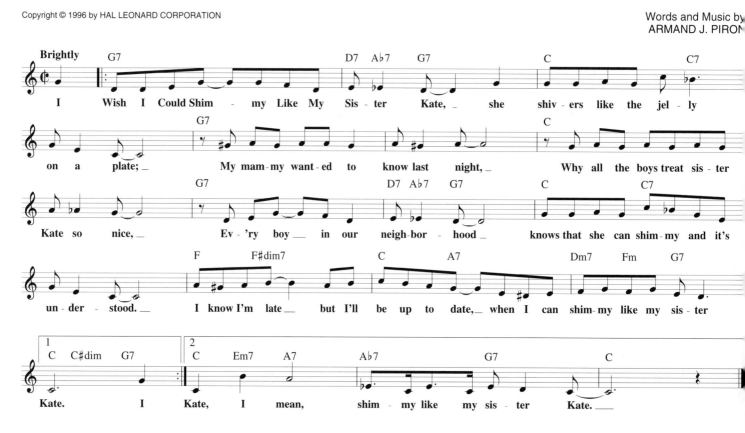

I Wish I Could Shim - my Like My Sis - ter Kate, she shiv - ers like the jel - ly
on a plate; My mam - my want - ed to know last night, Why all the boys treat sis - ter
Kate so nice, Ev - 'ry boy in our neigh - bor - hood knows that she can shim - my and it's
un - der - stood. I know I'm late but I'll be up to date, when I can shim - my like my sis - ter
Kate. I Kate, I mean, shim - my like my sis - ter Kate.

I'LL BE WITH YOU IN APPLE BLOSSOM TIME

Words by NEVILLE FLEESON
Music by ALBERT VON TILZER

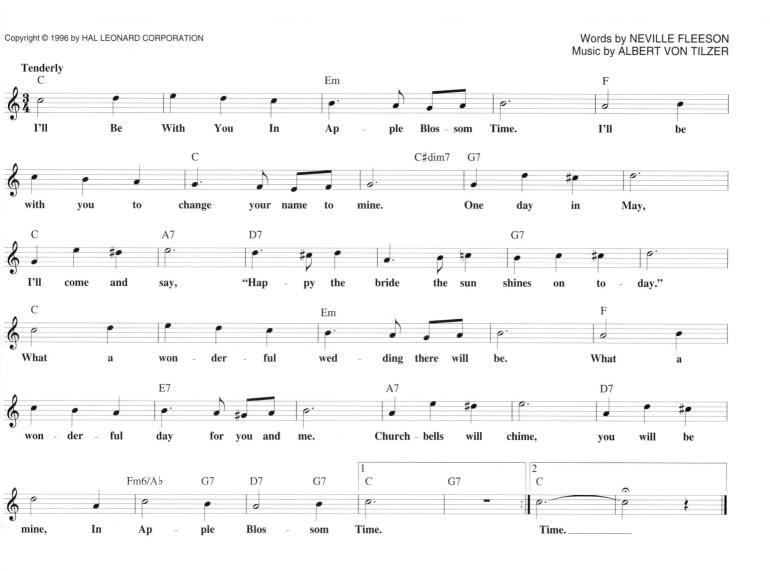

I'll Be With You In Ap - ple Blos - som Time. I'll be
with you to change your name to mine. One day in May,
I'll come and say, "Hap - py the bride the sun shines on to - day."
What a won - der - ful wed - ding there will be. What a
won - der - ful day for you and me. Church - bells will chime, you will be
mine, In Ap - ple Blos - som Time. Time.

I'LL BUILD A STAIRWAY TO PARADISE
from GEORGE WHITE'S SCANDALS

Words by B.G. DeSYLVA and IRA GERSHWIN
Music by GEORGE GERSHWIN

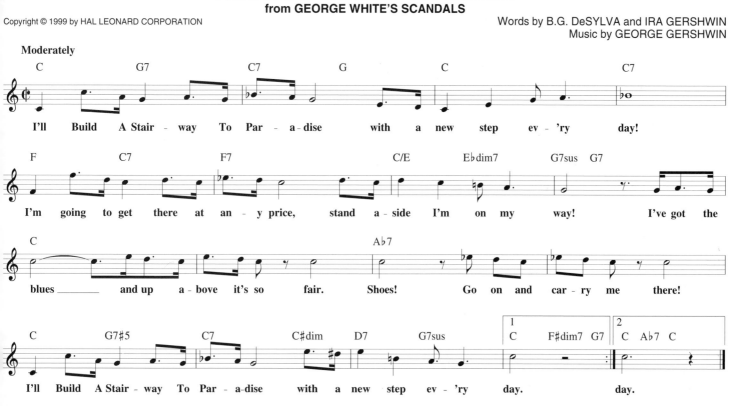

I'll Build A Stair - way To Par - a - dise with a new step ev - 'ry day!
I'm going to get there at an - y price, stand a - side I'm on my way! I've got the
blues and up a - bove it's so fair. Shoes! Go on and car - ry me there!
I'll Build A Stair - way To Par - a - dise with a new step ev - 'ry day. day.

I'M ALWAYS CHASING RAINBOWS

Words by JOSEPH McCARTHY
Music by HARRY CARROLL

I'M FOREVER BLOWING BUBBLES

Words and Music by JEAN KENBROVIN
and JOHN WILLIAM KELLETTE

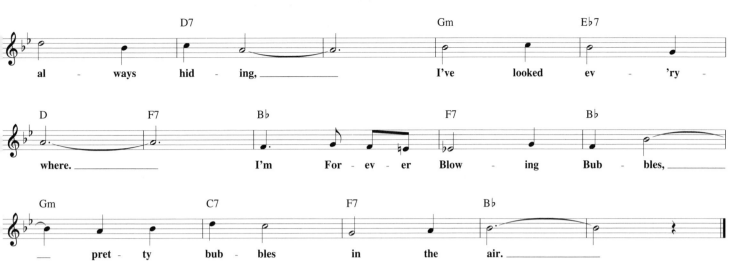

al - ways hid - ing, _____ I've looked ev - 'ry - where. _____ I'm For - ev - er Blow - ing Bub - bles, _____ ____ pret - ty bub - bles in the air. _____

I'M JUST WILD ABOUT HARRY

Words and Music by NOBLE SISSLE
and EUBIE BLAKE

I'm just wild a - bout Har - ry, _____ and Har - ry's wild ____ ____ a - bout me. _____ The heav'n - ly bliss - es of his kiss - es fill me with ec - sta - sy. ____ He's sweet, just like _____ choc - 'late can - dy, _____ and just like hon - ey from the bee, _____ Oh, I'm just wild ____ ____ a - bout Har - ry and he's just wild ____ a - bout, can - not do ____ with - out, he's just wild ____ a - bout me. me. _____

IF I KNOCK THE "L" OUT OF KELLY
(It Would Still Be Kelly to Me)

Words by SAM M. LEWIS and JOE YOUNG
Music by BERT GRANT

IF YOU WERE THE ONLY GIRL IN THE WORLD

Words by CLIFFORD GREY
Music by NAT D. AYER

lov - ing in the same old way. A Gar - den of E - den just made for two, With

noth - ing to mar our joy. _____ I would say such won-der-ful things to

you, There would be such won-der-ful things to do, If {You Were / I was} The On - ly

Girl In The World And {I was / you were} the on - ly boy. If boy. _____

IN THE GARDEN

Words and Music by
C. AUSTIN MILES

I come to the gar - den a - lone _____ while the dew is still on the
He speaks, and the sound of His voice _____ is so sweet the birds hush their
I'd stay In The Gar - den with Him _____ though the night a - round me be

ros - es, and the voice I hear fall - ing on my ear, the
sing - ing, and the mel - o - dy that He gave to me with -
fall - ing, but He bids me go; thru the voice of woe His

Son of God dis - clos - es. } And He walks with me, and He
in my heart is ring - ing. }
voice to me is call - ing. }

talks with me, and He tells me I am His own; _____ and the

joy we share as we tar - ry there, none oth - er has ev - er _____ known. _____

INDIAN SUMMER

By VICTOR HERBER

INDIANA
(Back Home Again in Indiana)

Words by BALLARD MacDONALD
Music by JAMES F. HANLEY

IRELAND MUST BE HEAVEN
(For My Mother Came from There)

Music by FRED FISHER
Words by JOSEPH McCARTHY
and HOWARD JOHNSON

Moderately

Chords: Bb F7/C C#dim7 Bb/D D7 Eb Edim7 Bb/F F7

Ire - land Must Be Heav - en, for an an - gel came from there. I

Chords: Bb Bb/D Eb Bb/D Db7 F/C Gm7 C7 F F7 Bb F7 Bb G7

nev - er knew a liv - ing soul one half as sweet __ or __ fair. For her eyes are like the star - light, and the

Chords: C7 F7 C#dim7 Bb/D F7/C C#dim7 Bb/D Fm6/Ab G7 C9 Ebm/Gb F7 Bb

white clouds match her hair. Sure __ Ire - land Must Be Heav - en, for my moth - er came from there.

THE JAPANESE SANDMAN

Words by RAYMOND EGAN
Music by RICHARD WHITING

Moderately

Chords: F D7

Here's The Jap - a - nese Sand - man __ sneak-ing on with the dew __ just an old sec - ond

Chords: G7 C7 F

hand man __ he'll buy your old day from you. He will take ev - 'ry sor - row __

Chords: A E7 A Adim

__ of the day that is through, __ and he'll give you to - mor - row just to start life a - new. __

Chords: Gm7 C7 F F7 Bb Bbm

__ Then you'll be a bit old - er __ in the dawn when you wake, __ and you'll be a bit bold - er __

Chords: Gm7 C7 F

__ with the new day you make. __ Here's The Jap - a - nese Sand - man __ trade him sil - ver for

Chords: Dm Dm#5 G7 N.C. G7 C7

gold __ just an old sec - ond hand man __ trad - ing new days for old.

1.
F

2.
Chords: Bb C Fm Edim7 Fm Db9 B9 F

Here's The Jap - a - nese old. __

THE JAZZ-ME BLUES

Words and Music by
TOM DELANEY

Down in Lou-is-ian-a in that sun-ny clime, __ they play a class of mu-sic that is su-per fine. __ And it
sounds so pe-cu-liar __ 'cause the mu-sic's queer. How its sweet vi-bra-tion seems to fill the air. __

makes no dif-fer-ence if it's __ rain or shine, __ you can hear that jazz band mu-sic play-ing
Then to you the whole world seems to be in rhyme. __ You want noth-ing else but jazz band mu-sic

1
all the time. __ It

2
all the time. __ Ev-'ry-one that's nigh nev-er seems __ to sigh, hear them loud-ly

cry; Oh! Jazz - man __ don't stop that mu-sic it's __ Jazz - man. __ (Jazz - man) __ You
Rag - time __ please sir will you play it in Jazz - time. __ (Jazz - time) __ You

1
know I want to hear it both __ day and night. __ And if you don't blow it hot then I don't feel right. __ Now if it's

2
Don't want it fast don't want it slow take your time don't rush it play it

sweet and low. __ I've got those dog-gone real-gone jazz band "Jazz - Me" Blues. _____

JELLY ROLL BLUES

By FERDINAND "JELLY ROLL" MORTON

JOHNSON RAG

Words by JACK LAWRENCE
Music by GUY HALL and HENRY KLEINKAUF

Hep Hep There goes the John-son Rag __ Hoy Hoy there goes the lat-est shag __ Ho Ho It real-ly

is-n't a gag __ Hep Hep There goes the John-son Rag __ Jump Jump Don't let your left foot drag __ Jeep

Jeep It's like a game of tag __ Juke Juke It's e-ven good for a stag __ Jump jump And do the

John-son Rag __ If you're feel-in' in the groove __ It sends you out of the world __

Fun-ny how it makes you move __ I don't wan-na coax __ But don't be a "Mokes" Zig

Zig Then add a Zig Zig Sag __ Zoop Zoop Just let your shoul-ders wag __ Zoom

Zoom And now it's right in the bag __ Get hep __ and get hap-py with the John-son Rag. __

KA-LU-A

Words by ANNE CALDWELL
Music by JEROME KERN

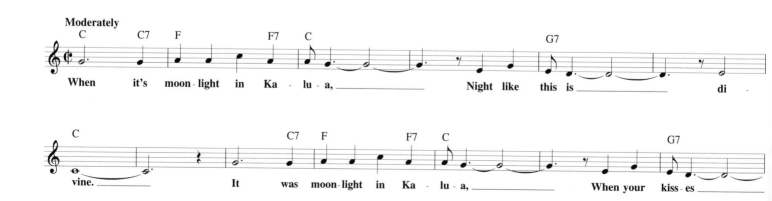

When it's moon-light in Ka-lu-a, __ Night like this is __ di

vine. __ It was moon-light in Ka-lu-a, __ When your kiss-es __

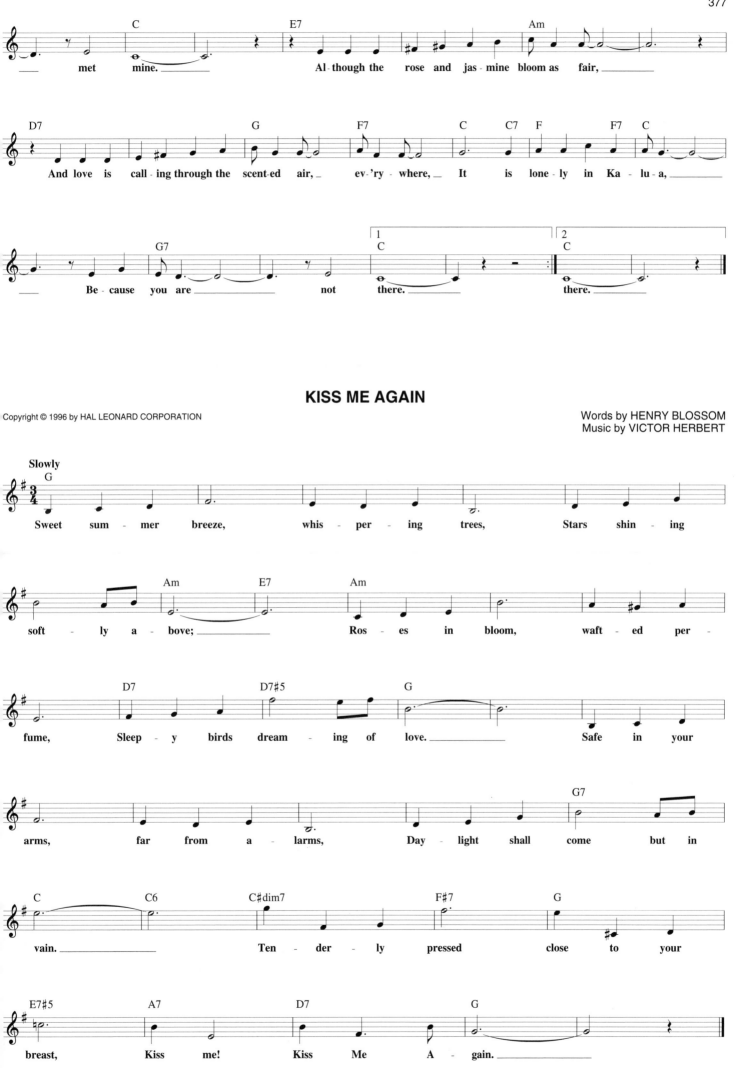

KISS ME AGAIN

Words by HENRY BLOSSOM
Music by VICTOR HERBERT

378

A KISS IN THE DARK

Copyright © 1996 by HAL LEONARD CORPORATION

By VICTOR HERBERT

Moderate Waltz

Oh, that kiss in ____ the dark was ____ to him just ____ a lark, but ____ to me 'twas ____ a thrill su - preme! ____

Just A Kiss In ____ The Dark but ____ it kin - dled ____ the spark, the ____ a - wak - 'ning ____ of love's young dream!

KISS WALTZ

Copyright © 1996 by HAL LEONARD CORPORATION

By JOHANN STRAUSS, Jr.

K-K-K-KATY

Words and Music by
GEOFFREY O'HARA

"K - K - K - Ka - ty, beau - ti - ful Ka - ty, You're the

on - ly g - g - g - girl that I a - dore; ___ When the m - m - m - moon shines, O - ver the

cow - shed, I'll be wait - ing at the k - k - k - kitch - en door." ___

KITTEN ON THE KEYS

By ZEZ CONFREY

Moderately

LADY OF THE EVENING
from the 1922 Stage Production MUSIC BOX REVUE

Words and Music by
IRVING BERLIN

LA CINQUANTAINE
(Golden Wedding)

By J. GABRIEL-MARIE

LA CUMPARSITA

Music by G.H. MATOS RODRIGUEZ

'TIS THE LAST ROSE OF SUMMER

Words by THOMAS MOORE
Music by RICHARD ALFRED MILLIKEN

LET THE REST OF THE WORLD GO BY

Words by J. KEIRN BRENNAN
Music by ERNEST R. BALL

LI'L LIZA JANE

Words and Music by
COUNTESS ADA DE LACHAU

LIMEHOUSE BLUES
from ZIEGFELD FOLLIES

Words by DOUGLAS FURBER
Music by PHILIP BRAHAM

LITTLE SIR ECHO

Words by LAURA R. SMITH
Music by J. S. FEARIS

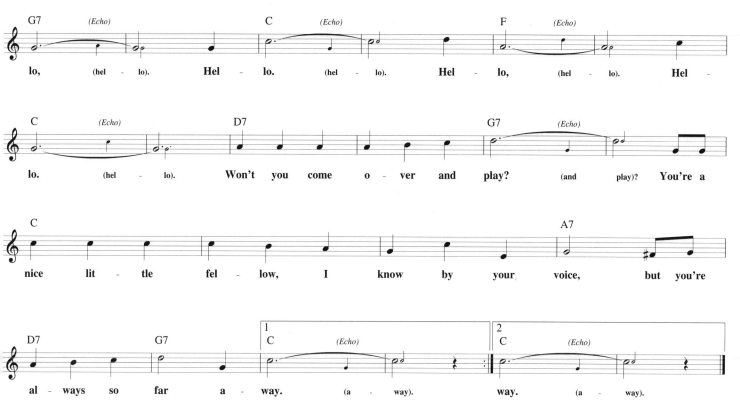

LOOK FOR THE SILVER LINING

Words by BUDDY DeSYLVA
Music by JEROME KERN

THE LOVE NEST

Words by OTTO HARBACH
Music by LOUIS A. HIRSCH

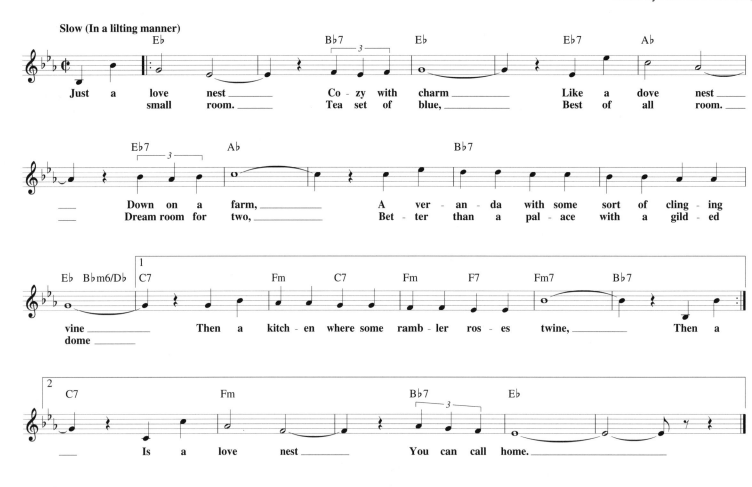

Slow (In a lilting manner)

Just a love nest _____ Co - zy with charm _____ Like a dove nest _____
small room. _____ Tea set of blue, _____ Best of all room. _____

Down on a farm, _____ A ver - an - da with some sort of cling - ing
Dream room for two, _____ Bet - ter than a pal - ace with a gild - ed

vine _____ Then a kitch - en where some ramb - ler ros - es twine, _____ Then a
dome _____

Is a love nest _____ You can call home. _____

LOVESICK BLUES

Words by IRVING MILLS
Music by CLIFF FRIEND

Moderately

I got a feel - in' called the blues, _____ o oh lawd since my ba - by said good - bye. _____ Lawd I

don't know what I'll do. _____ All I do is sit and sigh, _____ that last long

day she said good - bye. Well Lawd I tho't ___ I would cry _____ She'd

do me, she'd do you, she's got that kind of lov - in'. Lawd I love to hear her when she calls me sweet dad

MA

(He's Making Eyes at Me)

Words by SIDNEY CLARE
Music by CON CONRAD

MacNAMARA'S BAND

Words by JOHN J. STAMFORD
Music by SHAMUS O'CONNOR

Lively

G   A7/C#   D7sus   G

Oh! me name is Mc-Na-ma-ra, I'm the lead-er of the band,_____ Al-
Now we are re-hear-sin' for a ver-y swell af-fair,_____ The

Am7   D7   G/B   Em7   A9   G/B Cm A7/C# D7   G

though we're few in num-ber, we're the fin-est in the land. We play at wakes and
an-nual cel-e-bra-tion, all the gen-try will be there. When Gen-eral Grant to

A7/C# D7sus G G/F C/E Cm/Eb G/D Em7 A9 D7

wed-dings and at ev-'ry fan-cy ball,_____ And when we play at fu-ner-als we play the march from
Ire-land came he took me by the hand,_____ Says he, "I nev-er saw the likes of Mc-Na-ma-ra's

G   D7   G   D7 G Am7 D7

Saul.
band." } Oh! the drums go bang, and the cym-bals clang and the horns they blaze a-way;_____ Mc-Car-thy pumps the

G/B Em7 A9   D7   G

old ba-zoon while I the pipes do play; and, Hen-nes-sey Ten-nes-see toot-les the flute, and the mu-sic is some-thing

G G/F C/E Cm/Eb G/D Em7 A9 D7 | 1. G   D7 | 2. G

grand;_____ A cre-dit to old I-re-land is Mc-Na-ma-ra's Band. Band.

MANDY
from YIP, YIP, YAPHANK

Words and Music by
IRVING BERLIN

Moderately

F   C   A7   D7

Man-dy,_____ there's a min-is-ter hand-y._____ And it sure would be dan-dy,

G9   G7#5 C   C7b5 C7 C7#5 F

_____ if we'd let him make a fee._____ So don't you lin-ger,_____ here's the ring for your

C   A7   D7   G9   G7#5

fin-ger._____ Is-n't it a hum-din-ger?_____ Come a-long and let the

C Cdim G7 C Am   D9   G7 | 1. C   C7 | 2. C

wed-ding chimes bring hap-py times, for Man-dy and me. me._____

MARGIE

Words by BENNY DAVIS
Music by CON CONRAD
and J. RUSSELL ROBINSON

MEMORIES

Words by GUS KAHN
Music by EGBERT VAN ALSTYNE

MIYA SAMA
from THE MIKADO

Words by W.S. GILBERT
Music by ARTHUR SULLIVAN

Allegro moderato

Mi - ya Sa - ma,

Mi - ya Sa - ma, On - n'm - ma no ma - yé ni Pi - ra - Pi - ra su - ru no wa

Nan — gia — na ———— To - ko ton - ya - ré ton - ya - ré na!

Mi - ya Sa - ma,

Mi - ya Sa - ma, On - n'm - ma no ma - yé ni Pi - ra - Pi - ra su - ru no wa

Nan — gia — na ———— To - ko ton - ya - ré ton - ya - ré na!

MY BUDDY

Lyrics by GUS KAHN
Music by WALTER DONALDSON

Slowly

Nights are long since you went a - way, I think a - bout you
Miss your voice, the touch of your hand, I just long to know you that

all thru the day; } My Bud - dy, My Bud - dy, { No
you un - der - stand; } { Your

1 Bud - dy quite so true. ———

2 miss - es you. ———

M-O-T-H-E-R
(A Word That Means the World to Me)

Words by HOWARD JOHNSON
Music by THEODORE MORSE

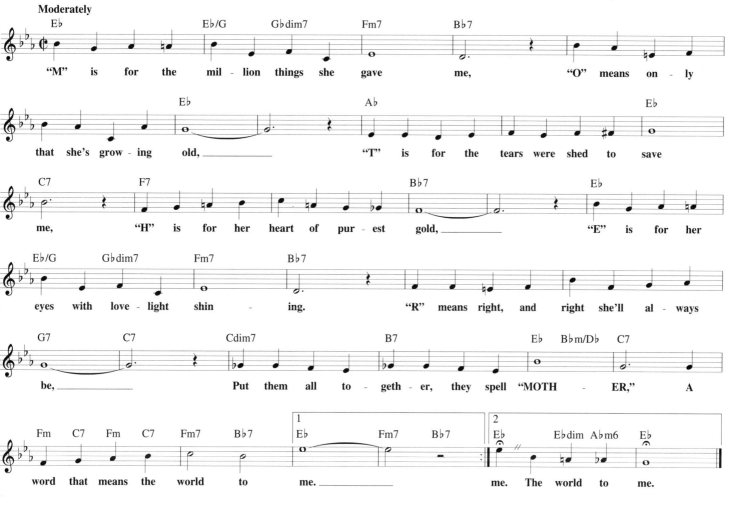

Moderately

"M" is for the mil-lion things she gave me, "O" means on-ly that she's grow-ing old, _____ "T" is for the tears were shed to save me, "H" is for her heart of pur-est gold, _____ "E" is for her eyes with love-light shin - ing. "R" means right, and right she'll al-ways be, _____ Put them all to-geth-er, they spell "MOTH - ER," A word that means the world to me. _____ me. The world to me.

MY HONEY'S LOVING ARMS

Words by HERMAN RUBY
Music by JOSEPH MEYER

Bouncy

I love your lov-in' arms; _ they hold a world of charms, _ a place to nes-tle when _ I am lone - ly. A co-zy Mor-ris chair, _ oh, what a hap-py pair! _ One ca-ress, hap-pi-ness, _ seems to bless my lit-tle hon-ey. I love you more each day; _ when years have passed a-way, _ you'll find my love be-longs _ to you on - ly; 'Cause when the world seems wrong, _ I know that I be-long _ right in My Hon-ey's Lov-in' Arms. _____

MY LITTLE GIRL

Words by SAM M. LEWIS and WILLIAM DILLO
Music by ALBERT VON TILZE

Cheerfully
B♭
My Lit - tle Girl, You know I love you, And I
B♭/D D♭dim7 F7
long for you each day My Lit - tle Girl, I'm dream - ing
F+ B♭
of you, Tho' you're man - y miles a - way.
I see the lane down in the wild - wood, Where you
Fm7 B♭7 B♭7♯5 E♭ G7/D Cm G7♯5 C7
prom - ised to be true. My Lit - tle Girl, I know you're wait - ing,
F7 1 B♭ Bdim7 F7 2 B♭ E♭m6 B♭6
And I'm com - ing back to you. My Lit - tle you.

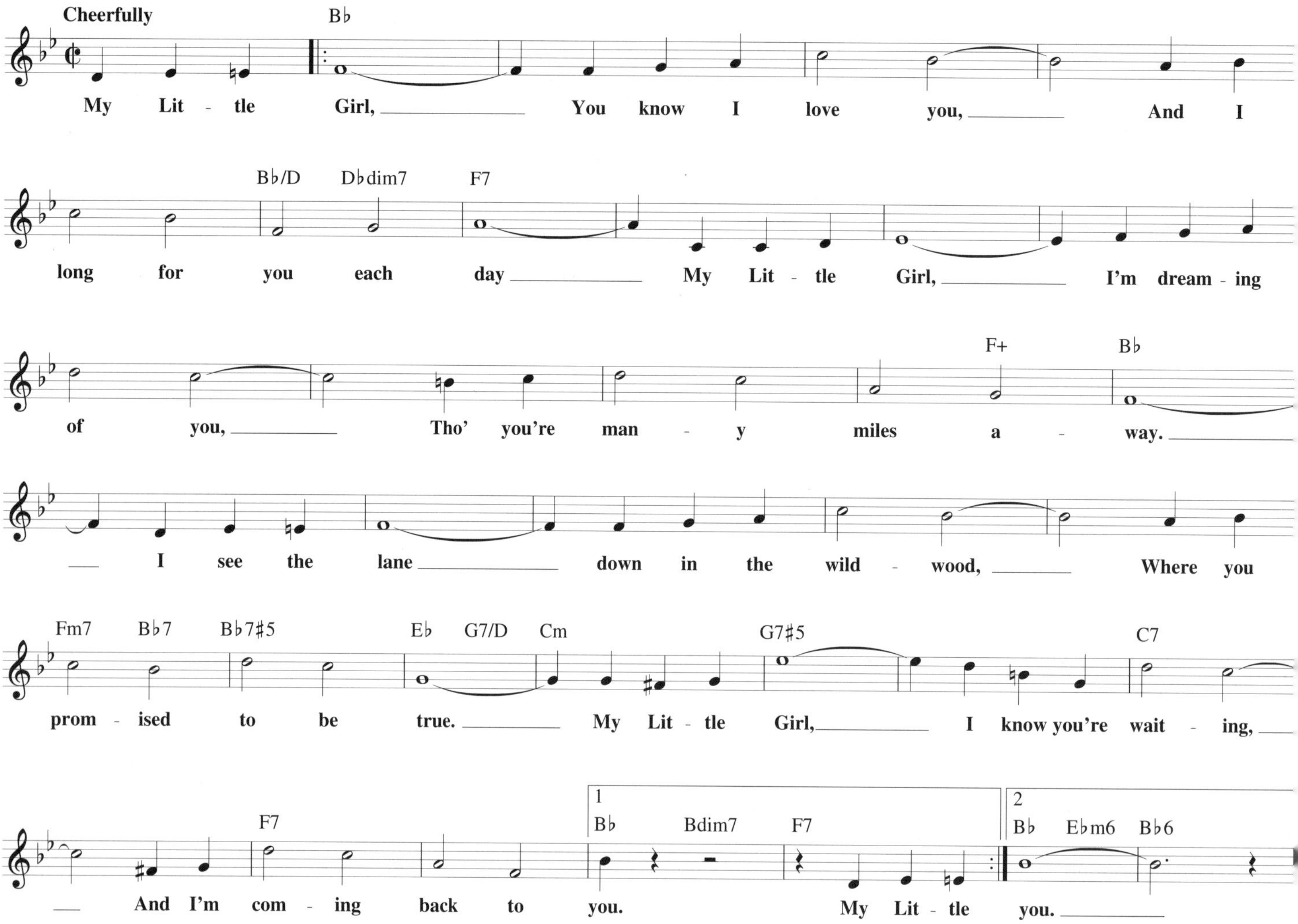

MY ISLE OF GOLDEN DREAMS

Words by GUS KAHN
Music by WALTER BLAUFUSS

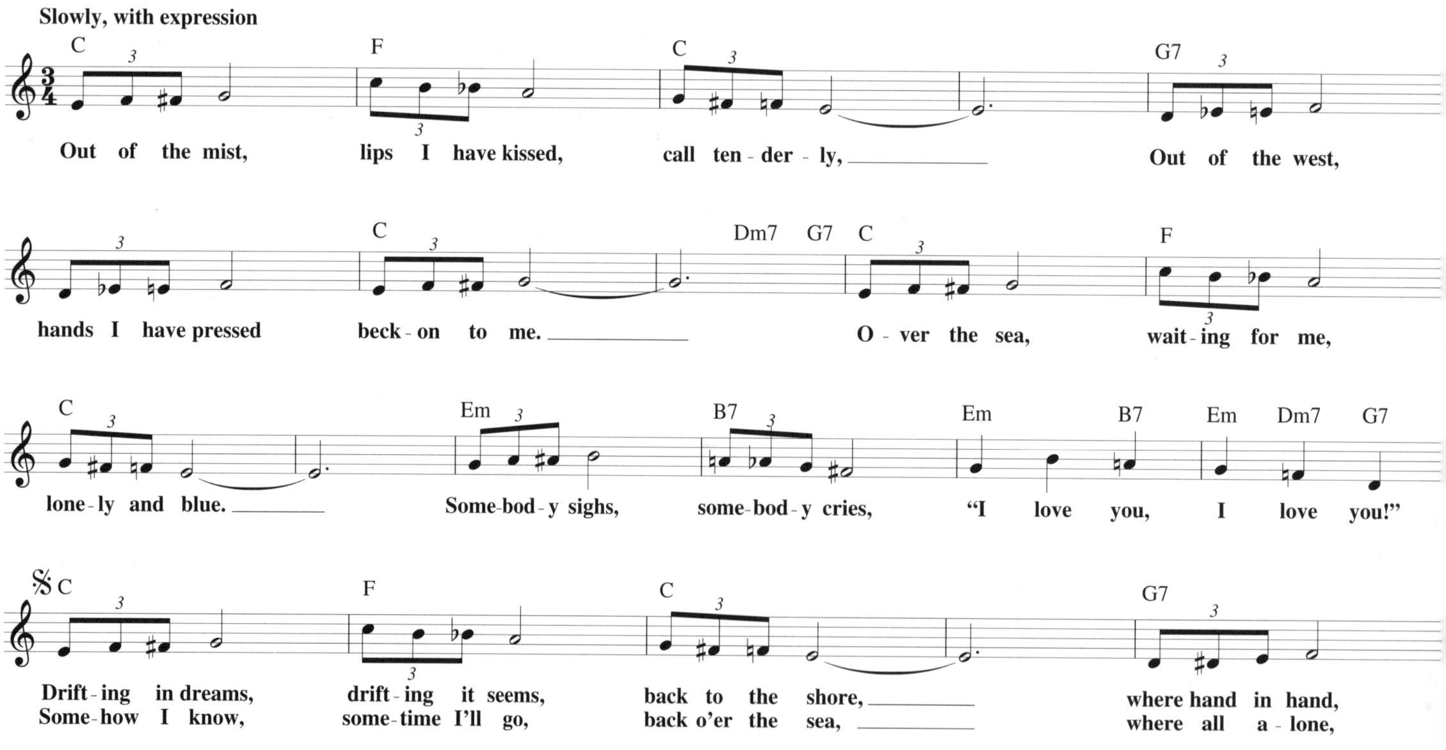

Slowly, with expression
C F C G7
Out of the mist, lips I have kissed, call ten - der - ly, Out of the west,
C Dm7 G7 C F
hands I have pressed beck - on to me. O - ver the sea, wait - ing for me,
C Em B7 Em B7 Em Dm7 G7
lone - ly and blue. Some - bod - y sighs, some - bod - y cries, "I love you, I love you!"
C F C G7
Drift - ing in dreams, drift - ing it seems, back to the shore, where hand in hand,
Some - how I know, some - time I'll go, back o'er the sea, where all a - lone,

MY MAMMY

Words by SAM M. LEWIS and JOE YOUNG
Music by WALTER DONALDSON

MY MAN
(Mon homme)
from ZIEGFELD FOLLIES

Words by ALBERT WILLEMETZ and JACQUES CHARLE
English Words by CHANNING POLLOC
Music by MAURICE YVA

NOLA

Music by
FELIX ARNDT

NEAPOLITAN LOVE SONG

Words by HENRY BLOSSO
Music by VICTOR HERBER

Moderately

Sweet one! _____ How my heart is yearn - ing _____ Ev - er _____
T'a - mo _____ fan - ci - ul - la tan - to Piu del -

_____ with _ you to be! Love - light _____ in your dear eyes burn - ing,
- la _ vi - ta mia Ar - do per te sol - tan -

stead - fast, faith - ful _____ and true _ to me! Tell _____ me!
to d'a mor _____ di ge - los - sia! T'a - mo!

When shall _____ I a - gain ca - ress you? _____ Kiss you? On - ly tell me
Dim - mi _ che _ mi vuoi be - ne _____ Ba - Ciami _____ un - a vol - ta'an -

when? _____ Ah, me! _____ I long to press you,
cor _____ Vie - ni sor - diam le pe - ne

Dar - ling, fond - ly _____ with - in my arms a - gain! _____
so - gne re - mo _____ an - cor, an - cor d'a - mor!

O MIO BABBINO CARO
from GIANNI SCHICCHI

By GIACOMO PUCCINI

O Mio Bab - bi - no Ca - ro, mi pia - ce,è bel - lo, bel - lo; vo'an -

da - re in Por - ta Ros - sa a com - pe - rar l'a - nel - lo! Sì,

sì, ci vo - glio an - da - re! E se l'a - mas - si in dar - no, an -

OH JOHNNY, OH JOHNNY, OH!

Words by ED ROSE
Music by ABE OLMAN

Dedicated to my friend "Private Howard Friend"
who occupies the cot next to mine and feels as I do about the "bugler"

OH! HOW I HATE TO GET UP IN THE MORNING
from the Stage Production YIP, YIP YAPHANK

Words and Music by
IRVING BERLIN

THE OLD REFRAIN

Music by
FRITZ KREISLER

Flowing

I oft - en think of home, dee - oo - lee - ay, when I am all a - lone and far a -
passed and gone, dee - oo - lee - ay, and though my heart is young my head is

way. I sing an old re - frain: dee - oo - le - ay, for it re - calls to me a by - gone
gray. Yet still the e - choes ring dee - oo - le - ay, and dear old mem - o - ries for - ev - er

day. It takes me back a - gain to mea - dows fair, where sun - light's gol - den rays beam ev' - ry - where. My child - hood
stay. My song can bring me vi - sions full of light, and sweet - est dreams through - out the dark - est night. Of all that

joys a - gain come back to me, my moth - er's face in fan - cy, too I see. It was my
life can give that song is best. I'll take it with me when I go to rest. And when at

moth - er taught me how to sing, and to that mem - o - ry my heart will cling. I'm nev - er
last my jour - ney here is o'er, t'will ring more joy - ful - ly than e'er be - fore. For up to

sad and lone while on my way, as long as I can sing dee - oo - lee - ay! **Though years have**
heav - en I will take my lay, the an - gels too will sing dee - oo - lee - ay!

ON THE BEACH AT WAIKIKI

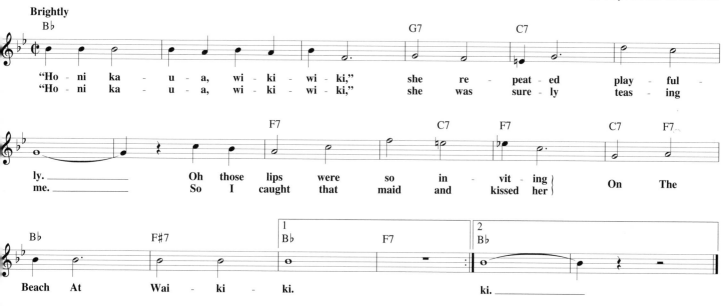

Words by G.H. STOVER
Music by HENRY KAILIMAIE

Brightly

"Ho - ni ka - u - a, wi - ki wi - ki," she re - peat - ed play - ful -
"Ho - ni ka - u - a, wi - ki wi - ki," she was sure - ly teas - ing

ly. _____ Oh those lips were so in - vit - ing
me. _____ So I caught that maid and kissed her } On The

Beach At Wai - ki - ki. ki. _____

OVER THERE

Words and Music by
GEORGE M. COHAN

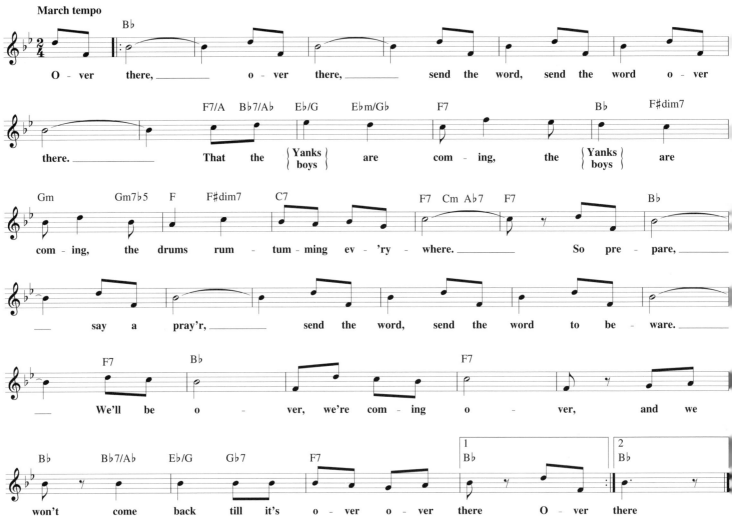

PACK UP YOUR TROUBLES IN YOUR OLD KIT BAG AND SMILE, SMILE, SMILE

Words by GEORGE ASAF
Music by FELIX POWELL

PAPER DOLL

Words and Music by
JOHNNY S. BLACK

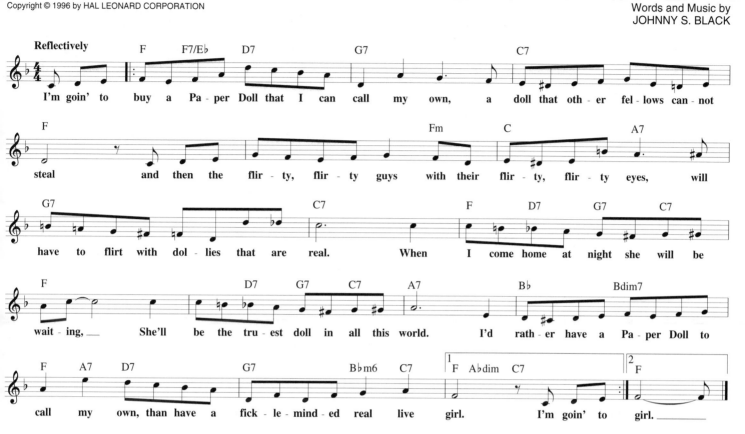

POOR BUTTERFLY

Words by JOHN L. GOLDEN
Music by RAYMOND HUBBELL

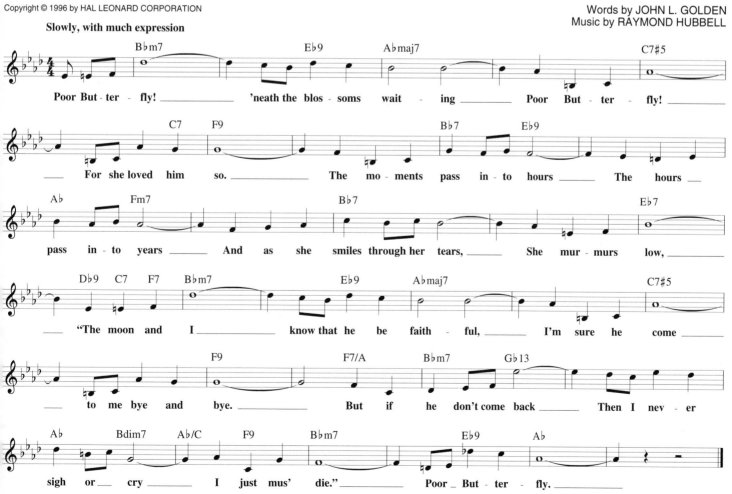

PARADE OF THE WOODEN SOLDIERS

English Lyrics by BALLARD MacDONALD
Music by LEON JESSEL

A PRETTY GIRL IS LIKE A MELODY
from the 1919 Stage Prodcution ZIEGFELD FOLLIES

Words and Music by
IRVING BERLIN

ROCK-A-BYE YOUR BABY WITH A DIXIE MELODY

Words by SAM M. LEWIS and JOE YOUNG
Music by JEAN SCHWARTZ

ROSE ROOM

Words by HARRY WILLIAMS
Music by ART HICKMAN

all the ros - es are sway - ing, Danc - ing _____ while the mead - ow brook flows. _____ The moon when shin - ing is more than ev - er de - sign - ing, For 'tis ev - er then I am pin - ing, Pin - ing _____ to be sweet - ly re - clin - ing, Some - where in Rose - land, Be - side a beau - ti - ful rose. _____ In sun - ny rose. _____

ROSES OF PICARDY

Words by FRED E. WEATHERLY
Music by HAYDN WOOD

Slowly

Ro - ses are shin - ing in Pi - car - dy in the hush of the sil - ver dew.

Ro - ses are flow'r - ing in Pi - car - dy, but there's nev - er a rose like you! And the

ro - ses will die with the sum - mer - time, and our roads may be far _____ a - part, but there's

one rose that dies not in Pi - car - dy! 'Tis the rose that I keep in my heart! _____

ROYAL GARDEN BLUES

Words and Music by CLARENCE WILLIAMS
and SPENCER WILLIAMS

RUNNIN' WILD

Words by JOE GREY and LEO WOODS
Music by A. HARRINGTON GIBBS

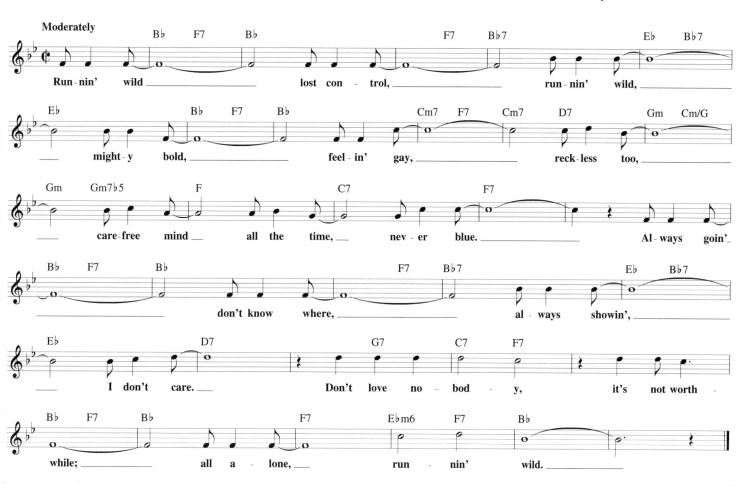

Run-nin' wild ___ lost con-trol, ___ run-nin' wild, ___ might-y bold, ___ feel-in' gay, ___ reck-less too, ___ care-free mind ___ all the time, nev-er blue. ___ Al-ways goin' ___ don't know where, ___ al-ways showin', ___ I don't care. ___ Don't love no-bod-y, it's not worth - while; ___ all a - lone, ___ run-nin' wild.

THE SHEIK OF ARABY

Words by HARRY B. SMITH and FRANCIS WHEELER
Music by TED SNYDER

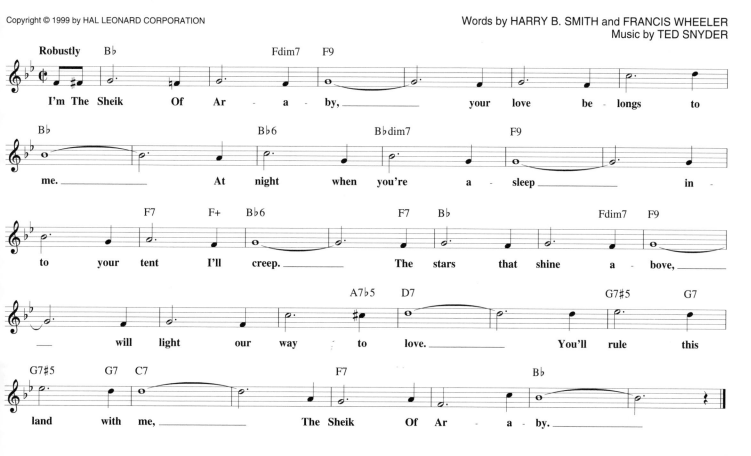

I'm The Sheik Of Ar - a - by, ___ your love be-longs to me. ___ At night when you're a-sleep ___ in - to your tent I'll creep. The stars that shine a-bove, will light our way to love. ___ You'll rule this land with me, ___ The Sheik Of Ar - a - by. ___

SAY IT WITH MUSIC
from the 1921 Stage Production MUSIC BOX REVUE

Words and Music b
IRVING BERLI

Moderately

Mu - sic is a lang - uage lov - ers un - der - stand. Mel - o - dy and
There's a ten - der mes - sage deep down in my heart. Some - thing you should

ro - mance wan - der hand in hand. Cu - pid nev - er fails as - sis - ted by a
know, but how am I to start? Sen - ti - men - tal speech - es nev - er could im -

band. So if you have some - thing sweet to tell her: Say it with
part just ex - act - ly what I want to tell you: Say it with

mu - sic, beau - ti - ful mu - sic, Some - how they'd

rath - er be kissed ___ to the strains of Cho - pin or Liszt. ___ A mel -

o - dy mel - low played on a cel - lo

helps mis - ter Cu - pid a - long. ___ So say it with a

beau - ti - ful song ___   beau - ti - ful song ___

SECOND HAND ROSE

Words by GRANT CLARKE
Music by JAMES F. HANLEY

Moderately, not too slow

I'm wear - ing sec - ond hand hats ___ sec - ond hand clothes ___ that's why they call ___ me
sec - ond hand shoes ___ sec - ond hand hose ___ all the girls hand ___ me their

Sec - ond Hand Rose. ___ E - ven our pi - a - no in the par - lor fa - ther bought for
sec - ond hand beaux. ___ E - ven my pa - ja - mas when I don 'em have some - bod - y

SMILES

Words by J. WILL CALLAHAN
Music by LEE S. ROBERTS

SOMEBODY STOLE MY GAL

Words and Music by
LEO WOO

SONG OF THE ISLANDS

Words and Music by
CHARLES E. KING

STUMBLING

Words and Music by
ZEZ CONFREY

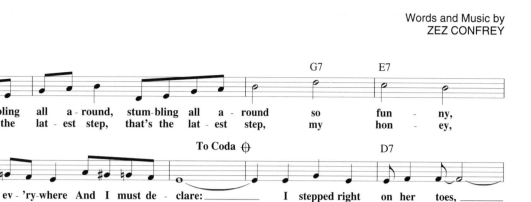

Moderately

G
Stum-bling all a - round, stum-bling all a - round, stum-bling all a - round so **G7** fun - **E7** ny,
that's the lat - est step, that's the lat - est step, that's the lat - est step, my hon - ey,

A7
stum-bling here and there, stum-bling ev - 'ry-where And I must de - clare:_____ I stepped right on her **D7** toes,_____
no - tice all the pep, no - tice all the pep, no - tice all the pep._____

To Coda ⊕

Adim **Em**
_____ and when she bumped my nose,_____ I fell and when I **A7** rose,_____ I felt a -

D7 Em7 Fdim7 D7/F♯   **D+**
shamed._____ And told her

D.C. al Coda

CODA
⊕
Cm6
She said, "Stop mum - bling,_____ tho' you are stum-

G D7 G   **A7**   **D7**   **G**
- bling._____ I like it just a lit - tle bit, just a lit - tle bit, quite a lit - tle bit."_____

SUGAR BLUES

Words by LUCY FLETCHER
Music by CLARENCE WILLIAMS

Moderate Blues

C
Sug - ar Blues,_____ ev - 'ry-bod - y's sing - ing the **G7** Sug - ar Blues._____ The

whole town is ring - ing. {My lov - in' man's___ sweet as he can **Dm7** be,_____ but the **G7**
{I love my cof - fee, I love my tea,_____ but the

C
dog - gone fool turned so - ur on me._____} I'm so un - hap - py, I
dog - gone cream turned so - ur on me._____}

C7
feel so bad _____ I could **Gm7** lay me down and **C7** die. **F A7/E Dm** You can

F6 F♯dim7   **C E7 A7**   **D7**   **G7**
say what you choose ___ but I'm all con - fused, I've got the sweet, sweet Sug - ar

C E7 A7   **D7 G7**   **C**
Blues, more sug - ar I've got the sweet, sweet Sug - ar Blues._____

SWANEE

Words by IRVING CAESAR
Music by GEORGE GERSHWIN

SWEET LITTLE BUTTERCUP

Words by ALFRED BRYAN
Music by HERMAN PALEY

THAT NAUGHTY WALTZ

Words by EDWIN STANLEY
Music by SOL P. LEVY

TAIN'T NOBODY'S BIZ-NESS IF I DO

Words and Music by PORTER GRAINGER
and EVERETT ROBBINS

THAT TUMBLE DOWN SHACK IN ATHLONE

Words by RICHARD W. PASCOE
Music by MONTE CARLO and ALMA M. SANDERS

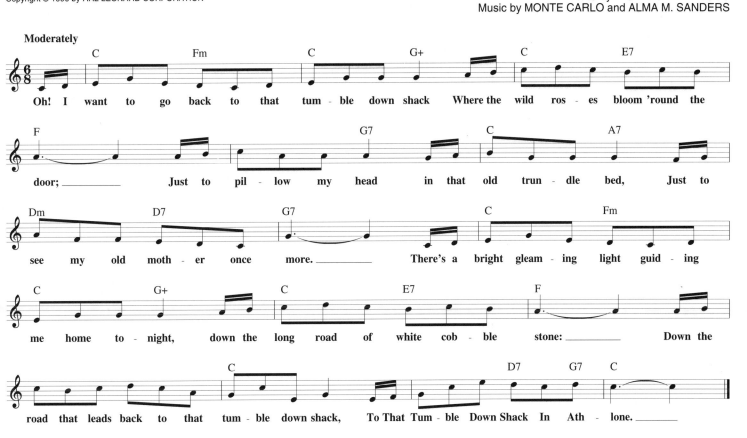

THREE O'CLOCK IN THE MORNING

Words by DOROTHY TERRISS
Music by JULIAN ROBLEDO

TIGER RAG
(Hold That Tiger)

Words by HARRY DECOSTA
Music by ORIGINAL DIXIELAND JAZZ BAND

TILL WE MEET AGAIN

Words by RAYMOND B. EGAN
Music by RICHARD A. WHITING

TISHOMINGO BLUES

By SPENCER WILLIAMS

I'm goin' to Tish-o-min-go be-cause I'm sad to-day, ___
I wish to lin-ger 'way down old Dix-ie way. ___
Oh my wea-ry heart cries out in pain, ___ oh how I wish that I was
back a-gain ___ with a race ___ in a place ___ where they make you wel-come all the
time. 'Way down in Mis-si-sip-pi a-mong the cy-press trees, ___
they get you dip-py, with their strange mel-o-dies. ___ To re-
sist temp-ta-tion, I just can't re-fuse, in Tish-o-min-go
I wish to lin-ger, where they play the wea-ry blues. I'm blues.

TILL THE CLOUDS ROLL BY

Words by P.G. WODEHOUSE
Music by JEROME KERN

Oh, the rain ___ comes a pit-ter, pat-ter, ___ and I'd like ___
to be safe in bed. Skies are weep-ing ___ while the world is sleep-ing ___
trou-ble heap-ing on our head. ___ It is vain ___ to re-main and
chat-ter, ___ and to wait ___ for a clear-er sky. Hel-ter-skel-ter ___
I must fly for shel-ter ___ Till The Clouds Roll By. ___

TOOT, TOOT, TOOTSIE! (GOODBYE!)
from THE JAZZ SINGER

Words and Music by GUS KAHN, ERNIE ERDMAN
DAN RUSSO and TED FIORITO

WABASH BLUES

Words by DAVE RINGLE
Music by FRED MEINKEN

THE WANG WANG BLUES

Words and Music by LEO WOOD, GUS MUELLER,
BUSTER JOHNSON and HENRY BUSSE

Moderately

Wang,   Wang   Blues. ____ She's gone and left me with The Wang,
Wang,   Wang   Blues, ____ I've got the ev - er - last - ing Wang,

Wang   Blues; ____ And let me tell you, mis - ter, I
Wang   Blues; ____ I'm on - ly ask - ing that my Sweet

nev - er   knew I'd be so blue un - til she went a -
Sweet - ie   will come back and chase a - way those

way. ____   Wang,   Wang   Blues. ____

'WAY DOWN YONDER IN NEW ORLEANS

Words and Music by HENRY CREAMER
and J. TURNER LAYTON

Moderate bounce

'Way down yon - der in New Or - leans ____ in the land ____ of dream - y scenes ____ there's a gar - den of

E - den   that's what I mean. ____ Cre - ole ba - bies with flash - ing eyes ____

soft - ly whis - per with ten - der sighs, ____ "Stop! Oh! won't you give your la - dy fair ____

a lit - tle smile?" Stop! you bet your life you'll lin - ger there ____ a lit - tle

while.   There is Hea - ven right here on earth ____ with those beau - ti - ful queens
They've got an - gels right here on earth ____ wear - ing lit - tle blue jeans

'way down yon - der in New Or - leans.   leans. ____

422

WHEN MY BABY SMILES AT ME

Words and Music by HARRY VON TILZER
ANDREW B. STERLING, BILL MUNRO and TED LEWIS

WHERE DID ROBINSON CRUSOE GO WITH FRIDAY ON SATURDAY NIGHT?

Words and Music by JOE YOUNG
SAM LEWIS and GEORGE W. MEYER

WHISPERING

Words and Music by RICHARD COBURN,
JOHN SCHONBERGER and VINCENT ROSE

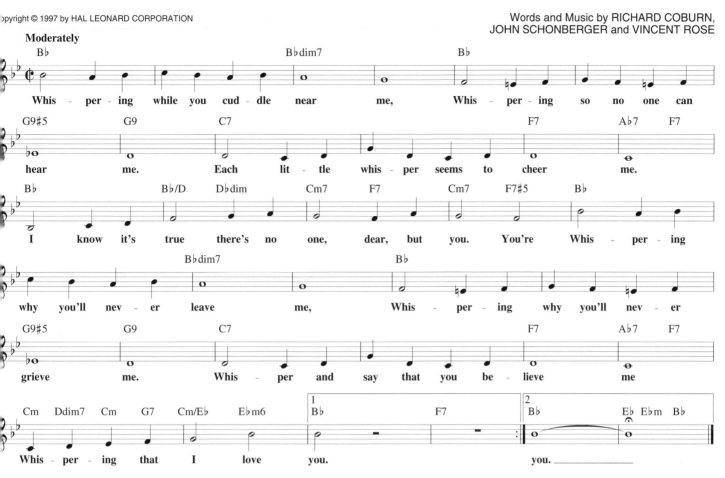

THE WORLD IS WAITING FOR THE SUNRISE

Words by EUGENE LOCKHART
Music by ERNEST SEITZ

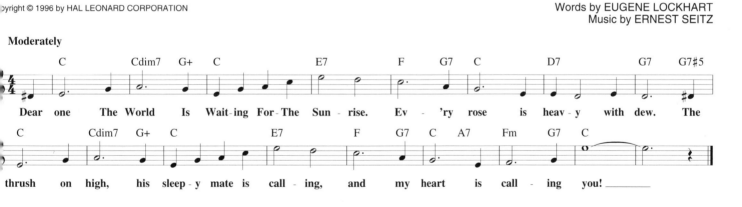

YAAKA HULA HICKEY DULA

Words and Music by RAY GOETZ,
JOE YOUNG and PETER WENDLING

YOU BELONG TO ME

Copyright © 1996 by HAL LEONARD CORPORATION

Words by HARRY B. SM
Music by VICTOR HERBE